CAPTIVATING
CROSSWORDS

Bath · New York · Cologne · Melbourne · Delhi
Hong Kong · Shenzhen · Singapore · Amsterdam

This edition published by Parragon Books Ltd in 2015
and distributed by

Parragon Inc.
440 Park Avenue South, 13th Floor
New York, NY 10016
www.parragon.com

ISBN 978-1-4748-1509-3

Printed in China

No 1

Across
1 - Bring forth (6)
5 - Foodstuff (3)
7 - Ungainly (5)
8 - Body of water (7)
9 - Male aristocrat (5)
10 - Least heavy (8)
12 - Proverb (6)
14 - Snarls (6)
17 - Greeting an officer (8)
18 - Supersedes (5)
20 - Not modern (7)
21 - Allowed by official rules (5)
22 - Bind (3)
23 - Rowing oars (6)

Down
2 - Unpleasantly (7)
3 - Sections of a book (8)
4 - White aquatic bird (4)
5 - Facial hair (7)
6 - First book of the Bible (7)
7 - Rover (5)
11 - Relating to sound (8)
12 - Type of sword (7)
13 - Struggle (7)
15 - Pertaining to the tongue (7)
16 - Area in South Africa (5)
19 - Heroic tale (4)

No 2

Across
1 - Uses again (8)
5 - Cook (4)
9 - Manor (anag) (5)
10 - Person of exceptional importance (5)
11 - Impossible to manage (10)
14 - Pronouncement (6)
15 - Quick sleep (6)
17 - Fine points of something (3,3,4)
20 - Fabric with parallel ribs (5)
21 - Live by (5)
22 - Take dinner (4)
23 - Hand woven pictorial design (8)

Down
1 - Unusual (4)
2 - Toothed implement for the hair (4)
3 - Therefore (12)
4 - Withstand (6)
6 - Greenhouse (8)
7 - Comedian (8)
8 - Standard equipment (5-2-5)
12 - Allowed in (8)
13 - Division (8)
16 - Region of the sun's atmosphere (6)
18 - Cheerful tune (4)
19 - Extremely (4)

No 3

Across

1 - Clown (6)
4 - Starve with hunger (6)
7 - Aromatic bark (8)
8 - Pointed missile (4)
9 - Get beaten (4)
11 - Suffers (4)
12 - Patient (7)
13 - Hurried (3)
15 - Apply (3)
17 - Clumsy (7)
19 - Remnant (4)
20 - Engrave with acid (4)
21 - Donated (4)
22 - Left over substance (8)
24 - Playground structure (6)
25 - Had corresponding sounds (6)

Down

1 - Cheerful (7)
2 - Colors lightly (6)
3 - Edge (3)
4 - Pecuniary (9)
5 - Average (6)
6 - Walks (7)
10 - Bottle opener (9)
14 - Put into action (7)
16 - Respired (7)
17 - Superior of a nunnery (6)
18 - Lethal (6)
23 - Polite title for a man (3)

No 4

Across
1 - Ballet skirt (4)
3 - Impending (8)
9 - Sharply (7)
10 - Roman country house (5)
11 - Pen-like tools (5)
12 - Appropriately (7)
13 - Scoundrel (6)
15 - Swiss city (6)
17 - Hanging (7)
18 - Scoundrel (5)
20 - Units (5)
21 - Competitor (7)
22 - Propose candidate (8)
23 - Renounce (4)

Down
1 - Musical arrangement (13)
2 - Genuinely (5)
4 - Distress signal (6)
5 - Without a backbone (12)
6 - Surpass (7)
7 - Clearly (13)
8 - Food shop (12)
14 - Ray (7)
16 - Bear witness (6)
19 - Irritate (5)

No 5

Across
1 - Make thirsty (5)
4 - Understand (5)
10 - Paper folding (7)
11 - Ruffle (5)
12 - Resistance units (4)
13 - Find (8)
16 - Top aim (anag) (6)
17 - Rarely (6)
20 - Boating (8)
21 - Thwart (4)
23 - Renown (5)
25 - Quantity (7)
26 - Written agreements (5)
27 - Spirited horse (5)

Down
2 - Containing aphorisms (9)
3 - Decapod that has pincers (4)
5 - Castoff (8)
6 - Cry (3)
7 - Elaborate form of decoration (6)
8 - Watch (5)
9 - Move (4)
14 - Recording of visual images (9)
15 - Purple quartz (8)
18 - Aria (6)
19 - Gold block (5)
20 - Exercise form (4)
22 - Curved (4)
24 - Eggs (3)

No 6

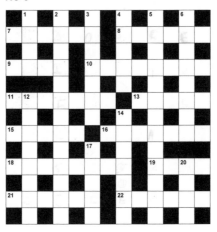

Across
7 - Mountain chain (6)
8 - Musical ensembles (6)
9 - Coalition (4)
10 - Red fruits eaten as vegetables (8)
11 - Reintegrate (7)
13 - Emirate on the Persian Gulf (5)
15 - Discharged (5)
16 - Toured (7)
18 - Recurring with regularity (8)
19 - Duration (4)
21 - Idle (6)
22 - Disrespects (6)

Down
1 - Tablet (4)
2 - Bias (13)
3 - Thrown away (4,3)
4 - Rascal (5)
5 - Denial (13)
6 - Software provided without charge (8)
12 - Expressions (8)
14 - Bishop's jurisdiction (7)
17 - Brown earth pigment (5)
20 - Fix (4)

No 7

Across
1 - Face (anag) (4)
3 - Fantasy in the mind (8)
9 - Recharges (7)
10 - Trims (5)
11 - Circumstance (5)
12 - Stain (7)
13 - Appease (6)
15 - Give in (6)
17 - Provoked or teased (7)
18 - Underground railway (5)
20 - Show (5)
21 - Internal organs (7)
22 - Convey from one place to another (8)
23 - Depend (4)

Down
1 - Journalist (13)
2 - Wrong (5)
4 - Support; help (6)
5 - Removal (12)
6 - Missive (7)
7 - Naughtily (13)
8 - Loyalty (12)
14 - Suspension (7)
16 - Tips and instruction (6)
19 - Trio (5)

No 8

Across
1 - Freshest (6)
7 - Watcher (8)
8 - Tropical constrictor (3)
9 - Very pure glass (6)
10 - Volcanic rock (4)
11 - Spread out (5)
13 - Dullness (7)
15 - Stiff coarse hair (7)
17 - Long ___ owl (5)
21 - Tribute (4)
22 - Set out on (6)
23 - Frozen water (3)
24 - Largest of the Canary Islands (8)
25 - Tiny bag (6)

Down
1 - Royal people (6)
2 - Small carnivorous mammal (6)
3 - A poison (5)
4 - From the East (7)
5 - Formerly Ceylon (3,5)
6 - Departs (6)
12 - Pardons (8)
14 - Country in North Africa (7)
16 - Firmly implanted (6)
18 - Jaunty (6)
19 - Dispirit (6)
20 - Double-reed instruments (5)

No 9

Across

1 - Childlike (4-4)
5 - Skin mark (4)
9 - New Zealand aboriginal (5)
10 - Golf clubs (5)
11 - Household management (10)
14 - Legume (6)
15 - Mix with (6)
17 - Having three sides (10)
20 - Express words by letters (5)
21 - Accustom (5)
22 - Utters (4)
23 - Least old (8)

Down

1 - Ten cent coin (4)
2 - Courts (4)
3 - Intermittently (12)
4 - Decays (6)
6 - Calvin ___ : 30th US President (8)
7 - Gave up one's job (8)
8 - Deterioration (12)
12 - Siltiest (anag) (8)
13 - Improbable (8)
16 - Sheep (6)
18 - Silent (4)
19 - Preparation for Easter (4)

No 10

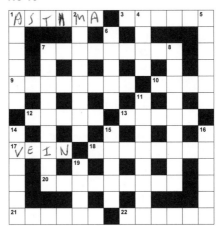

Across
1 - Respiratory disorder (6)
3 - Writings (6)
7 - Lovable (9)
9 - Makes larger (8)
10 - Thin strip of wood (4)
12 - Notices (5)
13 - Assisted (5)
17 - Blood vessel (4)
18 - Breaks (8)
20 - Desires (9)
21 - Bird of prey (6)
22 - First occasions (6)

Down
1 - Assert (6)
2 - Reflect (8)
4 - Drink greedily (4)
5 - Comfort (6)
6 - Show off (5)
7 - Illustrate (9)
8 - Inelegant (9)
11 - Space between two objects (8)
14 - Calls forth (6)
15 - Compact mass (5)
16 - Examines (6)
19 - Chat (4)

No 11

Across

1 - Relating to stars (6)
5 - Supplanted (6)
8 - Complain unreasonably (4)
9 - Appended textual matter (8)
10 - Repository (5)
11 - Go before (7)
14 - Expert in numerical calculations (13)
16 - Twirl (7)
18 - Boat (5)
20 - Adhering to closely (8)
22 - Fruit pie (4)
23 - Flesh of sheep (6)
24 - Flee (6)

Down

2 - Bird frightener (9)
3 - Harmonious relation (7)
4 - Incline (4)
5 - Unyielding (8)
6 - Pertaining to sound (5)
7 - Flightless bird (3)
12 - Unsafe structure (9)
13 - Oil and water mix (8)
15 - Disordered (7)
17 - Former gold coin (5)
19 - Look at amorously (4)
21 - Nineteenth Greek letter (3)

No 12

Across

7 - Administrative body (6)
8 - Married woman (6)
9 - Jaunty (4)
10 - Discourtesy (8)
11 - Flee (7)
13 - Level of a building (5)
15 - Self-indulgence (5)
16 - Incredible events (7)
18 - Thrown at a wedding (8)
19 - No part or amount (4)
21 - Diviner (6)
22 - Igneous rock (6)

Down

1 - Electrical safety device (4)
2 - Correct to the last detail (6-7)
3 - Hits (7)
4 - Change (5)
5 - Consideration for others (13)
6 - Bodily (8)
12 - Closet with shelves (8)
14 - Musical instrument (7)
17 - Spread by scattering (5)
20 - Egypt's river (4)

No 13

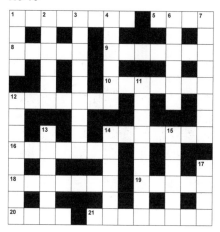

Across

1 - Submissive to authority (8)
5 - Recess (4)
8 - Enraged (5)
9 - Eg the West Indies (7)
10 - Snobbish (7)
12 - Compensation (7)
14 - Imprecise (7)
16 - Oriental (7)
18 - Recently wealthy person (7)
19 - Sheet (anag) (5)
20 - Cuts woods (4)
21 - Pattern of symptoms (8)

Down

1 - Look at amorously (4)
2 - Wanted; desired (6)
3 - Laziness (9)
4 - Equine sounds (6)
6 - Mexican cloak (6)
7 - Writer of literary works (8)
11 - Not deserved (9)
12 - Income (8)
13 - Written agreement (6)
14 - Physical wound (6)
15 - Ratio of reflected light (6)
17 - Celebration (4)

No 14

Across
1 - Relaxed (4-4)
6 - ___ cola (drink) (4)
8 - Cell centers (6)
9 - Walk very quietly (6)
10 - Allow (3)
11 - Entry devices (4)
12 - Leavening fungi (6)
13 - Far from the intended target (6)
15 - Remove color from (6)
17 - Twisted (6)
20 - State in the W United States (4)
21 - Sheep (3)
22 - Renovate (6)
23 - Decline (6)
24 - Chances of winning (4)
25 - Pile of fodder (8)

Down
2 - Charms (7)
3 - Girl's toys (5)
4 - In a nimble manner (7)
5 - Money pot (5)
6 - Small cake (7)
7 - Punch hard (5)
14 - Players (anag) (7)
15 - Totally without moisture (4-3)
16 - Traditional example (7)
18 - In front (5)
19 - Extent (5)
20 - Disturb (5)

No 15

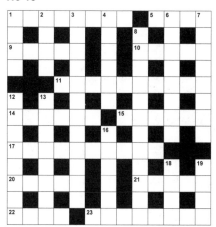

Across
1 - Reversed; changed order (8)
5 - Sell (4)
9 - Besmirch (5)
10 - Gives out (5)
11 - Self-governing (10)
14 - Struck by overwhelming shock (6)
15 - Tempt (6)
17 - Investigated (10)
20 - Pertaining to sound (5)
21 - Cancel (5)
22 - Consumes (4)
23 - Sculptured figures (8)

Down
1 - Cloth belt (4)
2 - Wild mountain goat (4)
3 - A particular incident (12)
4 - Implant deeply (6)
6 - Intermittent (8)
7 - Catastrophe (8)
8 - Condemnation (12)
12 - Native American game (8)
13 - Dark reddish-brown horse (8)
16 - Hidden (6)
18 - Priest (4)
19 - Resist (4)

No 16

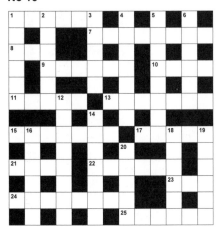

Across
1 - Desires (6)
7 - Sorting (8)
8 - Pasture (3)
9 - Shooting star (6)
10 - Apes (anag) (4)
11 - Impress on paper (5)
13 - Trespass (7)
15 - Erupt in an uncontrolled manner (4,3)
17 - Fastening (5)
21 - Poem (4)
22 - Superhuman (6)
23 - Hotel (3)
24 - Midwestern state of USA (8)
25 - Instigate (6)

Down
1 - Beat soundly (6)
2 - Prawns (6)
3 - Bottoms of shoes (5)
4 - Loving (7)
5 - Possessions (8)
6 - Not made explicit (6)
12 - Broadcast report (8)
14 - Curving outward (7)
16 - Fatty (6)
18 - Stimulate (6)
19 - Hard glassy mineral (6)
20 - Dominant theme (5)

No 17

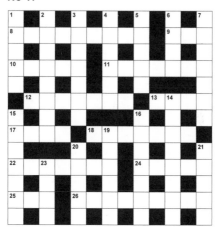

Across
8 - Mediate (9)
9 - Beer (3)
10 - Rice dish (5)
11 - Powerful dog (7)
12 - Data input devices (7)
13 - Causes; reasons (4)
17 - Too (4)
18 - Edible mollusk (7)
22 - Highest female voice (7)
24 - Rouse from sleep (5)
25 - Mud channel (3)
26 - Being in agreement (9)

Down
1 - Chilly (5)
2 - Huntsmen (8)
3 - Victory (7)
4 - Swarmed (6)
5 - Cooking fungus (5)
6 - Republic in W Africa (4)
7 - Greedy (7)
14 - Jewish festival (8)
15 - Artist of consummate skill (7)
16 - Eg roses (7)
19 - Blemish (6)
20 - Aircraft detection system (5)
21 - Joins together (5)
23 - Shame (4)

No 18

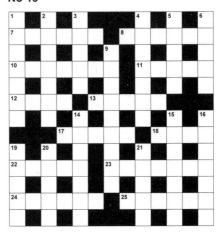

Across

7 - Assertion (6)
8 - Carriage (6)
10 - Appearance (7)
11 - Silk or thin fabric (5)
12 - Forefather (4)
13 - Go away (5)
17 - Talons (5)
18 - Religious leader (4)
22 - Puff up (5)
23 - Equilateral parallelogram (7)
24 - Starter (6)
25 - Cease to remember (6)

Down

1 - String player (7)
2 - Travelers (7)
3 - Four wheeled vehicle (5)
4 - Gossip (7)
5 - Musical instrument (5)
6 - Adolescents (5)
9 - Tagline (9)
14 - Paper used to absorb ink (7)
15 - Back pain (7)
16 - Groups within (7)
19 - Monks' superior (5)
20 - Functions (5)
21 - Large intestine (5)

No 19

Across

1 - Too (4)
3 - Signal (8)
9 - Shortened (7)
10 - Paint (anag) (5)
11 - Cheat the result (3)
12 - Clean (5)
13 - Toy bear (5)
15 - Principle of morality (5)
17 - Bring on oneself (5)
18 - Residue; tree (3)
19 - Fill with high spirits (5)
20 - Notwithstanding (7)
21 - Boating (8)
22 - Temporary outside shelter (4)

Down

1 - In place of (13)
2 - Hurt; smart (5)
4 - Pushed gently (6)
5 - Eccentricity (12)
6 - Rearranged word (7)
7 - Institution (13)
8 - Resentment (12)
14 - Antiquated (7)
16 - Face-to-face (4-2)
18 - Nimble (5)

No 20

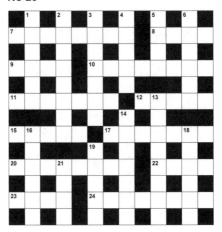

Across

7 - Hot and humid (8)
8 - Sports group (4)
9 - Decay (4)
10 - Struggle (8)
11 - Tell (7)
12 - Jeweled headdress (5)
15 - Analyze syntactically (5)
17 - Beetles (7)
20 - Busiest time on the roads (4,4)
22 - Seeds (4)
23 - Endure (4)
24 - Upper part of the intestines (8)

Down

1 - Psychological state (6)
2 - Disagreeable people (8)
3 - Put into action (7)
4 - Burst of light (5)
5 - Performs (4)
6 - Jogger (6)
13 - Came up with (8)
14 - Eating house (7)
16 - Insightfulness (6)
18 - Chemical indicator (6)
19 - Head coverings (5)
21 - Male red deer (4)

No 21

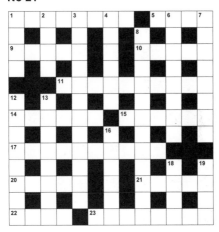

Across
1 - Flowering (8)
5 - Top tennis serves (4)
9 - Make crisp by heating (5)
10 - Certain to fail (2-3)
11 - Exaggerate (10)
14 - Small tucks in clothing (6)
15 - Skiing race (6)
17 - Cocoa based sweet products (10)
20 - Ray (5)
21 - Web-footed bird (5)
22 - Negatives (4)
23 - Having no wires (8)

Down
1 - Use these in baseball (4)
2 - Gemstone (4)
3 - Inspirational (12)
4 - Essential qualities (6)
6 - Craven (8)
7 - Rays of light (8)
8 - Generally agreed upon (12)
12 - Sample plant or animal (8)
13 - Deny (8)
16 - Gambling den (6)
18 - Ripped; rote (anag) (4)
19 - Stitches (4)

No 22

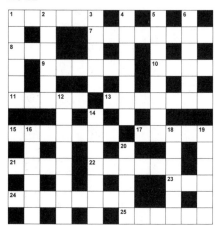

Across
1 - Fraternize (6)
7 - Judges (8)
8 - Goal (3)
9 - Republic in E Africa (6)
10 - Cut of meat (4)
11 - Iron alloy (5)
13 - Relate (7)
15 - Experienced serviceman (7)
17 - Practice (5)
21 - State of USA (4)
22 - Old Portuguese coin (6)
23 - Small green vegetable (3)
24 - Raised horizontal surface (8)
25 - Chase (6)

Down
1 - Stores (6)
2 - Bewilder (6)
3 - Announcement of a marriage (5)
4 - Attempted; tested (7)
5 - Separates out (8)
6 - Sign of the zodiac (6)
12 - Canine (3,5)
14 - King Arthur's home (7)
16 - Breathe out (6)
18 - Takes up (6)
19 - Diversion (6)
20 - Rascal (5)

No 23

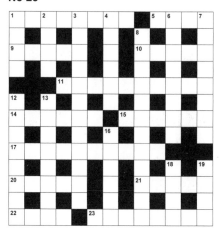

Across
1 - Huge sums of money (8)
5 - Ship's complement (4)
9 - Effects (5)
10 - Boasts about (5)
11 - Act in opposition to (10)
14 - Long legged rodent (6)
15 - Administrative body (6)
17 - Shortened by omitting notes (10)
20 - Type of music (5)
21 - Period of time (5)
22 - Consumes (4)
23 - Riders (8)

Down
1 - Obscures (4)
2 - Protective cover (4)
3 - Without official permission (12)
4 - Make beloved (6)
6 - Appreciates (8)
7 - Doomed to extinction (6-2)
8 - Completeness (12)
12 - Recording device (8)
13 - Least old (8)
16 - Coarse cloth (6)
18 - Bubble (4)
19 - Subsequently (4)

No 24

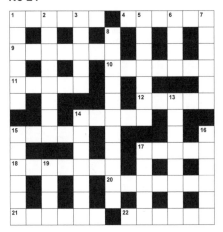

Across

1 - Traveling on horseback (6)
4 - Semitic language (6)
9 - Spanish Mediterranean island (7)
10 - Vote in again (7)
11 - Money; revenues (5)
12 - South American animal (5)
14 - Dog like mammal (5)
15 - Container for storing items (5)
17 - Homo sapiens (5)
18 - Stipulation (7)
20 - Make an explosive sound (7)
21 - Chain mail (6)
22 - Soul (6)

Down

1 - Reverberate (6)
2 - Low-spirited (8)
3 - Norwegian (5)
5 - German measles (7)
6 - Restrain; moderate (4)
7 - Against (6)
8 - Most distant (11)
13 - Having a strong smell (8)
14 - Sanitariness (7)
15 - Managing (6)
16 - False (6)
17 - Periods of 60 minutes (5)
19 - Resistance units (4)

No 25

Across

1 - Suspends; prevents (6)
5 - Law enforcers (6)
8 - Throb (4)
9 - Silly mistakes (8)
10 - Mattress used on frame (5)
11 - Foretell (7)
14 - Executive officer (4,9)
16 - Scent; smell (7)
18 - Songbird (5)
20 - Food of the gods (8)
22 - Entice (4)
23 - Ancient or well established (3-3)
24 - Observing (6)

Down

2 - Incompatible (9)
3 - Solvent; adhesive (7)
4 - Slender (4)
5 - Garden flower (8)
6 - Weaved (5)
7 - Stimulus (3)
12 - Modifying circumstance (9)
13 - Declared (8)
15 - Trickle (7)
17 - Do away with (5)
19 - Water storages (4)
21 - Periodic publication (abbrev) (3)

No 26

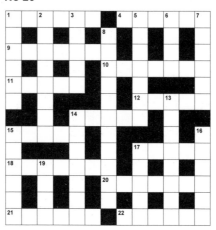

Across
1 - Pressed (6)
4 - Impress deeply (6)
9 - Friendly goodbye (7)
10 - Musical instrument (7)
11 - Attribute (5)
12 - Join together (5)
14 - Small lakes (5)
15 - Dough-like mixture (5)
17 - Voting compartment (5)
18 - Grotesque monster (7)
20 - Robbers (7)
21 - Circumstances (6)
22 - Tenant (6)

Down
1 - Linear units (6)
2 - Warm to excess (8)
3 - Acquires (5)
5 - Disposed to love (7)
6 - Move rapidly (4)
7 - Compare (6)
8 - Large globular fruit (11)
13 - Includes (8)
14 - Prepare for printing (7)
15 - Preserved cucumber (6)
16 - Morally pure (6)
17 - Illegal payment (5)
19 - Lazy (4)

No 27

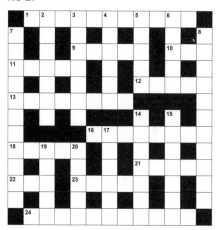

Across
1 - Rural areas (11)
9 - Lifting tools (5)
10 - Zero (3)
11 - Dairy product (5)
12 - Reports (5)
13 - Allocated (8)
16 - Unauthorized writing on walls (8)
18 - Bunches (5)
21 - Not concealed (5)
22 - Male sheep (3)
23 - Speak (5)
24 - Someone on radio or television (11)

Down
2 - Front of a coin (7)
3 - Small nuts (7)
4 - Fester (6)
5 - Impudent (5)
6 - Giver (5)
7 - Emphatic (11)
8 - Unwilling to part with money (11)
14 - Yields (7)
15 - Striped (7)
17 - Country person (6)
19 - Thighbone (5)
20 - Underwater apparatus (5)

No 28

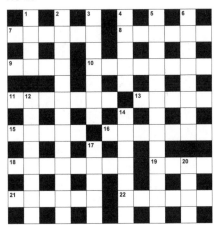

Across

7 - Sudden in action (6)
8 - Emblem of victory (6)
9 - Flightless bird (4)
10 - Unable to appreciate music (4-4)
11 - Obscurity (7)
13 - Axis (5)
15 - Gave out cards (5)
16 - Disentangle (7)
18 - Setting (8)
19 - Part of a roof (4)
21 - Entertains (6)
22 - Leads (6)

Down

1 - The King ___ / ___ : musical (3,1)
2 - Liveliness (13)
3 - Large shellfish (7)
4 - Fail badly (5)
5 - Having four sides (13)
6 - Pest controlling worm (8)
12 - Prevail over (8)
14 - Financial statement (7)
17 - Timber frame (5)
20 - Extremely (4)

No 29

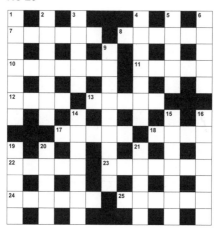

Across
7 - Winner (6)
8 - Blue semi precious gem (6)
10 - Quick musical tempo (7)
11 - Inspire anew (5)
12 - Comply (4)
13 - Light meal (5)
17 - Summons (5)
18 - Couple (4)
22 - Belief in God (5)
23 - Taught (7)
24 - Hidden (6)
25 - Performing (6)

Down
1 - Pilot (7)
2 - Told off (7)
3 - Tool for cutting channels (5)
4 - Materials (7)
5 - Male cattle (5)
6 - Plastic (5)
9 - One-piece garment (9)
14 - Injuring (7)
15 - Sheikdom in the Persian Gulf (7)
16 - Genius (7)
19 - Mature (5)
20 - Elevators (5)
21 - Plant stem (5)

No 30

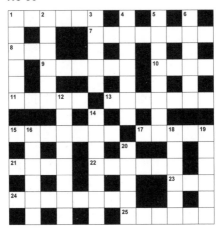

Across
1 - Part of the eye (6)
7 - Calm under pressure (8)
8 - Four wheel vehicle (3)
9 - Implement change (6)
10 - Slippery fish (4)
11 - Aristocrats (5)
13 - Whenever (7)
15 - Pertaining to fire (7)
17 - Non-standard speech (5)
21 - Heat up (4)
22 - Symbolic figures; shapes (6)
23 - Unit of current (3)
24 - Sheets and pillowcases (8)
25 - Assert (6)

Down
1 - Remember (6)
2 - Intense fear (6)
3 - Stage performer (5)
4 - A self-governing body (7)
5 - Set in from margin (8)
6 - Shelter (6)
12 - Fancifully (8)
14 - Pushing in a direction (7)
16 - Kitchen utensil (6)
18 - Crazy (6)
19 - Hoarding bird (6)
20 - Dog like mammal (5)

No 31

Across

1 - Eager (4)
3 - Musical composition (8)
9 - Capital of Kenya (7)
10 - Upright (5)
11 - Unpleasant (12)
13 - Strong (6)
15 - Swimmers (6)
17 - Refusal to recognize (4,8)
20 - Four wheeled vehicle (5)
21 - Pursues (7)
22 - Littlest (8)
23 - Nothing (4)

Down

1 - Royal countries (8)
2 - Transgressions (5)
4 - Young cow (6)
5 - Insecurely (12)
6 - Positioned on top of (7)
7 - Legendary creature (4)
8 - Running lengthwise (12)
12 - Strong coffee (8)
14 - State in the SE United States (7)
16 - Felonies (6)
18 - Male bee (5)
19 - Inspires fear (4)

No 32

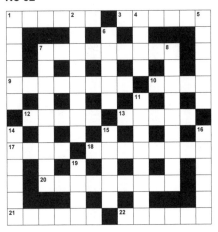

Across
1 - User's environment (6)
3 - Removes from property (6)
7 - Stealing (9)
9 - Easy chair (8)
10 - Eg T S Eliot (4)
12 - Out of fashion (5)
13 - Citrus fruit (5)
17 - Vessel (4)
18 - Great circle via poles (8)
20 - Heavy Winter garment (9)
21 - Trip (6)
22 - Perish (6)

Down
1 - Light beers (6)
2 - Most fortunate (8)
4 - Blood vessel (4)
5 - Calm (6)
6 - Regenerate (5)
7 - Wrapping (9)
8 - Specialist in the earth's structure (9)
11 - Airport for choppers (8)
14 - Modify (6)
15 - Thaws (5)
16 - Instep (6)
19 - Legume (4)

No 33

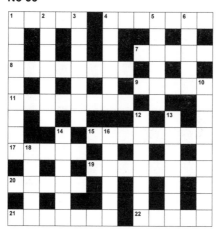

Across

1 - Top degree mark (5)
4 - Interpreting (7)
7 - Enemy (5)
8 - State of being born (8)
9 - Remains (5)
11 - Pertaining to ships (8)
15 - Refer to famous people (8)
17 - Seabirds (5)
19 - Expression of gratitude (5,3)
20 - Bring on oneself (5)
21 - Ape (7)
22 - Gets less difficult (5)

Down

1 - Strangeness (9)
2 - Tranquil (7)
3 - Burdensome work (7)
4 - Sacred writing (6)
5 - Indicates a direction (6)
6 - Nursemaid (5)
10 - Superabundances (9)
12 - Get back together (7)
13 - Wax drawing sticks (7)
14 - Blue semi precious gem (6)
16 - Greek goddess of wisdom (6)
18 - Japanese form of fencing (5)

No 34

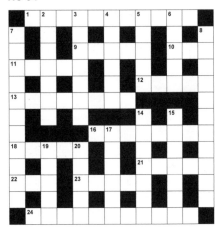

Across

1 - Junction of highways (11)
9 - Margin (5)
10 - King (3)
11 - Silly (5)
12 - Move sideways (5)
13 - Spend wastefully (8)
16 - Daydream (8)
18 - Cake decoration (5)
21 - Ancient Greek style (5)
22 - Vase (3)
23 - Vines (5)
24 - Spread rapidly (11)

Down

2 - Render utterly perplexed (7)
3 - Desiring (7)
4 - Shade of red (6)
5 - Regions (5)
6 - Pierced by bull (5)
7 - Diligent (11)
8 - Things that happen to you (11)
14 - Boxer (7)
15 - Sincere (7)
17 - Indirect tax (6)
19 - Interior (5)
20 - Cook food; broil (5)

No 35

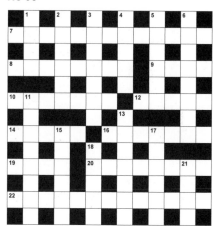

Across

7 - Fashionable (2-2-3-6)
8 - Overabundances (8)
9 - Child's plastic construction set (4)
10 - Moral rightness (7)
12 - Customary (5)
14 - Paces (5)
16 - Added up (7)
19 - Modify (4)
20 - Distinctively (8)
22 - Legerdemain (7,2,4)

Down

1 - Extreme point (4)
2 - Land covered with trees (6)
3 - Science of matter and energy (7)
4 - Wrong (5)
5 - Fishes (6)
6 - Stop progressing (8)
11 - Messily (8)
13 - Display unit (7)
15 - Slang; dialect (6)
17 - Nothing (6)
18 - Soft and comfortable (5)
21 - Solitary (4)

No 36

Across
1 - Pieces of evidence (6)
5 - Bristlelike appendage (3)
7 - Finished (5)
8 - Feared (7)
9 - Searches without warning (5)
10 - Resoluteness (8)
12 - Begins (6)
14 - Move faster than (6)
17 - Precarious (8)
18 - English royal house (5)
20 - Foretell (7)
21 - Lose consciousness (5)
22 - Beam of light (3)
23 - Tropical fly (6)

Down
2 - Cheese on toast (7)
3 - Form a union of states (8)
4 - Smell (4)
5 - A suitor (7)
6 - Communicators (7)
7 - Develop (5)
11 - Fairness (8)
12 - Suffocate (7)
13 - Make sour (7)
15 - Opens (7)
16 - Maladroit (5)
19 - Devastation (4)

No 37

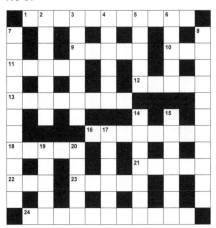

Across

1 - Manufacture (11)
9 - Thin biscuit (5)
10 - Double (3)
11 - More recent (5)
12 - Small nails (5)
13 - Pain in the neck (8)
16 - Projectile rebound (8)
18 - Comedian (5)
21 - Start (5)
22 - Nervous twitch (3)
23 - Jewel (5)
24 - Bullying (11)

Down

2 - Clumsy (7)
3 - Amended (7)
4 - Cotton or silk garment (6)
5 - Fortune telling card (5)
6 - Nerve in the eye (5)
7 - Declaim (11)
8 - Logical coherence (11)
14 - Person who mends shoes (7)
15 - Feeling of vexation (7)
17 - Breathe in (6)
19 - Extremely small (5)
20 - Island in the Bay of Naples (5)

No 38

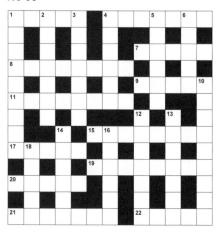

Across
1 - Succulent (5)
4 - Affluent (7)
7 - Propel forwards (5)
8 - Curiosity (8)
9 - Push away (5)
11 - Exemption (8)
15 - Gregarious bird (8)
17 - Information (5)
19 - Cane sugar (8)
20 - Flat-bottomed boat (5)
21 - Title of respect (7)
22 - Role; office (5)

Down
1 - Prejudiced; envious (9)
2 - Annoying (7)
3 - Expressing boredom (7)
4 - Compensate (6)
5 - Bigger (6)
6 - Brightening stars (5)
10 - Gloomy (4-5)
12 - Debts (7)
13 - Provide money for (7)
14 - Martial art (4,2)
16 - Grow teeth (6)
18 - Collect large quantities (5)

No 39

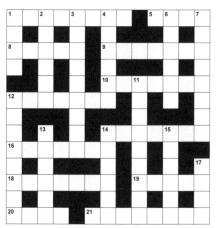

Across
1 - Assumed (8)
5 - Remove water from a boat (4)
8 - Not heavy (5)
9 - Terse (7)
10 - Restrain (7)
12 - Learns (7)
14 - Eccentricity (7)
16 - Supposed (7)
18 - Hot fire (7)
19 - Mix up (5)
20 - Facial feature (4)
21 - Judges (8)

Down
1 - Tablet (4)
2 - Hosiery (6)
3 - Doddering (9)
4 - Principles (6)
6 - Yearly (6)
7 - Permits (8)
11 - Person who seeks an office (9)
12 - German Shepherd dog (8)
13 - Steep faces of rock (6)
14 - Detestable (6)
15 - Escapes (6)
17 - Chief god of ancient Greece (4)

No 40

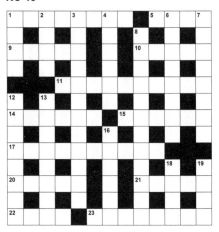

Across
1 - Resembling a tree (8)
5 - Intellectual faculty (4)
9 - Indian of Mexico (5)
10 - Pertaining to warships (5)
11 - Conveying to destination (10)
14 - Not uniform (6)
15 - Thrown about (6)
17 - A written record (5,5)
20 - Muscular strength (5)
21 - Accustom (5)
22 - Sweet potatoes (4)
23 - Small spined mammal (8)

Down
1 - Unfortunately (4)
2 - Flying mammals (4)
3 - Swindling (12)
4 - Nimble (6)
6 - Financial statements (8)
7 - Industrious (8)
8 - Amusing (12)
12 - Guiltily (8)
13 - New growth (8)
16 - Sweet dish (6)
18 - Sentimentality (4)
19 - Mass of floating ice (4)

No 41

Across

1 - Colorless flammable gas (6)
4 - Small chicken (6)
9 - Dark pigment in skin (7)
10 - Washing and finishing (7)
11 - Sound (5)
12 - Kinswoman (5)
14 - Utilizing (5)
15 - Pertaining to bees (5)
17 - Upper part of the leg (5)
18 - Pasta pockets (7)
20 - Stimulated (7)
21 - Even paced (6)
22 - Remarks (6)

Down

1 - Fur (6)
2 - Capital of Finland (8)
3 - The present occasion (5)
5 - Mixing up (7)
6 - Cab (4)
7 - Injure severely (6)
8 - Shoddiness (11)
13 - Allowed (8)
14 - Relaxed (7)
15 - Projectiles (6)
16 - Protects from heat (6)
17 - Tortilla wraps (5)
19 - Ballot choice (4)

No 42

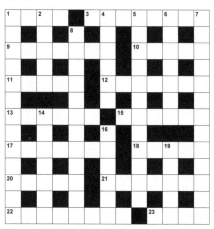

Across

1 - Domesticated (4)
3 - Ornamental climbing plant (8)
9 - Postpone (7)
10 - Group of shots (5)
11 - Rides waves (5)
12 - Scientist (7)
13 - Loud noise (6)
15 - Starting point (6)
17 - Schedule of activities (7)
18 - Fight (3-2)
20 - Decorative filling (5)
21 - Adaptable garden plants (7)
22 - Denominated (8)
23 - Catch sight of (4)

Down

1 - Musical arrangement (13)
2 - Army rank (5)
4 - Insanity (6)
5 - Falsify (12)
6 - Bending (7)
7 - Impulsively (13)
8 - Short poem for children (7,5)
14 - Dilemma (7)
16 - Pierce (6)
19 - Receptacles (5)

No 43

Across
1 - Change gradually (6)
3 - Interfere (6)
7 - Stylishness (9)
9 - Mechanize (8)
10 - Spaces (4)
12 - Environment (5)
13 - Be (5)
17 - Soothing remedy (4)
18 - Cookies (8)
20 - Criterion (9)
21 - Most secure (6)
22 - Self-centered person (6)

Down
1 - Make beloved (6)
2 - Essential nutrients (8)
4 - Saw; observed (4)
5 - Create raised lettering (6)
6 - Long narrow estuary (5)
7 - Inherently (9)
8 - Boisterous comedy (9)
11 - Ask (8)
14 - Church buildings (6)
15 - In the middle of (5)
16 - Characteristic (6)
19 - Makes mistakes (4)

No 44

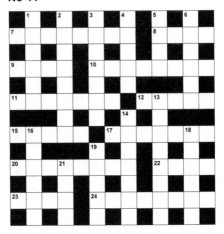

Across

7 - Immediately after this (8)
8 - Device for securing (4)
9 - Sure (anag) (4)
10 - Capability (8)
11 - Mischief (7)
12 - Opposite of lows (5)
15 - Push (5)
17 - Area of ground (7)
20 - Fervid (5-3)
22 - Depart from (4)
23 - System (4)
24 - Defector (8)

Down

1 - Tenant (6)
2 - Discovering (8)
3 - Connoisseur (7)
4 - Awkward (5)
5 - Coalition (4)
6 - Put an end to (6)
13 - Large bodies of frozen water (8)
14 - Solvent; adhesive (7)
16 - Maintain (6)
18 - Wears down (6)
19 - Carnivorous fish (5)
21 - Makes brown (4)

No 45

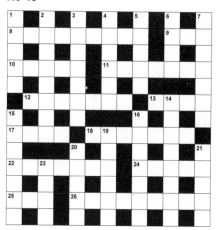

Across

8 - Place side by side (9)
9 - Residue of a fire (3)
10 - Body of water (5)
11 - Vagrant (7)
12 - Keepsake; reminder (7)
13 - Freshwater game fish (4)
17 - Solely (4)
18 - Dispute (7)
22 - Shoulder bone (7)
24 - Thrash (5)
25 - Seed (3)
26 - Removing particles (9)

Down

1 - Go swiftly (5)
2 - Wild flower (8)
3 - Speak in response (7)
4 - Outlaw (6)
5 - Strange and mysterious (5)
6 - Ultimate (4)
7 - Thus (7)
14 - Pertaining to Spain (8)
15 - Chats about someone else (7)
16 - Manned (7)
19 - Diviner (6)
20 - Forelock of hair (5)
21 - Bring into a line (5)
23 - Swiss mountains (4)

No 46

Across
1 - Venison meat (4)
3 - Strong coffee (8)
9 - Male laborers (7)
10 - Decrease; quench (5)
11 - Recurrently (12)
13 - Slovenly (6)
15 - Contort (6)
17 - Useless (12)
20 - Palpitate (5)
21 - Optician (7)
22 - Illnesses (8)
23 - Lose grip (4)

Down
1 - Heavy rain (8)
2 - Fault (5)
4 - Naturally illuminated (6)
5 - Eating place proprietor (12)
6 - Bright red color (7)
7 - Comply (4)
8 - Uncertainty (12)
12 - Returned to type (8)
14 - Slender stemlike appendage (7)
16 - Exertion (6)
18 - Clay block (5)
19 - Volcano in Sicily (4)

No 47

Across
1 - Roman god of fire (6)
4 - Very milky (6)
7 - Piece for a soloist and orchestra (8)
8 - Content word (4)
9 - Official language of Pakistan (4)
11 - Greek god of love (4)
12 - Hit hard (7)
13 - Timid (3)
15 - Belonging to him (3)
17 - Slanted characters (7)
19 - Color properties (4)
20 - Entering (4)
21 - Sharp bristle (4)
22 - Warm to excess (8)
24 - Hankers after (6)
25 - Infuriate (6)

Down
1 - Empty spaces (7)
2 - Desert plant (6)
3 - And not (3)
4 - Held together by cultural ties (5-4)
5 - Wanted; desired (6)
6 - Radio pioneer (7)
10 - Spacious (9)
14 - Towage (7)
16 - Lessen (7)
17 - Line of equal pressure (6)
18 - Let out breath (6)
23 - Tree (3)

No 48

Across
1 - Beer (5)
4 - Part of telephone (7)
7 - Burning (5)
8 - Impending (8)
9 - Altar stone (5)
11 - Engrave (8)
15 - Intelligentsia (8)
17 - Once more (5)
19 - Overflowing (8)
20 - Up and about (5)
21 - Normally (7)
22 - Kitchen appliance (5)

Down
1 - State in the S United States (9)
2 - A look (7)
3 - Competitors in a race (7)
4 - Fraternize (6)
5 - Holds out (6)
6 - Acquires (5)
10 - Height-measuring instrument (9)
12 - Perplexed (7)
13 - Scared (7)
14 - Smallest quantities (6)
16 - Dishonor (6)
18 - Strong winds (5)

No 49

Across

7 - Pivot (6)
8 - Barbed (6)
9 - Smell (4)
10 - Scruffily (8)
11 - Blaze fighters (7)
13 - Apart from (5)
15 - Norwegian (5)
16 - Most crinkled (7)
18 - Shipwrecked person (8)
19 - Encourage in wrongdoing (4)
21 - Cowardly (6)
22 - Empty (6)

Down

1 - Inspired by reverence (4)
2 - Unduly thin-skinned (13)
3 - Splashed water (7)
4 - Role; office (5)
5 - In a grandiose manner (13)
6 - Incorporates (8)
12 - Worship (8)
14 - Bulrush (7)
17 - ___ flu: form of influenza (5)
20 - Test (4)

No 50

Across
7 - Flower (13)
8 - Divine manifestation (8)
9 - Halt (4)
10 - Tightly framed camera shot (5,2)
12 - ___ Ababa: Ethiopian capital (5)
14 - Shadow (5)
16 - Documents (7)
19 - Midge (4)
20 - Precipitation (8)
22 - Consideration for others (13)

Down
1 - Male (4)
2 - Larvae (6)
3 - Short-tailed monkey (7)
4 - Remains (5)
5 - Familiarized (6)
6 - Writer with an amusing style (8)
11 - Layered material (8)
13 - Ameliorate (7)
15 - Decayed (6)
17 - Near future (6)
18 - Soup; liquid meal (5)
21 - Final (4)

No 51

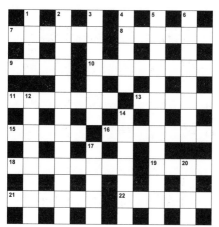

Across

7 - Alcoholic beverage (6)
8 - Flight of steps (6)
9 - Essential substance (4)
10 - Reflect (8)
11 - Disdained (7)
13 - Written form of music (5)
15 - Rides horseback (5)
16 - Biting with teeth (7)
18 - Short lyric poem (8)
19 - Accent (4)
21 - Scented ointment (6)
22 - Loses consciousness (6)

Down

1 - Prefix for small (4)
2 - Tyrannical person (13)
3 - Brass wind instrument (7)
4 - Apart from (5)
5 - Involvement (13)
6 - Brothers (8)
12 - Rhizomatous herb (8)
14 - Uncovered (7)
17 - Concur (5)
20 - Religious women (4)

No 52

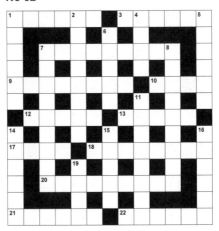

Across
1 - Confirm (6)
3 - Wading birds (6)
7 - Banal statement (9)
9 - Act a part (8)
10 - Having pains (4)
12 - Small egg (5)
13 - Savor (5)
17 - Fit of shivering (4)
18 - A Roman emperor (8)
20 - Entry gate (9)
21 - Post (6)
22 - Ancient (3-3)

Down
1 - Electorate (6)
2 - Tall staff (8)
4 - Larva (4)
5 - Spreads out (6)
6 - Spring tree (5)
7 - Jumping competition (4,5)
8 - Stockade (9)
11 - Alluring (8)
14 - Order to report for duty (4,2)
15 - Stern (5)
16 - Elevated (6)
19 - Killer whale (4)

No 53

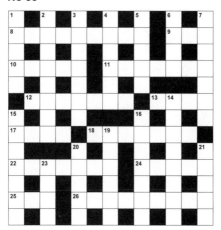

Across

8 - Less well behaved (9)
9 - Scarf of feathers or fur (3)
10 - Many times (5)
11 - Combined (7)
12 - Elevate (7)
13 - Long poem (4)
17 - Singles (4)
18 - Licentious (7)
22 - Motor home (7)
24 - Rides horseback (5)
25 - Vitality (3)
26 - Memory (9)

Down

1 - Negative ion (5)
2 - Several (8)
3 - Gossip (7)
4 - Sofas (6)
5 - Adornment (5)
6 - Skillfully (4)
7 - Fish (7)
14 - Free from sensual desire (8)
15 - Make up (7)
16 - Foreshadow (7)
19 - Memorandum (6)
20 - Forestall (5)
21 - Utilizing (5)
23 - Fresh water (4)

No 54

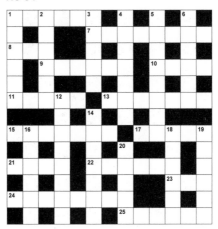

Across
1 - Violin (6)
7 - Unbranded range animal (8)
8 - Positive answer (3)
9 - Insertion points (6)
10 - Intellect (4)
11 - Eg oxygen and nitrogen (5)
13 - Developed gradually (7)
15 - Ceremonial staff (7)
17 - Select; choose (5)
21 - Storage barn (4)
22 - Infinitesimally small (6)
23 - Possesses (3)
24 - Christmas season (8)
25 - Donors (anag) (6)

Down
1 - Traveling by air (6)
2 - Dances (6)
3 - Last light of fire (5)
4 - Elusive (7)
5 - Creased (8)
6 - Charge (6)
12 - Worker (8)
14 - Dark pigment in skin (7)
16 - Exclusive circle (6)
18 - Flowering plant (6)
19 - Deforms (6)
20 - Comedian (5)

No 55

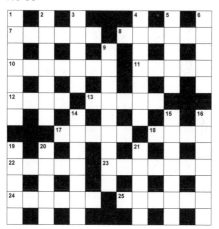

Across

7 - Capital of Canada (6)
8 - Look through casually (6)
10 - Dry red table wine of Italy (7)
11 - Initial item; beginning (5)
12 - Set up (4)
13 - Curve (5)
17 - Tries out (5)
18 - Trademark (4)
22 - Weary (5)
23 - Cloths (7)
24 - Self-supporting structures (6)
25 - Rough shelter (4-2)

Down

1 - Refuse to sponsor (7)
2 - Marks of a zebra (7)
3 - Large white birds (5)
4 - Fabled monster (7)
5 - Give merit (5)
6 - Spiritual being (5)
9 - Shaft of a weapon (9)
14 - Person who interferes (7)
15 - Toiletries (7)
16 - Active part of fire (7)
19 - Plant fiber (5)
20 - Short written work (5)
21 - Church building (5)

No 56

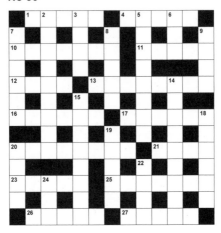

Across

1 - Apart from (5)
4 - Own up to (5)
10 - Proclaim (7)
11 - Major African river (5)
12 - Smudge (4)
13 - Spacecraft (8)
16 - Chooses (6)
17 - Deliberately catch out (6)
20 - Associated with employment (2-3-3)
21 - Nothing (4)
23 - Ticked over (5)
25 - Circling around (7)
26 - Secret agents (5)
27 - Compositions in verse (5)

Down

2 - Juicy (9)
3 - Transaction (4)
5 - Particular policy taught (8)
6 - Hotel (3)
7 - Fit for consumption (6)
8 - Petulant (5)
9 - Poultry enclosure (4)
14 - Keyboard instrument (9)
15 - Participant in a meeting (8)
18 - Solemn promise (6)
19 - Loses heat (5)
20 - Roman poet (4)
22 - Training hall (4)
24 - Cut away (3)

No 57

Across
1 - Sanitary (8)
6 - Doubtful (4)
8 - Beepers (6)
9 - Yield (6)
10 - Young child; small quantity (3)
11 - First man (4)
12 - Herb with oil rich seeds (6)
13 - Cord (6)
15 - Continue (6)
17 - Candy (6)
20 - Cool and collected (4)
21 - Of recent origin (3)
22 - Exertion (6)
23 - Crazy (6)
24 - Vases (4)
25 - Relinquishing (8)

Down
2 - A long time ago (4,3)
3 - Small intestine (5)
4 - Tensing (anag) (7)
5 - Converses (5)
6 - Fills with (7)
7 - Meeting (5)
14 - Influxes (7)
15 - Beverage made from grapes (3,4)
16 - Dark pigment in skin (7)
18 - Suggest (5)
19 - Written account (5)
20 - Enclosed (5)

No 58

Across
1 - Fairness (6)
5 - Burrowing marsupial (6)
8 - Helps (4)
9 - Repaired (8)
10 - Motionless (5)
11 - Merit (7)
14 - Capable of being understood (13)
16 - Fashion anew (7)
18 - Group together (5)
20 - Greek meat casserole (8)
22 - Incline (4)
23 - Biochemical catalyst (6)
24 - Displays (6)

Down
2 - Fivefold (9)
3 - Narrowly restricted in scope (7)
4 - Three feet length (4)
5 - Genre of movies (8)
6 - Deer (5)
7 - Affirmative vote (3)
12 - Done by free choice (9)
13 - Fellow crew member (8)
15 - Used by asthma sufferers (7)
17 - Hurried (5)
19 - A laugh (2,2)
21 - Possess (3)

No 59

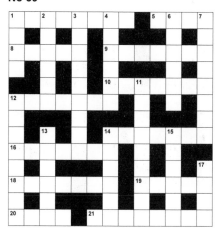

Across
1 - Make fun of (8)
5 - Confine (4)
8 - Requirements (5)
9 - Court game (7)
10 - Shuns (7)
12 - Traveler (7)
14 - With an oblique glance (7)
16 - Plots (7)
18 - Put into action (7)
19 - Rustic (5)
20 - 24 hour periods (4)
21 - Surreptitious traveler (8)

Down
1 - Outer covering (4)
2 - Showy (6)
3 - Reprimand severely (9)
4 - For more time (6)
6 - Moved about aimlessly (6)
7 - Fence of stakes (8)
11 - Bottle opener (9)
12 - Front of an advancing army (8)
13 - Sandy (6)
14 - Feature (6)
15 - Of little width (6)
17 - Associate (4)

No 60

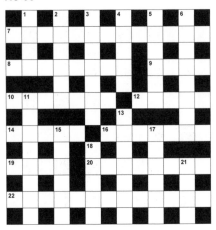

Across

7 - Obsoletely (13)
8 - Traveling too fast (8)
9 - Curse; solemn promise (4)
10 - Creaky (7)
12 - Halts (5)
14 - Small salamanders (5)
16 - Dishonest (7)
19 - Displace (4)
20 - Eland (8)
22 - Absence (13)

Down

1 - Break (4)
2 - Reproductive cell (6)
3 - Gets smaller (7)
4 - Red cosmetic (5)
5 - Highly seasoned stew (6)
6 - Monotreme (8)
11 - Interrogative sentence (8)
13 - First letter (7)
15 - Weave (6)
17 - Roman god of fire (6)
18 - Freshwater fish (5)
21 - Brownish purple (4)

No 61

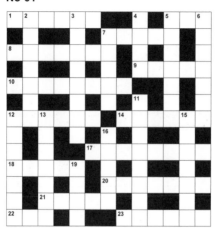

Across
1 - Happens (6)
5 - Vitality (3)
7 - Haze (5)
8 - Bolero rhythm dance (7)
9 - Farm (5)
10 - Form of precipitation (8)
12 - Weakly (6)
14 - Falls down (6)
17 - Woolen clothing (8)
18 - Submerged ridges of rock (5)
20 - Stupid (7)
21 - Musical movement (5)
22 - Fairy (3)
23 - Had in common (6)

Down
2 - Remove impurities (7)
3 - Precipitation (8)
4 - Box lightly (4)
5 - Flinched away (7)
6 - Narrow strip of land (7)
7 - Concealing garments (5)
11 - Eg plaice (8)
12 - Walking stick cap (7)
13 - Become less intense (4,3)
15 - Analyze (7)
16 - Remove binding (5)
19 - Heroic tale (4)

No 62

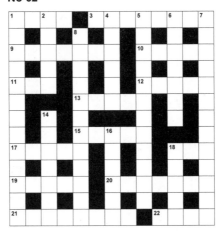

Across
1 - ___ Ruth: baseball star (4)
3 - Bivalve mollusks (8)
9 - Insanity (7)
10 - Of the nose (5)
11 - Era (anag) (3)
12 - Accustom (5)
13 - Thorax (5)
15 - Recorded (5)
17 - Small woodland (5)
18 - Affirmative vote (3)
19 - Iterations (5)
20 - Multi-span structure (7)
21 - Longing (8)
22 - Resist (4)

Down
1 - In a grandiose manner (13)
2 - Form of identification (5)
4 - Trigonometrical ratio (6)
5 - Running lengthwise (12)
6 - Unknown (7)
7 - Obviously (4-9)
8 - Food shop (12)
14 - Certificate (7)
16 - Established as true (6)
18 - Give pleasure (5)

No 63

Across

7 - Assailed (8)
8 - Very small (4)
9 - Irritation (4)
10 - Pest in the roof (8)
11 - Title of respect (7)
12 - Horned ruminant mammal (5)
15 - Extra terrestrial (5)
17 - Planned (7)
20 - Extraordinarily good (8)
22 - Crazy (4)
23 - None (anag) (4)
24 - Rays of light (8)

Down

1 - Prestige (6)
2 - Asylum (8)
3 - Long pins (7)
4 - Supplementary component (3-2)
5 - Pack (4)
6 - Food starter (6)
13 - Hotel-keeper (8)
14 - Graceful in form (7)
16 - Hired out (6)
18 - Live in a tent (6)
19 - Wash off soap or dirt (5)
21 - Large quantities (4)

No 64

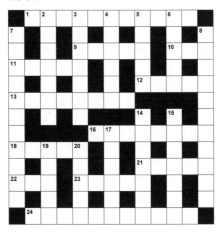

Across
1 - Gallant (11)
9 - Customary (5)
10 - An edible mushroom (3)
11 - Loans (anag) (5)
12 - Very simple (5)
13 - Eternal (8)
16 - Envy (8)
18 - Public transport vehicles (5)
21 - Dessert (5)
22 - Airtight container (3)
23 - Big cats (5)
24 - Pointlessly (11)

Down
2 - Symbols (7)
3 - Roll (7)
4 - Escapes (6)
5 - Spontaneous remark (2-3)
6 - Laps up with tongue (5)
7 - Transfer responsibility (4,3,4)
8 - Prophetic of devastation (11)
14 - School groups (7)
15 - Universal remedy (4-3)
17 - Register (6)
19 - From a specified time (5)
20 - Grain stores (5)

No 65

Across

1 - Rocks (6)
5 - British currency (plural) (6)
8 - Tool (4)
9 - Extreme bitterness (8)
10 - Equipment (5)
11 - Nonconformist (7)
14 - Opposing (13)
16 - Portable enclosure for infants (7)
18 - Involuntary muscle contraction (5)
20 - Printmaking technique (8)
22 - Before long (4)
23 - Miserly (6)
24 - Bear witness (6)

Down

2 - Speedboat (9)
3 - Citadel of Moscow (7)
4 - Heat; burn (4)
5 - Grated Italian cheese (8)
6 - Unwarranted (5)
7 - Small spot (3)
12 - Capitalists (9)
13 - Reassign (8)
15 - Prepare for printing (7)
17 - Long for (5)
19 - Tiny amount (4)
21 - Seed (3)

No 66

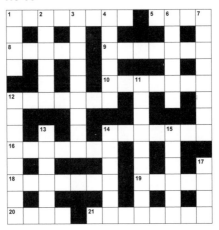

Across
1 - Lavish (8)
5 - Capital of Norway (4)
8 - Enters on a keyboard (5)
9 - Coatings (7)
10 - Hard white substances (7)
12 - Prevented (7)
14 - Disposed to love (7)
16 - Examined hastily (7)
18 - Let out (7)
19 - Live (5)
20 - Soaks up (4)
21 - Fated (8)

Down
1 - Essential substance (4)
2 - Obligate (6)
3 - A stopping (9)
4 - Taxed (6)
6 - Israeli monetary unit (6)
7 - Preoccupies (8)
11 - Tending to take in (9)
12 - Unit of length (8)
13 - Order to report for duty (4,2)
14 - Stick to (6)
15 - Choice (6)
17 - Horse breeding stable (4)

No 67

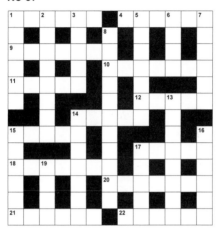

Across
1 - Strong (6)
4 - Deep pit (6)
9 - Hide (7)
10 - Excessive freedom (7)
11 - External (5)
12 - Tests (5)
14 - Respect (5)
15 - Dog like mammal (5)
17 - Big (5)
18 - Present for acceptance (7)
20 - Shut in (7)
21 - Holds up (6)
22 - Throws away (6)

Down
1 - Millionth of a meter (6)
2 - Grammatical case (8)
3 - Belonging to them (5)
5 - Farmer (7)
6 - Substantive word (4)
7 - Foot travelers (6)
8 - Poorly behaved (3-8)
13 - Plane's control surfaces (8)
14 - Midpoint (7)
15 - Jumped on one leg (6)
16 - Spirited horses (6)
17 - Lizard (5)
19 - Translucent mineral (4)

No 68

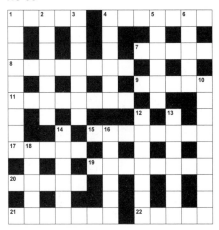

Across
1 - Exhaust gases (5)
4 - Mundane (7)
7 - Worthy principle or aim (5)
8 - Intrinsically (8)
9 - Precious stone (5)
11 - Period during which you live (8)
15 - Playful (8)
17 - Not as expected (5)
19 - Male child of your child (8)
20 - Fragile (5)
21 - Big cat (7)
22 - Declamations (5)

Down
1 - Unproductive (9)
2 - Enlarge (7)
3 - Enactment (7)
4 - Examination (6)
5 - Capital of New South Wales (6)
6 - Republic in S Europe (5)
10 - Gracefulness (9)
12 - Smasher (7)
13 - Task (7)
14 - Tips and instruction (6)
16 - Brandy distilled from cherries (6)
18 - Stern (5)

No 69

Across
1 - Small wave (6)
5 - Speak solemnly (6)
8 - Encourage in wrongdoing (4)
9 - Cookies (8)
10 - Engross oneself in (5)
11 - Letter (7)
14 - Strengthening (13)
16 - Annulling (7)
18 - Interior (5)
20 - Green vegetable (8)
22 - Skating venue (4)
23 - Opposite of greater (6)
24 - Bullet (6)

Down
2 - Intermediate (2-7)
3 - Template (7)
4 - Falls back (4)
5 - Inclination (8)
6 - Hits (5)
7 - Negative (3)
12 - Revenge (9)
13 - Heavy rain (8)
15 - Ore (7)
17 - Killer whales (5)
19 - Speech defect (4)
21 - Fish eggs (3)

No 70

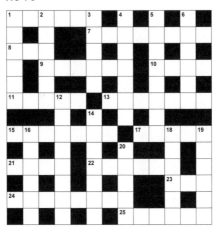

Across
1 - Dwarfed tree (6)
7 - Delay (8)
8 - And not (3)
9 - Improvise (4,2)
10 - Support (4)
11 - Dole out (5)
13 - Loving (7)
15 - Mislead (7)
17 - Aromatic resin (5)
21 - Blemish (4)
22 - Rational thought (6)
23 - Sticky substance (3)
24 - An unscheduled contact (4,4)
25 - Violent weather phenomena (6)

Down
1 - Yellow fruit (6)
2 - Standard (6)
3 - Did nothing (5)
4 - Has financial means (7)
5 - Correctly (8)
6 - Strand (6)
12 - Countermand (8)
14 - Cover (7)
16 - Holding of funds (6)
18 - Person who tolls bell (6)
19 - Wading birds (6)
20 - Shopping areas (5)

No 71

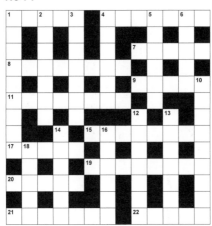

Across
1 - Simpleton (5)
4 - Revolving (7)
7 - Neck warmer (5)
8 - Pre Christian belief (8)
9 - Sniff (5)
11 - Write notes (8)
15 - Left to one's choice (8)
17 - Undersea swimmer (5)
19 - Spacecraft (8)
20 - Any finger or toe (5)
21 - Decisions (7)
22 - Levels out (5)

Down
1 - Showed (9)
2 - Pestering (7)
3 - Issue forth (7)
4 - Compensate (6)
5 - Money coming in (6)
6 - Fourth month (5)
10 - Round sweets on sticks (9)
12 - Chemical fertilizer (7)
13 - Excite (7)
14 - Third sign of the zodiac (6)
16 - Flower parts (6)
18 - Inhabitants of Ireland (5)

No 72

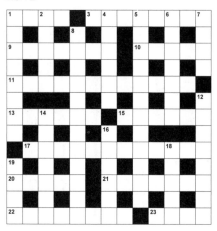

Across
1 - Titled peer (4)
3 - Bodily structure (8)
9 - Mediterranean resort area (7)
10 - Repasts (5)
11 - Praise (12)
13 - Untamed (6)
15 - Skin stain (6)
17 - Rarely (12)
20 - Rice dish (5)
21 - Artistic movement (3,4)
22 - Cosmic particles (8)
23 - Opposite of front (4)

Down
1 - Writer of song words (8)
2 - Large crow (5)
4 - Playing cards suit (6)
5 - Concurrency (12)
6 - Four singers (7)
7 - Otherwise (4)
8 - Amusement park ride (5-2-5)
12 - Exterior of a motor vehicle (8)
14 - Flavoring prepared from pods (7)
16 - Leg exercises (6)
18 - Eighth Greek letter (5)
19 - Musical composition (4)

No 73

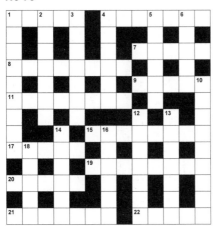

Across
1 - Due to someone (5)
4 - Manservant (7)
7 - Joyous (5)
8 - Water-resistant jacket (8)
9 - Incites (5)
11 - Juvenile (8)
15 - Green vegetable (8)
17 - Rank (5)
19 - Abnormal (8)
20 - Up and about (5)
21 - Matter (7)
22 - Kingdom (5)

Down
1 - Functioning (9)
2 - Provokes (7)
3 - Icy (7)
4 - Rummage (6)
5 - Vibration (6)
6 - Bitterly pungent (5)
10 - Leftism (9)
12 - Staff (7)
13 - Musical composition (7)
14 - Suggest (6)
16 - Child's toy (6)
18 - Decays (5)

No 74

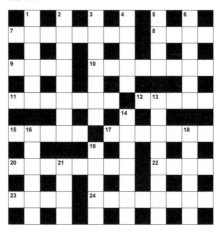

Across

7 - Acrimoniously (8)
8 - Ellipse (4)
9 - Domesticated ox (4)
10 - Tack with a large head (8)
11 - Witty saying (7)
12 - Bring into a line (5)
15 - Disturbed (5)
17 - Creamy chocolate candy (7)
20 - Small spined mammal (8)
22 - Soothing remedy (4)
23 - Hilltop (4)
24 - Legal instruments (8)

Down

1 - Abandon; drop out (4,2)
2 - Strive (8)
3 - Not sudden (7)
4 - Textile (5)
5 - Content word (4)
6 - Betting (6)
13 - Sea rescue vessel (8)
14 - Fire breathers (7)
16 - Metrical writing (6)
18 - Drooped (6)
19 - Gong (5)
21 - Gape (4)

No 75

Across

1 - Office table (4)
3 - Morally compel (8)
9 - Eastern governors (7)
10 - Fleshy (5)
11 - Personal pride (3)
12 - Stated (5)
13 - Recorded (5)
15 - Region (5)
17 - Defense (5)
18 - Correlation coefficient (3)
19 - Inactive (5)
20 - Machine workers (7)
21 - Observing (8)
22 - Group of women (4)

Down

1 - Circulation (13)
2 - Fight (3-2)
4 - Spiritual head of a diocese (6)
5 - Uncertain (12)
6 - Living in water (7)
7 - Efficiently (13)
8 - Favoring private ownership (12)
14 - Plain (7)
16 - Sovereign's bodyguards (6)
18 - Historical local official (5)

No 76

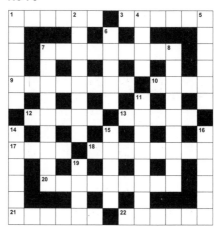

Across

1 - Characteristic of a young male (6)
3 - Place of education (6)
7 - Bird frightener (9)
9 - Separating the notes (8)
10 - Piece of land (4)
12 - Links together (5)
13 - Valleys (5)
17 - Fourth Gospel (4)
18 - Messily (8)
20 - Young racehorses (9)
21 - Foul-smelling (6)
22 - Confirm (6)

Down

1 - Look through casually (6)
2 - Deficiency (8)
4 - Suppress (4)
5 - Women (6)
6 - Openings (5)
7 - Loyally (9)
8 - Trivial deceptions (5,4)
11 - Cheerful brightness (8)
14 - Expels (6)
15 - Hill (5)
16 - Exemplify (6)
19 - Prepare for holiday (4)

No 77

Across

1 - In the prevailing musical key (8)
6 - Catwalk posture (4)
8 - Third sign of the zodiac (6)
9 - Wonder at (6)
10 - Vitality (3)
11 - Avoid; be without (4)
12 - Lines up (6)
13 - Scanty (6)
15 - Lots of (6)
17 - Chest (6)
20 - Plant with flavor (4)
21 - Nevertheless (3)
22 - Say again (6)
23 - Eagles' nests (6)
24 - Puts down (4)
25 - Driver (8)

Down

2 - Tool for the Arctic (3-4)
3 - Neatens (5)
4 - Innocently (7)
5 - Punctuation mark (5)
6 - Hoggish (7)
7 - Shininess (5)
14 - Social exchange structures (7)
15 - Defend (7)
16 - Goals at work (7)
18 - Dog like mammal (5)
19 - Plant tissue (5)
20 - Employer (5)

No 78

Across
1 - Calculating machine (6)
5 - Enclosure (3)
7 - Empty spaces (5)
8 - Skill (7)
9 - Shrub (5)
10 - Early period of human culture (5,3)
12 - Top; positive gain (6)
14 - Arithmetic operators (6)
17 - Weak part (4,4)
18 - Not concealed (5)
20 - Expertise (4-3)
21 - Striped animal (5)
22 - Downhill snow shoe (3)
23 - A metrical foot (6)

Down
2 - Peopled with settlers (5-2)
3 - Unstable (8)
4 - Having pains (4)
5 - Mends (7)
6 - Works against (7)
7 - Margin (5)
11 - Excess (8)
12 - Supports (7)
13 - Musical movements (7)
15 - Efficiency (7)
16 - Russian liquor (5)
19 - Hollow conduit (4)

No 79

Across
1 - Sample of cloth (6)
5 - Confer (6)
8 - Ice (4)
9 - Amicable (8)
10 - Softly radiant (5)
11 - Flower shop (7)
14 - Things that are given (13)
16 - Transportation (7)
18 - Unconditional love (5)
20 - Detested person (8)
22 - Swiss mountains (4)
23 - Unemotional (6)
24 - Destitution (6)

Down
2 - Criminal (9)
3 - Transpire (4,3)
4 - Watering device (4)
5 - Rod-shaped bacterium (8)
6 - Elevated step (5)
7 - Night bird (3)
12 - Abrasive (9)
13 - Bonus (8)
15 - Fix deeply (7)
17 - Area in South Africa (5)
19 - Torch (4)
21 - Divides tennis court (3)

No 80

Across
1 - Fuss; harass (6)
4 - Afloat (6)
9 - Mythical firebird (7)
10 - Dyestuff (7)
11 - Borders (5)
12 - Hoarder (5)
14 - Travels in water (5)
15 - Procreate (5)
17 - Releases on payment (5)
18 - Stupid (7)
20 - Arabic domain (7)
21 - Frames (6)
22 - Restores (6)

Down
1 - Occur (6)
2 - Hitting very hard (8)
3 - Breathing organs (5)
5 - Fairground vehicles (7)
6 - Not in action (4)
7 - Stifled laugh (6)
8 - Things that happen to you (11)
13 - Be envious (8)
14 - Enactment (7)
15 - Building materials (6)
16 - Determine the value (6)
17 - Seawater (5)
19 - Hotels (4)

No 81

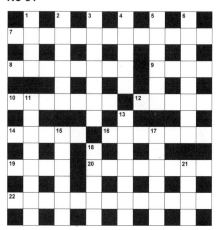

Across

7 - Admirably (13)
8 - Achieve maximum efficiency (8)
9 - Fever (4)
10 - Part of a gun (7)
12 - Ancient object (5)
14 - Insect larva (5)
16 - Affluent (7)
19 - Keep away from (4)
20 - Giving out (8)
22 - Prone to steal (5-8)

Down

1 - Turn over (4)
2 - Purchasing (6)
3 - Walks with long steps (7)
4 - Green citrus fruits (5)
5 - Component of natural gas (6)
6 - Thrive (8)
11 - Recurring with regularity (8)
13 - Functional drawings (7)
15 - Mexican cloak (6)
17 - Surface quality (6)
18 - Muscular (5)
21 - Change course (4)

No 82

Across
1 - Relating to wolves (6)
4 - Rectitude (6)
9 - Japanese dish of raw fish (7)
10 - Perform again (7)
11 - Ground (5)
12 - Cloak (5)
14 - Covered with water (5)
15 - Mound of stones (5)
17 - Linear units (5)
18 - Enhance (7)
20 - Respired (7)
21 - A series of prayers (6)
22 - Loops of rope (6)

Down
1 - Itemized (6)
2 - Highly seasoned smoked beef (8)
3 - Animal cry (5)
5 - Thoroughly (2,5)
6 - Garment of ancient Rome (4)
7 - Excitingly strange (6)
8 - Ornithologist (4,7)
13 - Low-cost travel package (2-6)
14 - Shaped like a ring (7)
15 - Where two streets meet (6)
16 - Remarks (6)
17 - Loutish male (5)
19 - Draws (4)

No 83

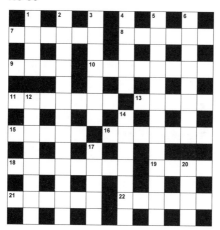

Across

7 - Drumbeat (6)
8 - Middle (6)
9 - Wizard (4)
10 - Increase in number (8)
11 - Induct (7)
13 - Musical note (5)
15 - Meat juices (5)
16 - Personal property (7)
18 - Crustacean (8)
19 - Hybrid animal (4)
21 - Botch (4-2)
22 - Possessors (6)

Down

1 - Main island of Indonesia (4)
2 - Consideration for others (13)
3 - Travel back and forth regularly (7)
4 - Parboil (5)
5 - Type of medication (13)
6 - Hour for eating (8)
12 - Reads out (8)
14 - What footwear comes in (7)
17 - Extent (5)
20 - Conceal (4)

No 84

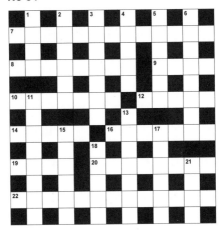

Across

7 - Curiously (13)
8 - Arenas (8)
9 - Deficiency (4)
10 - A person (7)
12 - More recent (5)
14 - Light downy particles (5)
16 - Postpone (7)
19 - Affirm with confidence (4)
20 - Advanced medical student (8)
22 - Private accommodation (8,5)

Down

1 - Midge (4)
2 - Group discussion (6)
3 - Supplying (7)
4 - Hiding place (5)
5 - Slender (6)
6 - Signal that danger is over (3,5)
11 - Total forgetfulness (8)
13 - Declare to be (7)
15 - Sudden outburst (6)
17 - Dark spotted wildcat (6)
18 - Belonging to them (5)
21 - Too (4)

No 85

Across
1 - Edible tuber (6)
4 - Areas of strong current (6)
7 - Refer to famous people (8)
8 - Ring (4)
9 - Lower the temperature (4)
11 - Orient (4)
12 - Multiplied by two (7)
13 - Measure of length (3)
15 - Sovereign government (3)
17 - Runs through (7)
19 - Ruse (anag) (4)
20 - Burn (4)
21 - Capital of Peru (4)
22 - Positive disposition (8)
24 - Wading birds (6)
25 - American inventor (6)

Down
1 - Elegance (7)
2 - Ancient (3-3)
3 - Used to row a boat (3)
4 - Reissue (9)
5 - Burst open (6)
6 - Very salty lake (4,3)
10 - Sumptuous (9)
14 - Enduring (7)
16 - Court panelists (7)
17 - Make (6)
18 - Prawns (6)
23 - Bind (3)

No 86

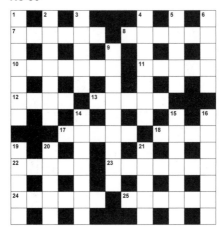

Across

7 - Harass (6)
8 - Trifles (6)
10 - Edible fruit (7)
11 - Take away by force (5)
12 - Slimy fish (4)
13 - Play a guitar (5)
17 - Homeless cat (5)
18 - Back of neck (4)
22 - Kingdom (5)
23 - Declaring (7)
24 - Required (6)
25 - Straying from the right course (6)

Down

1 - Broke the rules (7)
2 - Learning institutions (7)
3 - Sheep's sound (5)
4 - Closely cropped hairstyle (4,3)
5 - Climbing plants (5)
6 - Floating platforms (5)
9 - Representation (9)
14 - Speak haltingly (7)
15 - Uppercase (7)
16 - Elevations (7)
19 - Fork (5)
20 - Tangle; complicate (5)
21 - Excursions (5)

No 87

Across

7 - People who construct things (8)
8 - Contest between two persons (4)
9 - Lattice (4)
10 - Cultivated tufted grass (8)
11 - Important hormone (7)
12 - Stage (5)
15 - Emits a breath (5)
17 - Obtaining (7)
20 - Overflowing (8)
22 - Religious custom (4)
23 - Reflection of sound (4)
24 - Lens (8)

Down

1 - Serving dish (6)
2 - In spite of the fact (8)
3 - State in the SE United States (7)
4 - Twig of a willow tree (5)
5 - Smell (4)
6 - Lines of poetry (6)
13 - Banister (8)
14 - Chuckled (7)
16 - Effect; force (6)
18 - Observe (6)
19 - Acknowledged; assumed (5)
21 - A closed circuit (4)

No 88

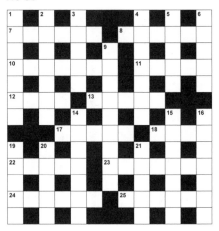

Across

7 - Workers' groups (6)
8 - Wreckage washed ashore (6)
10 - Light-hearted musical movements (7)
11 - Rips (5)
12 - Donkey and horse hybrid (4)
13 - Female garment (5)
17 - Old French currency (5)
18 - Continent (4)
22 - Loft (5)
23 - Business lecture (7)
24 - Showy pretense (6)
25 - Garnet (anag) (6)

Down

1 - Overdone (7)
2 - Justly (7)
3 - Lure (5)
4 - Risk (7)
5 - Customary (5)
6 - Give pleasure (5)
9 - Smoothness (9)
14 - Chirping insect (7)
15 - Into parts (7)
16 - Orange vegetables (7)
19 - Tawdry (5)
20 - Stretch (5)
21 - Hurt (5)

No 89

Across
1 - How audible a sound is (8)
5 - Outbuilding (4)
9 - Army cloth (5)
10 - Pursues an animal (5)
11 - Written symbols (10)
14 - Choice (6)
15 - Erase (6)
17 - Classic French dessert (5,5)
20 - Ballroom dance (5)
21 - Change (5)
22 - Young men (4)
23 - Overclouded (8)

Down
1 - Find pleasant (4)
2 - State in the W United States (4)
3 - District (12)
4 - Cuts off (6)
6 - Hampered (8)
7 - Catastrophe (8)
8 - Game board with 64 squares (12)
12 - Sanatorium (8)
13 - Achieved (8)
16 - Celestial point above you (6)
18 - Pack (4)
19 - Walked (4)

No 90

Across

1 - Followed orders (6)
5 - Deep anger (3)
7 - Pending (5)
8 - Mound made by insects (7)
9 - Objection (5)
10 - Of the third order (8)
12 - Agreement (6)
14 - Rain gently (6)
17 - Tonic (4-2-2)
18 - Precious stone (5)
20 - Awakening from sleep (7)
21 - Blackboard stand (5)
22 - Consume (3)
23 - Grinned (6)

Down

2 - Big posters; flags (7)
3 - Impressions (8)
4 - Male red deer (4)
5 - Unlawful (7)
6 - Ruler of an empire (7)
7 - Extreme (5)
11 - Where films are developed (8)
12 - Whenever (7)
13 - Fragment (7)
15 - Imitate (7)
16 - Last (5)
19 - Spiciness (4)

No 91

Across
1 - Infuriates (6)
4 - Lightweight jacket (6)
9 - Capable of being treated (7)
10 - Announcements (7)
11 - Plastic (5)
12 - Sticky tree sap (5)
14 - Connection; link (3-2)
15 - Punctuation mark (5)
17 - Rose (5)
18 - Mistake (7)
20 - Living in water (7)
21 - Decline to do something (6)
22 - Protects from heat (6)

Down
1 - Recess (6)
2 - Plant (8)
3 - Insurgent (5)
5 - Stand (7)
6 - Bluish white metallic element (4)
7 - Dried grape (6)
8 - Lady (11)
13 - Written (8)
14 - Plans (7)
15 - Roman general (6)
16 - Perennial flowering plant (6)
17 - Cleaning implement (5)
19 - Protective cover (4)

No 92

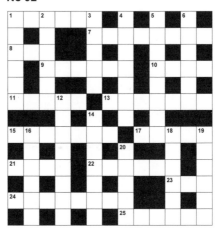

Across
1 - Chief component of sand (6)
7 - Explode (8)
8 - Very cold (3)
9 - Songbird (6)
10 - Guinea pig (4)
11 - Erect (3,2)
13 - Great courage (7)
15 - Exhausted (4,3)
17 - Past tense of stand (5)
21 - Periodic movement of the sea (4)
22 - Oddly picturesque (6)
23 - Edge of cup (3)
24 - Intelligentsia (8)
25 - French fashion designer (6)

Down
1 - Revolves around (6)
2 - Plan (6)
3 - Spanish for 'goodbye' (5)
4 - Become more precipitous (7)
5 - Stunning blow (8)
6 - Musical notations (6)
12 - Not necessary (8)
14 - Small orange colored fruit (7)
16 - Starting point (6)
18 - Move faster than (6)
19 - Pertaining to the skin (6)
20 - Insane (5)

Across

1 - Compromise (4-3-4)
9 - Command (5)
10 - Fix the result (3)
11 - Currently in progress (5)
12 - Herb (5)
13 - Reevaluate (8)
16 - Cheerful brightness (8)
18 - Travels (5)
21 - Chambers (5)
22 - Unit (3)
23 - Evil spirit (5)
24 - Austerely (11)

Down

2 - Licentious (7)
3 - Conceited person (7)
4 - Pokes gently (6)
5 - Palpitate (5)
6 - Four-wheeled vehicles (5)
7 - Presides over a meeting (11)
8 - Form into a cluster (11)
14 - Predatory South American fish (7)
15 - Breathing aid in water (7)
17 - Graduates of a college (6)
19 - Songs by two people (5)
20 - Rushlike plant (5)

No 94

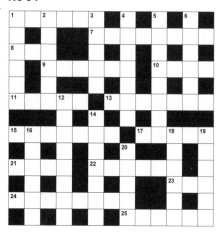

Across
1 - Large spiny lizard (6)
7 - Recoil (8)
8 - Level score (3)
9 - American inventor (6)
10 - Subsequently (4)
11 - Strength of a solution (5)
13 - Set apart (7)
15 - Modified (7)
17 - Island in the Bay of Naples (5)
21 - Greek spirit (4)
22 - Round object (6)
23 - Nineteenth Greek letter (3)
24 - Places in position (8)
25 - Chooses (6)

Down
1 - Deposit knowledge (6)
2 - Turbulence (6)
3 - Chasm (5)
4 - Coolness (7)
5 - Fleet (8)
6 - Characteristic (6)
12 - Accomplishments (8)
14 - Act of ceding (7)
16 - Misgivings (6)
18 - Having romantic imagery (6)
19 - Topics for debate (6)
20 - Period of time (5)

No 95

Across
1 - Shovels (6)
5 - Residential district (6)
8 - Outdoor pool (4)
9 - Part of the immune system (8)
10 - Relay device (5)
11 - Cools below zero (7)
14 - Assured (4-9)
16 - Seedily (anag) (7)
18 - Foam (5)
20 - Pasta (8)
22 - Blood vessel (4)
23 - Diminished in size (6)
24 - Terminate (6)

Down
2 - Not publicly (9)
3 - Deterioration (4-3)
4 - Exchange (4)
5 - Ascent (8)
6 - Piece of furniture (5)
7 - Marry (3)
12 - Appliances (9)
13 - Carpentry (8)
15 - Labored for (7)
17 - Camel like animal (5)
19 - Repeated jazz phrase (4)
21 - Fire residue (3)

No 96

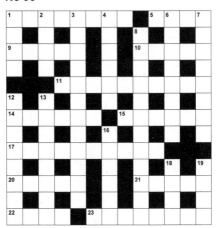

Across
1 - Diametric (8)
5 - Roman poet (4)
9 - Remit (anag) (5)
10 - Needs (5)
11 - Juveniles (10)
14 - Colorless flammable gas (6)
15 - Walk very quietly (6)
17 - Operating on land and water (10)
20 - Pointed projection (5)
21 - Interior (5)
22 - 24 hour periods (4)
23 - Mesmerism (8)

Down
1 - Upon (4)
2 - Wildcat (4)
3 - Environment (12)
4 - Crowd (6)
6 - Small illustrative sketch (8)
7 - Catastrophe (8)
8 - Exchange (12)
12 - Renovated (8)
13 - Musical composition (8)
16 - Securely (6)
18 - Hotels (4)
19 - Ancient boats (4)

No 97

Across
7 - Land covered with trees (6)
8 - Deviate suddenly (6)
9 - Desert in central China (4)
10 - Give new meaning to (8)
11 - Ancestry (7)
13 - Fast (5)
15 - Hold responsible (5)
16 - Acutely (7)
18 - Squid (8)
19 - Content word (4)
21 - Vendor (6)
22 - Trouble (6)

Down
1 - Indifferent (2-2)
2 - Selectively porous (13)
3 - Containers (7)
4 - Apart from (5)
5 - Self-knowledge (4-9)
6 - Momentous (8)
12 - Unlucky (3-5)
14 - Small persons (7)
17 - Block attack (5)
20 - Employs (4)

No 98

Across
1 - Broken fragments (6)
3 - View of the world (6)
7 - Inanity (9)
9 - Observing (8)
10 - Protective crust (4)
12 - Past tense of stand (5)
13 - Pure love (5)
17 - Prayer (4)
18 - Divine manifestation (8)
20 - Toiletry (9)
21 - Wishing (6)
22 - Powerful (6)

Down
1 - Not dense (6)
2 - Weakening (8)
4 - Fencing sword (4)
5 - Flaccid (6)
6 - Musical instrument (5)
7 - Play previously unseen music (5-4)
8 - Fawning parasite (9)
11 - Vegetable (8)
14 - Communication (6)
15 - Ghost (5)
16 - Man machine system (6)
19 - Layabout (4)

No 99

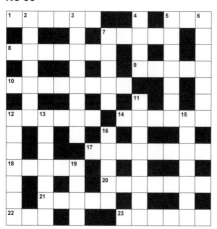

Across
1 - Covers little (6)
5 - Lay seed (3)
7 - Parrot (5)
8 - Mexican liquor (7)
9 - Cash registers (5)
10 - Short account (8)
12 - Currents (6)
14 - Eccentric (6)
17 - Resoluteness (8)
18 - Prologue (abbrev) (5)
20 - Layer of earth (7)
21 - Increment (5)
22 - Decline (3)
23 - Untamed (6)

Down
2 - Removed dirt (7)
3 - Twirled (8)
4 - Short tail (4)
5 - Suffer from oppressive heat (7)
6 - Liquor (7)
7 - Dullness (5)
11 - Residential district (8)
12 - Make amends (7)
13 - Move (7)
15 - Striking with the foot (7)
16 - Portly (5)
19 - Roman poet (4)

No 100

Across
1 - More likely than not (4-2)
5 - Writhe (6)
8 - Continent (4)
9 - Run over (8)
10 - Breathing organs of fish (5)
11 - Designated meal time (7)
14 - To suffice (3,3,7)
16 - Maybe (7)
18 - Cut of meat (5)
20 - Investigate (8)
22 - Metal fastener (4)
23 - Adornment (6)
24 - End of the vertebral column (6)

Down
2 - Penniless (9)
3 - Bright red (7)
4 - Cranny (4)
5 - Not genuine (8)
6 - Unsuitable (5)
7 - Seventeenth Greek letter (3)
12 - Routine (9)
13 - Relating to time (8)
15 - Of great size (7)
17 - Elevated shoes (5)
19 - Stylish (4)
21 - Period of time (3)

No 101

Across
7 - Bring back (8)
8 - Military (4)
9 - Wildcat (4)
10 - Forming lumps in milk (8)
11 - Updated (7)
12 - Gross (5)
15 - Spirited horse (5)
17 - Severely (7)
20 - Brought up (8)
22 - Memo (4)
23 - Sage (anag) (4)
24 - In rough pieces (8)

Down
1 - Hold in high esteem (6)
2 - A formal exposition (8)
3 - Chopping tool (7)
4 - Underground railway (5)
5 - Shopping venue (4)
6 - Revises (6)
13 - Pinkness (8)
14 - Tool for cutting wood (7)
16 - Tramp (6)
18 - Recently (6)
19 - Large motor vehicle (5)
21 - Work assignment (4)

No 102

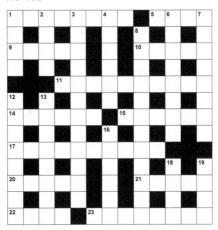

Across
1 - Blew up (8)
5 - Raced (4)
9 - Feeling (5)
10 - Pond dwelling amphibians (5)
11 - Decorative style of architecture (3,7)
14 - Container for keeping food cool (6)
15 - Cause resentment (6)
17 - Great brightness (10)
20 - Customary (5)
21 - Gets less difficult (5)
22 - Robust (4)
23 - Inexpensive snack (4,4)

Down
1 - Reflection of sound (4)
2 - Light shade of red (4)
3 - Dreamy (12)
4 - Increase in size (6)
6 - Consisting of fine particles (8)
7 - Deter (8)
8 - Inadequate (12)
12 - Paint sprayer (8)
13 - Remaining (8)
16 - Capital of the Philippines (6)
18 - Capital of Norway (4)
19 - Consumed (4)

No 103

Across
1 - Low-spirited (8)
6 - Agricultural implement (4)
8 - Resentment (6)
9 - Expresses opinion (6)
10 - Liquid used for washing (3)
11 - Display (4)
12 - Metamorphic rock (6)
13 - Dog like carnivores (6)
15 - Utilize wrongly (6)
17 - Tropical fly (6)
20 - Vex (4)
21 - Hard seed (3)
22 - Doles out (6)
23 - Reasons (6)
24 - Mission (4)
25 - Impressions (8)

Down
2 - Terrestrial (7)
3 - Equip (5)
4 - Lattice (7)
5 - Medication amounts (5)
6 - Attains (7)
7 - Leg joints (5)
14 - Communication system (7)
15 - Cocktail (7)
16 - Flavoring from crocus (7)
18 - Type of dance (5)
19 - Result (5)
20 - Civilian dress (5)

No 104

Across

7 - Appliances (8)
8 - Extol (4)
9 - The wise men (4)
10 - Scarceness (8)
11 - Shining (7)
12 - Precious stone (5)
15 - Feudal vassal (5)
17 - Bewilder (7)
20 - Distresses (8)
22 - Elegance (4)
23 - Time periods (4)
24 - Improves quality (8)

Down

1 - Desert in N Africa (6)
2 - Setting fire to (8)
3 - Putting away items (7)
4 - Aromatic resin (5)
5 - System (4)
6 - Chase (6)
13 - Well establish (8)
14 - Ugly building (7)
16 - Communicate (6)
18 - Former loves (6)
19 - Yellow-orange pigment (5)
21 - Failure (4)

No 105

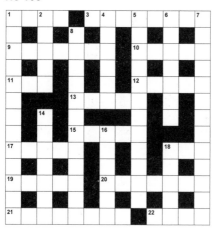

Across

1 - Finishes (4)
3 - Worried (8)
9 - Swiss houses (7)
10 - Hides (5)
11 - North American nation (1,1,1)
12 - Exclusive story (5)
13 - Paint (anag) (5)
15 - Small spot (5)
17 - Dissatisfaction (5)
18 - Mongrel dog (3)
19 - Crumble (5)
20 - Waterproof fabric (7)
21 - Delaying (8)
22 - Small piece of land (4)

Down

1 - Expression of approval (13)
2 - Stage play (5)
4 - World's largest country (6)
5 - Evidently (12)
6 - Teachings (7)
7 - Vanishing (13)
8 - Liberally (12)
14 - Line showing height (7)
16 - Veto; issue an injunction (6)
18 - Baked sweet desserts (5)

No 106

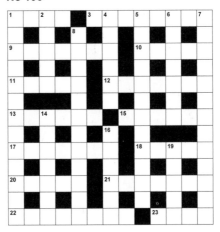

Across

1 - Birds of prey (4)
3 - Evening dress (5,3)
9 - Delivered a blow (7)
10 - Outdo (5)
11 - Aircraft detection system (5)
12 - Prior (7)
13 - Immature (6)
15 - Pronouncement (6)
17 - Resemble (7)
18 - Compare (5)
20 - Tines (anag) (5)
21 - End stations (7)
22 - Wool-clippers (8)
23 - Beat (4)

Down

1 - Chances for advancement (13)
2 - Covered (5)
4 - Tenant (6)
5 - Butterfly larvae (12)
6 - Traveler (7)
7 - Testing (13)
8 - Type of therapist (12)
14 - Print anew (7)
16 - Suppurate (6)
19 - Tiny crustaceans (5)

No 107

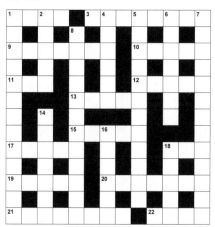

Across
1 - Hardens (4)
3 - Early bead calculators (8)
9 - Casual shoes (7)
10 - Spring flower akin to the primrose (5)
11 - Toothed wheel (3)
12 - Sea duck (5)
13 - Indifferent (5)
15 - Turn off and on (5)
17 - Hawaiian greeting (5)
18 - Sound of a cow (3)
19 - Not anyone (2,3)
20 - Children's carers (7)
21 - Dawn (8)
22 - Catch sight of (4)

Down
1 - Independent (4-9)
2 - Strong nasality in speech (5)
4 - Eating place (6)
5 - Tight but comfortable (5-7)
6 - Oblique stroke (7)
7 - Excessively (13)
8 - Eating place proprietor (12)
14 - Branch of biology (7)
16 - Lines of a poem (6)
18 - Female servants (5)

No 108

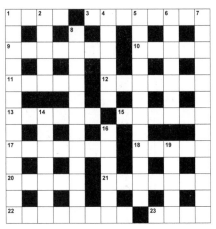

Across

1 - Elegance (4)
3 - Indoor footwear (8)
9 - Improves (7)
10 - Speak in a slow manner (5)
11 - Abhorrence (5)
12 - Flexible (7)
13 - Distinct being (6)
15 - Writing implement (6)
17 - Absolves (7)
18 - Hot pepper (5)
20 - Talked audibly (5)
21 - Woody plant (7)
22 - Guards (8)
23 - Hire (4)

Down

1 - Aimlessly (13)
2 - Civilian dress (5)
4 - Endured (6)
5 - Specialist in baby care (12)
6 - Precisely (7)
7 - Self-assured (4-9)
8 - Use of words that mimic sounds (12)
14 - Rapid repetition of a tone (7)
16 - Line of pressure (6)
19 - Suffuse with color (5)

No 109

Across

1 - Disintegrate (8)
6 - Elapsed time (4)
8 - Distant (3-3)
9 - Vent (6)
10 - Not (anag) (3)
11 - Pond (4)
12 - Annually (6)
13 - Coloring (6)
15 - Melodious (6)
17 - Somewhat ill (6)
20 - Retain (4)
21 - Not new (3)
22 - Remove (6)
23 - Intellectual giant (6)
24 - Respiratory organ of fish (4)
25 - Saw-like (8)

Down

2 - Representational process (7)
3 - Rock (5)
4 - Raising (7)
5 - Dark wood (5)
6 - Trap for the unwary (7)
7 - Wave (5)
14 - Writing fluid holder (7)
15 - Vessel to remove debris (7)
16 - Put in effect (7)
18 - Dissatisfaction (5)
19 - Adores (5)
20 - Republic in E Africa (5)

No 110

Across
1 - Cardinal point (4)
3 - Derisive (8)
9 - Coarsen (7)
10 - Linear units (5)
11 - Store selling men's clothes (12)
13 - Nocturnal arboreal marsupial (6)
15 - Capital of Austria (6)
17 - Insignificant detail (12)
20 - Aquatic mammal (5)
21 - Nymph; moon of Saturn (7)
22 - Pristine (5-3)
23 - Lids (anag) (4)

Down
1 - Adores (8)
2 - Noisy firework (5)
4 - Heavy fabric (6)
5 - Periodically (12)
6 - Precede (7)
7 - To a smaller extent (4)
8 - Pedigree (12)
12 - Infancy (8)
14 - Precast (anag) (7)
16 - Ringlike formation (6)
18 - Cause to (5)
19 - Toothed implement for the hair (4)

No 111

Across

1 - Word that qualifies (6)
7 - Herb (8)
8 - Mongrel dog (3)
9 - Third sign of the zodiac (6)
10 - Once more (4)
11 - Indoor game (5)
13 - Hopes to achieve (7)
15 - Armory (7)
17 - Concur with (5)
21 - Rebuff (4)
22 - Disliking intensely (6)
23 - Burnt wood (3)
24 - Inherited from a mother (8)
25 - Entangle (6)

Down

1 - Curved (6)
2 - Church official (6)
3 - Tender low-growing herb (5)
4 - Most gruesome (7)
5 - Process of removing dirt (8)
6 - Give in (6)
12 - Quivered (8)
14 - Beating (7)
16 - Airport take off strip (6)
18 - Entertain (6)
19 - After seventh (6)
20 - Manner (5)

No 112

Across
1 - Baker's dozen (8)
6 - Reverse (4)
8 - Emperor of Japan (6)
9 - Concept (6)
10 - Exclamation of contempt (3)
11 - Singles (4)
12 - Comfortable (6)
13 - Idle (6)
15 - Climbing tool (6)
17 - Early stage of animal (6)
20 - Roster (4)
21 - Statute (3)
22 - Seals (6)
23 - Nutlike kernel (6)
24 - Paradise garden (4)
25 - Relating to the stars (8)

Down
2 - Head piece (7)
3 - Highways (5)
4 - Passionate (7)
5 - Between eighth and tenth (5)
6 - Savage (7)
7 - Waggish (5)
14 - Rowers (7)
15 - Garment worn by dancers (7)
16 - Baltic country (7)
18 - Hushed (5)
19 - Fertile area in a desert (5)
20 - Gossip (5)

No 113

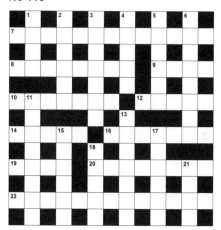

Across

7 - Benevolent (13)
8 - Majesty (8)
9 - On top of (4)
10 - Choose and follow (7)
12 - An unplanned speech (2-3)
14 - Flat circular plates (5)
16 - Not native (7)
19 - Augury (4)
20 - Periodical publication (8)
22 - Institution (13)

Down

1 - Show; gathering (4)
2 - Rough shelter (4-2)
3 - Ardent (7)
4 - Frighten (5)
5 - Distributed (6)
6 - Rotating (8)
11 - Fight (8)
13 - Clog (7)
15 - State in the central US (6)
17 - Biochemical catalyst (6)
18 - Sufficiently (5)
21 - Nothing (4)

No 114

Across

1 - Pronouncement (6)
3 - Opposite of wins (6)
7 - Pleasurable remembrance (9)
9 - Small part (8)
10 - Dairy product (4)
12 - Saturate (5)
13 - Units of heredity (5)
17 - Ship's complement (4)
18 - Relating to an empire (8)
20 - Book containing synonyms (9)
21 - Well-paid young professional (6)
22 - Game participant (6)

Down

1 - Towers over (6)
2 - Anonymous (8)
4 - Birds of prey (4)
5 - Furtive (6)
6 - Sing softly (5)
7 - Dwelling rooms (9)
8 - Trivial deceptions (5,4)
11 - Recommendation (8)
14 - Sharpness of vision (6)
15 - Besmirch (5)
16 - Flat (6)
19 - Legendary creature (4)

No 115

Across

1 - Glass filled to the brim (6)
4 - Stared at (6)
9 - Large island of Indonesia (7)
10 - Flowed (7)
11 - Artificial waterway (5)
12 - Native American tent (5)
14 - Golf shots on green (5)
15 - Musical times (5)
17 - Alleviate (5)
18 - Redwood tree (7)
20 - Universal remedy (4-3)
21 - Forces out (6)
22 - Loud noise (6)

Down

1 - Split into two (6)
2 - Impelling force or strength (8)
3 - Laud (5)
5 - Clinging shellfish (7)
6 - Small watercourse (4)
7 - Work hard (6)
8 - Commercial activity (11)
13 - Withdraw (4,4)
14 - Crucial (7)
15 - Scuffle (6)
16 - Small hole (6)
17 - Main artery (5)
19 - Remark (4)

No 116

Across
1 - Remarks (6)
5 - Softwood tree (6)
8 - Geographical region (4)
9 - Apprehended (8)
10 - Semiprecious quartz (5)
11 - Police detective (7)
14 - Lacking color (5-3-5)
16 - Kernel (7)
18 - Grass areas (5)
20 - Allocated (8)
22 - Symbol (4)
23 - Cake (6)
24 - Personal claims (6)

Down
2 - Strives (9)
3 - Severe (7)
4 - Stolen goods (4)
5 - Convince (8)
6 - Annoying insects (5)
7 - Wonder (3)
12 - Complete (3-3-3)
13 - Hawking (8)
15 - Warming up (7)
17 - Be (5)
19 - Smell (4)
21 - Health resort hotel (3)

No 117

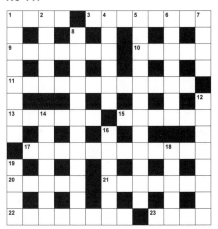

Across
1 - Satiate (4)
3 - Mishap (8)
9 - Countries (7)
10 - Cloaked (5)
11 - Involvement (12)
13 - Cleared a debt (6)
15 - Occupation or profession (6)
17 - Slowing down (12)
20 - Dole out (5)
21 - Crushed rock (7)
22 - Female house owner (8)
23 - Give up (4)

Down
1 - Capital of Australia (8)
2 - Group of eight (5)
4 - Fortified feudal residence (6)
5 - Matchless (12)
6 - Scope or area (7)
7 - Clean up (4)
8 - Occurring at the same time (12)
12 - Having dark hair (8)
14 - Devise beforehand (7)
16 - Ocean floor (6)
18 - Representation (5)
19 - Opposite of short (4)

No 118

Across

1 - Make a copy of (4,2)
7 - Assuages (8)
8 - Seventh Greek letter (3)
9 - Stupid person (6)
10 - Small social insects (4)
11 - Mountainous (5)
13 - Most active (7)
15 - Eccentricity (7)
17 - Repeat (5)
21 - Projecting edge (4)
22 - Domains (6)
23 - Used to open a door (3)
24 - Pepper plant (8)
25 - Preserved in brine (6)

Down

1 - Air inhaled and exhaled (6)
2 - French fashion designer (6)
3 - Go about stealthily (5)
4 - At top speed (4,3)
5 - Punish (8)
6 - Triangular river features (6)
12 - Large extent of land (8)
14 - Large flightless bird (7)
16 - Near the upper surface (6)
18 - Small box (6)
19 - Engaged in (6)
20 - Areas of agricultural land (5)

No 119

Across
1 - Bloodsucking insect (4)
3 - Unyielding (8)
9 - Operational home for planes (3,4)
10 - Male parent (5)
11 - Exemplar (12)
13 - Place inside (6)
15 - Dinner jacket (6)
17 - In a consoling manner (12)
20 - Earth (5)
21 - Plant of the parsley family (7)
22 - Most important (8)
23 - Conjoin (4)

Down
1 - Peaceful (8)
2 - Domestic dog (5)
4 - Fleshy white poultry meat (6)
5 - Unbiased (12)
6 - Prompting device (7)
7 - Real (anag) (4)
8 - Practical (6,2,4)
12 - Linguist (8)
14 - Flog (7)
16 - Costs (6)
18 - Acknowledged; assumed (5)
19 - Male deer (4)

No 120

Across
1 - Two of the same kind (4)
3 - Total nonsense (8)
9 - Disentangle (7)
10 - Ice home (5)
11 - Rational (5)
12 - Hair cleaner (7)
13 - Enlivening (6)
15 - Thoroughfare (6)
17 - Lift up (7)
18 - Cowboy display (5)
20 - Went down on one knee (5)
21 - Outlets (7)
22 - Explode (8)
23 - Biological unit (4)

Down
1 - Verified again (6-7)
2 - Loft (5)
4 - Most recent (6)
5 - Benevolence (12)
6 - Return (7)
7 - Corresponding (13)
8 - School for young children (12)
14 - Fundamental substance (7)
16 - Freshest (6)
19 - Song of mourning (5)

No 121

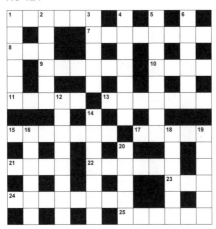

Across
1 - Crushes food (6)
7 - Is composed of (8)
8 - Finish first (3)
9 - Residential area (6)
10 - Effigy (4)
11 - Deep ravine (5)
13 - Declare to be (7)
15 - Alcoholic drinks (7)
17 - Undergarments (5)
21 - Body covering (4)
22 - Troublemaker (6)
23 - Unwell (3)
24 - Game of checkers (8)
25 - Degree (6)

Down
1 - Cat cry (6)
2 - Detecting device (6)
3 - Search rigorously for (5)
4 - Anyone (7)
5 - Make fun of (8)
6 - Powerful (6)
12 - Plant (8)
14 - Stiff and formal (7)
16 - Fire irons (6)
18 - Holy place (6)
19 - Naturally illuminated (6)
20 - Gray parasitic insect (5)

No 122

Across
1 - Away from the right path (6)
3 - Prawns (6)
7 - Interdependent existence (9)
9 - Harangue (8)
10 - Poem (4)
12 - Type of fashion (5)
13 - Small seat (5)
17 - Biblical garden (4)
18 - Hiking (8)
20 - Gently boiling (9)
21 - The land (6)
22 - Conceited person (6)

Down
1 - Prizes (6)
2 - Supporters (8)
4 - Actors (4)
5 - Charge (6)
6 - Eg arms and legs (5)
7 - Without form (9)
8 - In the event that (9)
11 - Franking (8)
14 - Mariner (6)
15 - Oatmeal dish (5)
16 - Struck by overwhelming shock (6)
19 - So be it (4)

No 123

Across

7 - Exercising influence or control (8)
8 - Geological time periods (4)
9 - Goes (anag) (4)
10 - Flight carriers (8)
11 - Judge (7)
12 - One more than seven (5)
15 - Money container (5)
17 - Country whose capital is Dublin (7)
20 - Shiny (8)
22 - Unit (4)
23 - Futile (4)
24 - Admitted (8)

Down

1 - Runner (6)
2 - Toward the center of a vessel (8)
3 - Pulled off; oversaw (7)
4 - Gaze fixedly (5)
5 - ___ Moore: Hollywood star (4)
6 - Entangle (6)
13 - Inopportune (3-5)
14 - Communicating with God (7)
16 - Empty (6)
18 - Required (6)
19 - Permeate gradually (5)
21 - Saltwater fish (4)

No 124

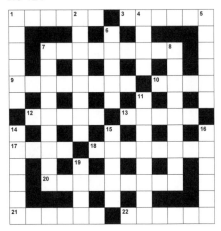

Across
1 - Bed linen (6)
3 - Outcome (6)
7 - Situation with unseen hazards (9)
9 - Thieves (8)
10 - Status (4)
12 - Slightly intoxicated (5)
13 - Covered with soft hairs (5)
17 - Kitchen appliance (4)
18 - One of the Channel Islands (8)
20 - Exhaustion (9)
21 - Revolves (6)
22 - Far from the intended target (6)

Down
1 - Run-down (6)
2 - Lacking in expression (8)
4 - At any time (4)
5 - Russian carriage (6)
6 - Burning (5)
7 - Hilarity (9)
8 - Medical analysis (9)
11 - Unpleasant flavor (8)
14 - Small drums (6)
15 - Exceed (5)
16 - Incidental activity (6)
19 - Increase in size (4)

No 125

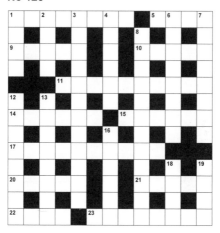

Across

1 - Inconceivably large (8)
5 - Young sheep (4)
9 - Part of small intestine (5)
10 - Nerve in the eye (5)
11 - Recurrently (10)
14 - Cringe (6)
15 - Sauce for fish (6)
17 - Urchin (10)
20 - Oak tree nut (5)
21 - Model; perfect (5)
22 - Nose (anag) (4)
23 - Always in similar role (8)

Down

1 - Pattern of lines (4)
2 - Right to hold property (4)
3 - Beginning (12)
4 - Arch of foot (6)
6 - Remedy to a poison (8)
7 - Ground behind a house (8)
8 - With the order reversed (12)
12 - Make sour (8)
13 - Breed of cattle (8)
16 - Inaccurate in pitch (3-3)
18 - Greek cheese (4)
19 - Mar; smudge (4)

No 126

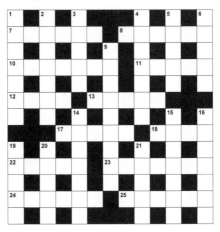

Across
7 - Through the mouth (6)
8 - Without ethics (6)
10 - Transgression (7)
11 - Exorbitant interest rate (5)
12 - Rank (4)
13 - Government (5)
17 - Erodes (5)
18 - Priest (4)
22 - Attribute (5)
23 - Indigenous people (7)
24 - Restaurant visitors (6)
25 - Criticizes (6)

Down
1 - Temporary stay (7)
2 - Crisp plain fabric (7)
3 - Heavy dull sound (5)
4 - Quantities (7)
5 - Plaster (5)
6 - Heavy soils (5)
9 - Repeating (9)
14 - Time off (7)
15 - Innocently (7)
16 - Singer with low voice (7)
19 - Interprets (5)
20 - Ring someone (5)
21 - Slender piece of wood (5)

No 127

Across

7 - Drumbeat (6)
8 - Large dark cloud (6)
9 - Famous Spanish painter (4)
10 - Where you park the car (8)
11 - Servile (7)
13 - Dye (5)
15 - Farm land (5)
16 - Corneas (anag) (7)
18 - Examined (8)
19 - Succulent plant (4)
21 - Rectitude (6)
22 - Rarely (6)

Down

1 - Aura (4)
2 - Accessibility (13)
3 - Clutching (7)
4 - Gastropod (5)
5 - Calm (13)
6 - Remedial (8)
12 - Legendary island (8)
14 - Female deity (7)
17 - Indian of Mexico (5)
20 - Smell (4)

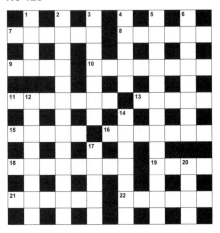

Across

7 - Mountain chain (6)
8 - Pertaining to the skin (6)
9 - Kitchen appliance (4)
10 - Virtue (8)
11 - Freezing (3-4)
13 - Gush forth; opening (5)
15 - Applying (5)
16 - Musician (7)
18 - Something easy or certain (8)
19 - Lofty (4)
21 - Adheres to (6)
22 - Exist in great numbers (6)

Down

1 - Capital of the Ukraine (4)
2 - Supremacy (13)
3 - Chiefly (7)
4 - Supplementary component (3-2)
5 - Exchange (13)
6 - Therapists (8)
12 - Victim of accident (8)
14 - Small Eurasian crow (7)
17 - Strong light wood (5)
20 - Slender (4)

No 129

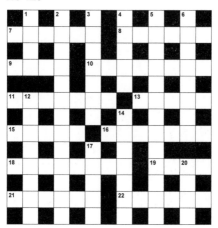

Across

7 - Artistic style (6)
8 - Church towers (6)
9 - Breaks; tears open (4)
10 - Pip-squeak (5,3)
11 - Muslim clerics (7)
13 - Effects (5)
15 - Injure (5)
16 - Contest (7)
18 - Monotreme (8)
19 - Support (4)
21 - Wading birds (6)
22 - Small hole (6)

Down

1 - ___ Spelling: American actress (4)
2 - Petrification (13)
3 - Russian soup (7)
4 - Customary (5)
5 - Compiler of lists of books (13)
6 - Be envious of (8)
12 - Unfurled (8)
14 - Support (7)
17 - Sudden contraction (5)
20 - Not closed (4)

No 130

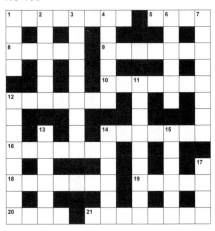

Across
1 - Person with authority over others (8)
5 - Engrave with acid (4)
8 - Not elaborate (5)
9 - Organic nutrient (7)
10 - Millionths of a meter (7)
12 - Edible root (7)
14 - Attendant (7)
16 - Not immediate (7)
18 - Unit of electric charge (7)
19 - Dark black wood (5)
20 - Utters (4)
21 - Thaws out (8)

Down
1 - Exclamation of mild dismay (4)
2 - Attract (6)
3 - Mercifully (9)
4 - Renovate (6)
6 - Type of drum (3,3)
7 - Truly (8)
11 - Employed to drive a car (9)
12 - Foretells (8)
13 - Indistinct (6)
14 - Fit for consumption (6)
15 - Armatures (6)
17 - Colors (4)

No 131

Across

1 - Inhabitant of Troy (6)
5 - Respectable (6)
8 - Without self-control (4)
9 - Separately issued article (8)
10 - Eg Sioux (5)
11 - Have (7)
14 - Untrained (13)
16 - Odd (7)
18 - Enraged (5)
20 - Ballroom dance (8)
22 - Morally very bad (4)
23 - Moorings (6)
24 - Had corresponding sounds (6)

Down

2 - Dutch painter (9)
3 - Automatic record player (7)
4 - Cranny (4)
5 - Yellow flower (8)
6 - Freshwater fish (5)
7 - Religious sister (3)
12 - Disinfect (9)
13 - Sergeant (anag) (8)
15 - Innocently (7)
17 - Allow (5)
19 - Sullen (4)
21 - Liquid used for washing (3)

No 132

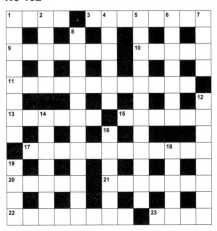

Across

1 - Heating fuel (4)
3 - When you are born (8)
9 - Catches (7)
10 - Republic in S Europe (5)
11 - Applied scientist (12)
13 - Judge (6)
15 - Fleet of ships (6)
17 - Prescience (12)
20 - Army cloth (5)
21 - Sediment (7)
22 - Creator (8)
23 - Remain (4)

Down

1 - Sumptuous (8)
2 - Loft (5)
4 - Emphatic form of it (6)
5 - Reckless (7-5)
6 - Very salty lake (4,3)
7 - Toy (4)
8 - Prayer expressing gratitude (12)
12 - Key player (8)
14 - Shoes (7)
16 - Center (6)
18 - Image within another (5)
19 - Slide (4)

No 133

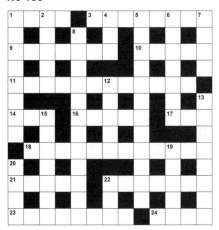

Across

1 - Belonging to us (4)
3 - Solids with regular structures (8)
9 - Propriety (7)
10 - Connection; link (3-2)
11 - Vain (12)
14 - To free (3)
16 - Cover with liquid (5)
17 - Ruction (3)
18 - Accepted behavior whilst dining (5,7)
21 - Ascend (5)
22 - Pale colors (7)
23 - Well establish (8)
24 - Sight organs (4)

Down

1 - Commonplace (8)
2 - Motorcar (5)
4 - Beam of light (3)
5 - Gratifyingly (12)
6 - Land mass of the New World (7)
7 - Beyond help (4)
8 - Lasting (12)
12 - Jostle (5)
13 - Is composed of (8)
15 - Writer of a journal (7)
19 - All (5)
20 - 4840 square yards (4)
22 - Intentionally so written (3)

No 134

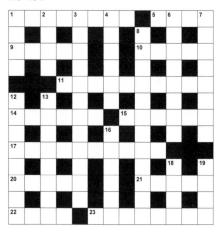

Across
1 - Lived in (8)
5 - From a distance (4)
9 - Exit (5)
10 - Rustic (5)
11 - Fear of heights (10)
14 - Semitic language (6)
15 - Cursive script (6)
17 - Restlessness (10)
20 - Greeting (5)
21 - Undo (5)
22 - Portion of medicine (4)
23 - Knee-length trousers (8)

Down
1 - Greasy (4)
2 - Nook (4)
3 - Medication (12)
4 - Implant deeply (6)
6 - Luminous meteor (8)
7 - Dependence (8)
8 - Building design (12)
12 - Disappeared (8)
13 - Larval frogs (8)
16 - Mental puzzle (6)
18 - Engrave with acid (4)
19 - Chickens (4)

No 135

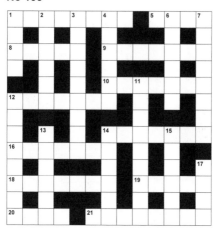

Across
1 - Part of the face (8)
5 - Den (4)
8 - Borough of New York City (5)
9 - Discontinues (7)
10 - Towards the side (7)
12 - Containing no liquid (7)
14 - Add up (7)
16 - Find the solution (7)
18 - Filer (7)
19 - Sharp-pointed spike (5)
20 - Fast flowing (4)
21 - Drugstore (8)

Down
1 - Tells a mistruth (4)
2 - Novice (6)
3 - Having six sides (9)
4 - Ancient (3-3)
6 - First light of day (6)
7 - Determined (8)
11 - Player of a brass instrument (9)
12 - Frightening (8)
13 - Remarks (6)
14 - Seek out (6)
15 - Long curly fleece (6)
17 - Solely (4)

No 136

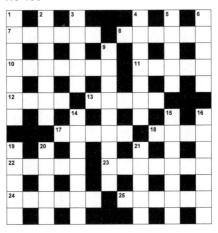

Across

7 - Takes the place of (6)
8 - Litter of pigs (6)
10 - Stock farmer (7)
11 - Very short time (5)
12 - Close by (4)
13 - Score (5)
17 - Try out (5)
18 - Story (4)
22 - Island in the Bay of Naples (5)
23 - Call before a court (7)
24 - Steers a vehicle (6)
25 - Foot levers (6)

Down

1 - Causing friction (7)
2 - Digit (7)
3 - Hand shovel (5)
4 - At speed (7)
5 - Cook with high heat (5)
6 - Clean with a brush (5)
9 - Flee (5,4)
14 - Voyages by boat (7)
15 - Contemptuous (7)
16 - Timidness (7)
19 - Sour substances (5)
20 - Greenfly (5)
21 - Eg from Athens (5)

No 137

Across

1 - Drills (6)
7 - Exercises authority (8)
8 - Our star (3)
9 - Goblin (6)
10 - Office table (4)
11 - Dimension (5)
13 - Challenges as false (7)
15 - Mistake (7)
17 - Gift (5)
21 - Verge (4)
22 - Bathing suit (6)
23 - Dry (of wine) (3)
24 - Surpass (8)
25 - Stagnation or inactivity (6)

Down

1 - Confer (6)
2 - Washed lightly (6)
3 - Break up (5)
4 - Saves (7)
5 - Redness of the skin (8)
6 - Individual (6)
12 - Journey across (8)
14 - Integers (7)
16 - Radioactive element (6)
18 - Gets up (6)
19 - Bumps into (6)
20 - Hops (5)

No 138

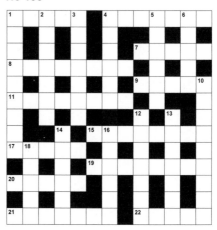

Across
1 - Draws into the mouth (5)
4 - Seems (7)
7 - Flies a plane (5)
8 - Unlucky (3-5)
9 - Recycle (5)
11 - Not acid (8)
15 - Squid (8)
17 - Praise (5)
19 - Comic opera (8)
20 - Fastening device (5)
21 - Pierces (7)
22 - Work out (5)

Down
1 - Card game for one (9)
2 - Feline (3-4)
3 - Scribbles (7)
4 - Backward direction (6)
5 - Banished (6)
6 - Tree anchors (5)
10 - Volatile (9)
12 - Transports (7)
13 - Incomplete (7)
14 - Domesticated llama (6)
16 - Fruits with pips (6)
18 - Plant tissue (5)

Across

7 - Expressing regret (6)
8 - Seaport in N Spain (6)
10 - Official sitting (7)
11 - Unwanted plants (5)
12 - Hotels (4)
13 - Eat quickly (5)
17 - Attempted (5)
18 - Group of three (4)
22 - Vigorous attack (5)
23 - Attempted; tested (7)
24 - Escapes (6)
25 - Deceives; fakes (6)

Down

1 - Mundane (7)
2 - Character (7)
3 - God of love (5)
4 - Childbirth assistant (7)
5 - Norwegian dramatist (5)
6 - Battle (5)
9 - Loosened by turning (9)
14 - Bishop's staff (7)
15 - Wax sticks used for drawing (7)
16 - Female deity (7)
19 - Double reed instruments (5)
20 - Nasal passageway (5)
21 - Steer (anag) (5)

No 140

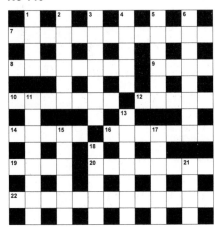

Across

7 - Written instructions (13)
8 - Prompt (8)
9 - Essential substance (4)
10 - From the United Kingdom (7)
12 - Urges (5)
14 - Cunningly (5)
16 - Calamity (7)
19 - Finish (4)
20 - Fondly (8)
22 - Put to trouble (13)

Down

1 - Bean curd (4)
2 - Melodious (6)
3 - Legacy (7)
4 - Coral reef (5)
5 - Increase (4,2)
6 - Altered; falsified (8)
11 - Narrating (8)
13 - Steering an automobile (7)
15 - Portable computer (6)
17 - Styles (6)
18 - Aromatic spice (5)
21 - Scottish lake (4)

No 141

Across
1 - Leg joint on horse (4)
3 - Yielded (8)
9 - Kingdom in NW Africa (7)
10 - Naming words (5)
11 - Calculations of dimensions (12)
13 - National flower of Mexico (6)
15 - Expels (6)
17 - Lacking beauty (12)
20 - Inert gas (5)
21 - Bonus (7)
22 - Religious residences (8)
23 - Among (4)

Down
1 - Domestic (8)
2 - Governing body (5)
4 - Covered (6)
5 - Evening dress for men (6,6)
6 - Harsh; corrosive (7)
7 - Flat circular plate (4)
8 - Someone you know (12)
12 - Prestigious (8)
14 - Pistol (7)
16 - Under the shoulder (6)
18 - Non-standard speech (5)
19 - Bathtime mineral (4)

No 142

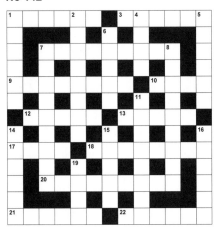

Across

1 - Sarcastic (6)
3 - Full of holes (6)
7 - Pardonably (9)
9 - Higher in rank (8)
10 - Geological periods (4)
12 - Gave away (5)
13 - Clean (5)
17 - Radar echo (4)
18 - Unidentified (8)
20 - Large land masses (9)
21 - Marshy (6)
22 - Straighten (6)

Down

1 - Speculate (6)
2 - Became liable (8)
4 - Spheres (4)
5 - Metamorphic rock (6)
6 - English horse racing track (5)
7 - Polite term (9)
8 - Skullcaps (9)
11 - Particular time (8)
14 - Lessens (6)
15 - Get together (5)
16 - Loved deeply (6)
19 - Cut of beef (4)

No 143

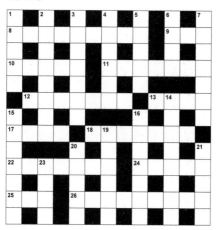

Across
8 - Call or ring (9)
9 - Naturally disposed toward (3)
10 - Requirements (5)
11 - Perfectly (7)
12 - Looking after (7)
13 - Cut of meat (4)
17 - Eurasian crow (4)
18 - Business venues (7)
22 - Scientist (7)
24 - U-shaped curve in a river (5)
25 - Taste (3)
26 - Rich butter cookie (9)

Down
1 - Smarted (5)
2 - Alternate personality (5,3)
3 - Occurrence (7)
4 - Magical brew (6)
5 - Less (5)
6 - Bucket (4)
7 - Remaining (7)
14 - Dominate (8)
15 - Exact (7)
16 - Italian rice dish (7)
19 - Come to understand (6)
20 - ___ Elliott: US rapper (5)
21 - Clean with a brush (5)
23 - Catch sight of (4)

No 144

Across
1 - Creatively (8)
6 - Letter (4)
8 - Open up (6)
9 - Desperate situations (6)
10 - Exclamation of surprise (3)
11 - Sharp blow (4)
12 - Chest (6)
13 - Stick to (6)
15 - Deceives; fakes (6)
17 - Warhorses (6)
20 - Breezy (4)
21 - Cinder (3)
22 - Grounds (6)
23 - Tray (6)
24 - Discharged a debt (4)
25 - Annual (8)

Down
2 - Renovated (7)
3 - Disregard (5)
4 - Pleasing (7)
5 - Water vessel (5)
6 - Capital of Kenya (7)
7 - Eighth Greek letter (5)
14 - Voted in (7)
15 - Bush shrub (7)
16 - Submarine weapon (7)
18 - Jeweled headdress (5)
19 - Impudent (5)
20 - Spontaneous remark (2-3)

No 145

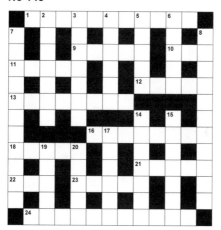

Across
1 - School chief (4,7)
9 - Stage play (5)
10 - Excavated soil (3)
11 - Hold on tight (5)
12 - Lumberjack (5)
13 - Bookish (8)
16 - Romantic and comic play (8)
18 - Extent (5)
21 - Spiritual leader (5)
22 - Slippery liquid (3)
23 - Poem (5)
24 - Beauty (11)

Down
2 - Joins the military (7)
3 - Cheaters (7)
4 - Item of stationery (6)
5 - Smash into (5)
6 - Equip (5)
7 - Not necessary (8-3)
8 - Gathering together (11)
14 - Part of a chair (7)
15 - Short and thick (7)
17 - Less well off (6)
19 - Rice dish (5)
20 - Disturbance (5)

No 146

Across
7 - Face-to-face (4-2)
8 - River in N South America (6)
10 - Proceeding by tens (7)
11 - Cancel out (5)
12 - Intellect (4)
13 - Telephones (5)
17 - Sneers (5)
18 - Kitchen utensil (4)
22 - Hair style (5)
23 - Unconventional (7)
24 - Apportion (6)
25 - Rugged (6)

Down
1 - Darkening (7)
2 - Strident (7)
3 - Develops (5)
4 - Friendly (7)
5 - Atmospheric layer (5)
6 - Knot of foot (5)
9 - Where coats are left (9)
14 - Atomic particle (7)
15 - Move apart (7)
16 - Sleep (7)
19 - Musical drama (5)
20 - Tattered and torn (5)
21 - Burning (5)

No 147

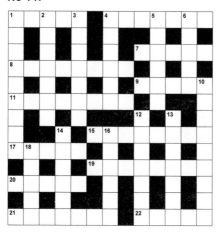

Across

1 - Emboldened (5)
4 - Acted (7)
7 - Cloth with crisscross pattern (5)
8 - Falling (8)
9 - Raise (5)
11 - Cultivated tufted grass (8)
15 - Large estate (8)
17 - Fur coats (5)
19 - Forbid (8)
20 - Big cats (5)
21 - Built up (7)
22 - Tapas (anag) (5)

Down

1 - Isotope of hydrogen (9)
2 - More spacious (7)
3 - US currency (plural) (7)
4 - Mixes together (6)
5 - Bursting into flower (6)
6 - Imposing poems (5)
10 - Large hairy spider (9)
12 - Illuminate (5,2)
13 - Helps to happen (7)
14 - Unpleasant people (6)
16 - In a foreign country (6)
18 - Non-standard speech (5)

No 148

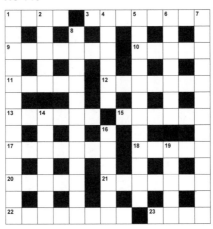

Across
1 - Pigs (4)
3 - Out-of-date (8)
9 - Expect (7)
10 - Inexpensive (5)
11 - Extent (5)
12 - Eg from Moscow (7)
13 - Part of the eye (6)
15 - Dwarfed tree (6)
17 - Russian novelist (7)
18 - Make right (5)
20 - Protective layer (5)
21 - Throb (7)
22 - Without affection (8)
23 - Applications (4)

Down
1 - Quibbling (13)
2 - Color of grass (5)
4 - Indistinct (6)
5 - Now and then (12)
6 - Antagonists (7)
7 - Ebullience (13)
8 - Occult (12)
14 - Large Israeli city (3,4)
16 - Immature water insects (6)
19 - Ellipses (5)

No 149

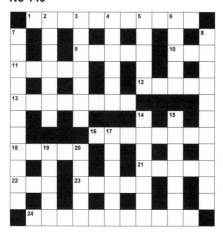

Across
1 - Faithfully (11)
9 - Denim (anag) (5)
10 - Hurried (3)
11 - Join together as one (5)
12 - Dry red wine (5)
13 - Overwhelmed with concern (8)
16 - Complete (8)
18 - Surpass (5)
21 - Unwarranted (5)
22 - Droop (3)
23 - Fertile spot in a desert (5)
24 - Promoting (11)

Down
2 - Coat; decorate lavishly (7)
3 - Vast (7)
4 - Electrify particles (6)
5 - Beneath (5)
6 - Dignified musical passage (5)
7 - Sound practical judgment (6,5)
8 - Expansion (11)
14 - Migratory grasshoppers (7)
15 - Dilapidated (7)
17 - Breed of hound (6)
19 - Enclosed (5)
20 - Free (5)

No 150

Across
7 - Act of breaking into (8)
8 - Seeds (4)
9 - Speed relative to sound (4)
10 - Emperor of Rome (8)
11 - Commercial undertaking (7)
12 - Newlywed (5)
15 - Tree (5)
17 - Polish (7)
20 - Luxurious (8)
22 - Slender (4)
23 - Entering (4)
24 - Rays of light (8)

Down
1 - Inborn (6)
2 - Pitiful (8)
3 - Parachute opener (7)
4 - Father's brother (5)
5 - Cozy (4)
6 - Unemotional (6)
13 - Ribbon or silk badges (8)
14 - People (7)
16 - Scholars (6)
18 - Self-evident truths (6)
19 - Wet thoroughly (5)
21 - Pigeon sounds (4)

No 151

Across

7 - Younger (6)
8 - Harsh (6)
9 - Show off; gloat (4)
10 - Presiding officer (8)
11 - Flash brightly (7)
13 - Principle of morality (5)
15 - Flower of remembrance (5)
16 - Boiling pots (7)
18 - Excessively emotional (6,2)
19 - Imprint (4)
21 - Remove the outer cover (6)
22 - Soundness of judgment (6)

Down

1 - Seed (4)
2 - Trickery (13)
3 - Sharp point (7)
4 - Common; regularly seen (5)
5 - Exaggeration (13)
6 - Become accustomed to town life (8)
12 - Advance (8)
14 - Storm (7)
17 - Good at (5)
20 - Decays (4)

No 152

Across
7 - Nerve cell (6)
8 - Deceive (6)
10 - Nerve impulses (7)
11 - Chats (5)
12 - Speech defect (4)
13 - Inner circle (5)
17 - Area shaded by trees (5)
18 - Leguminous plant (4)
22 - Unabridged (5)
23 - Quantities (7)
24 - Publish (3,3)
25 - Sheepskin (6)

Down
1 - One's own person (7)
2 - Most active (7)
3 - Specific location (5)
4 - In the middle (7)
5 - Trade association (5)
6 - Rent (5)
9 - Denial (9)
14 - Irritable (7)
15 - Rang (7)
16 - Herb (7)
19 - Squashy (5)
20 - Severe (5)
21 - Devout (5)

No 153

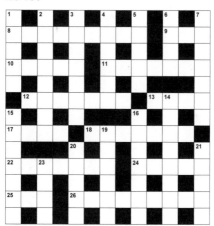

Across

8 - Sport played in a pool (5,4)
9 - Employ (3)
10 - Communicates (5)
11 - Weaves (7)
12 - Luminous beetle (7)
13 - Show; gathering (4)
17 - Capital of Italy (4)
18 - Fish hawks (7)
22 - Fixed in place (7)
24 - Decoration (5)
25 - Foodstuff (3)
26 - Amoral (9)

Down

1 - Wetland (5)
2 - Patience (8)
3 - Covered with icing (7)
4 - Relating to the mail system (6)
5 - Fret (5)
6 - Brass instrument (4)
7 - Hot water spouts (7)
14 - Anywhere (8)
15 - Discarded (7)
16 - Transport (7)
19 - Soaked thoroughly (6)
20 - Dreadful (5)
21 - Series (5)
23 - Fixes the result (4)

No 154

Across
1 - Children's entertainers (6)
4 - Cooks (6)
7 - Herb (8)
8 - House (4)
9 - Curd (4)
11 - Incline (4)
12 - Time off (7)
13 - Water barrier (3)
15 - To be unwell (3)
17 - Facial hair (7)
19 - Destroy (4)
20 - Beers (4)
21 - Official language of Pakistan (4)
22 - Electrical grounding (8)
24 - Walk nonchalantly (6)
25 - Dock for small yachts (6)

Down
1 - Intoned (7)
2 - Wretched (6)
3 - Snow blade (3)
4 - Detachment covering a retreat (9)
5 - For a short time (6)
6 - Very large drums (7)
10 - In various ways (9)
14 - Fish tanks (7)
16 - Layered pasta dish (7)
17 - Sufficient (6)
18 - Flat ring (6)
23 - Male sheep (3)

No 155

Across
1 - Swords (6)
4 - Word that qualifies (6)
9 - Pseudoscience (7)
10 - Forbear (7)
11 - Avoid (5)
12 - System of rules (5)
14 - Prune (5)
15 - Small woodland (5)
17 - Sticky tree sap (5)
18 - Liberate (7)
20 - Vast (7)
21 - Entice or attract (6)
22 - Removes wallpaper (6)

Down
1 - Neck warming garments (6)
2 - Rear curtain of a stage (8)
3 - Pass a rope through (5)
5 - Someone who wanders (7)
6 - Volcano in Sicily (4)
7 - Superhuman (6)
8 - Relating to fireworks (11)
13 - Capital of Finland (8)
14 - Legislator (7)
15 - Playing period in polo (6)
16 - Smiles contemptuously (6)
17 - Send money (5)
19 - Gyrate (4)

No 156

Across
1 - Capacity (6)
5 - Place (3)
7 - Sludgy (5)
8 - Temporary camp (7)
9 - Public square (5)
10 - Observing (8)
12 - Attack someone (6)
14 - File (6)
17 - Resoluteness (8)
18 - Ornamentation (5)
20 - Body of water (7)
21 - Confronts (5)
22 - Chatter (3)
23 - Copyist (6)

Down
2 - Starts (7)
3 - Large hill (8)
4 - Walk awkwardly (4)
5 - Polyhedron (7)
6 - Playhouse (7)
7 - Small rounded cake (5)
11 - Vigorously (8)
12 - Continuing (7)
13 - Yield (7)
15 - Repeat performances (7)
16 - Wind instruments (5)
19 - Deer (anag) (4)

No 157

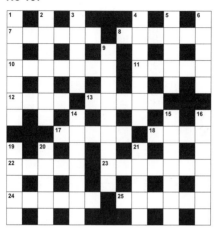

Across

7 - Scrape off (6)
8 - Apartment (6)
10 - Bring up (7)
11 - Sheet of paper (5)
12 - Book (4)
13 - Swerves off course (5)
17 - Card game (5)
18 - Tibetan priest (4)
22 - Touch on (5)
23 - Exposure of bedrock (7)
24 - Bird sounds (6)
25 - Borne on the water (6)

Down

1 - Iron attractors (7)
2 - Phoenician galley (7)
3 - Disgust (5)
4 - Wave riders (7)
5 - Cunningly (5)
6 - Laud (5)
9 - Withdrawing from organization (9)
14 - Medical care (7)
15 - What vultures eat (7)
16 - Course leading to battle (7)
19 - Seaweed (5)
20 - Attach (5)
21 - Personnel at work (5)

No 158

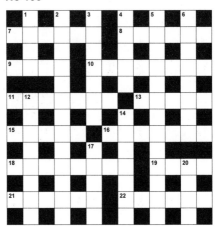

Across
7 - Blue semi precious gem (6)
8 - Language (6)
9 - Skin (4)
10 - Removed the interior of (8)
11 - High-flown (7)
13 - Neural structure (5)
15 - Untidy (5)
16 - Cut (7)
18 - Planning (8)
19 - Lazy (4)
21 - Put to the test (3,3)
22 - Flood (6)

Down
1 - Sheet of glass (4)
2 - State of being close together (13)
3 - Desirous (7)
4 - Motionless (5)
5 - Honest (13)
6 - Adolescent (8)
12 - Person with authority over others (8)
14 - Army unit (7)
17 - Leans (5)
20 - Child's plastic construction set (4)

No 159

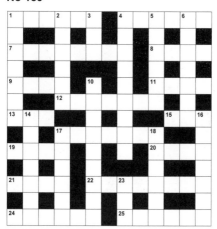

Across
1 - Large groups of people (6)
4 - Disturbs (6)
7 - Distresses (8)
8 - Red gem (4)
9 - Repeat again (4)
11 - Cattle; meat (4)
12 - Unit of sound in a language (7)
13 - Apply (3)
15 - Container (3)
17 - Persecute (7)
19 - Hind part (4)
20 - Semester (4)
21 - Niche (4)
22 - Canine (3,5)
24 - Bangle; bracelet (6)
25 - Number of Apostles (6)

Down
1 - Country house (7)
2 - Hit hard (6)
3 - Pouch (3)
4 - Loosened by turning (9)
5 - Playwright (6)
6 - Still image; dramatic scene (7)
10 - Part (9)
14 - Become more precipitous (7)
16 - Police detective (7)
17 - Trying experience (6)
18 - Minion (6)
23 - Consume (3)

No 160

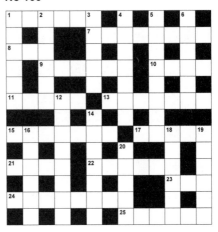

Across
1 - Japanese robe (6)
7 - Lessened (8)
8 - Toward the stern (3)
9 - Continue (6)
10 - Ark builder (4)
11 - Mother-of-pearl (5)
13 - Loud enough to be heard (7)
15 - Insanitary (7)
17 - Graceful young woman (5)
21 - Medicine (4)
22 - The lower side of anything (6)
23 - Auction offer (3)
24 - Horse of light tan color (8)
25 - Regular customer (6)

Down
1 - Mythical sea monster (6)
2 - A standard of measurement (6)
3 - Widespread unpopularity (5)
4 - Perplexed (5-2)
5 - Personality (8)
6 - Nitty gritty (6)
12 - Faith; belief (8)
14 - Cook briefly (7)
16 - Standard (6)
18 - Cut timber (6)
19 - Concealed (6)
20 - Condescend (5)

No 161

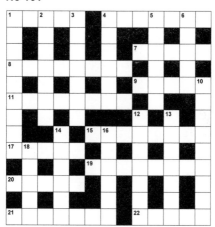

Across
1 - Very small (5)
4 - Outdoor game (7)
7 - Musical half note (5)
8 - Abandoned hulk (8)
9 - Mouselike mammal (5)
11 - Transport systems (8)
15 - Instructed (8)
17 - Attractively stylish (5)
19 - Sieve (8)
20 - Smells (5)
21 - Tend (4-3)
22 - Country in NE Africa (5)

Down
1 - Custom (9)
2 - Endless (7)
3 - Fall colors (7)
4 - Easily remembered (6)
5 - Tart with savory filling (6)
6 - Upper crust (5)
10 - Carpentry (9)
12 - Foot pedal (7)
13 - Equality of political rights (7)
14 - Robust (6)
16 - Powerful (6)
18 - Republic in S Asia (5)

No 162

Across

1 - Mode of standing (6)
5 - Touch gently (3)
7 - Cause; create (5)
8 - Irrigated (7)
9 - Dye (5)
10 - Scents (8)
12 - Make beloved (6)
14 - Large semiaquatic rodent (6)
17 - Body of related information (8)
18 - Not concealed (5)
20 - Occurring every evening (7)
21 - Start of (5)
22 - Swallow (3)
23 - Doing nothing (6)

Down

2 - Part exchange (5,2)
3 - Revelry (8)
4 - A great deal (4)
5 - Large Israeli city (3,4)
6 - Indicator (7)
7 - Borders (5)
11 - Mad (8)
12 - Sells abroad (7)
13 - Bring to fruition (7)
15 - Fifth Greek letter (7)
16 - Holy person (5)
19 - Work assignment (4)

No 163

Across

7 - Environmental condition (6)
8 - Man's wig (6)
9 - Capital of the Ukraine (4)
10 - Game bird (8)
11 - Atrocious act (7)
13 - Sink; sag (5)
15 - Cinders (5)
16 - Capture (7)
18 - Moved to tears (8)
19 - Set up (4)
21 - Stretches (6)
22 - Polish composer and pianist (6)

Down

1 - Prefix for small (4)
2 - 25th anniversary (6,7)
3 - Back pain (7)
4 - Cigarette ends (5)
5 - Official permission (13)
6 - In the adjacent residence (4,4)
12 - Disagreeable people (8)
14 - Outcome (7)
17 - Plant with aromatic seeds (5)
20 - Long poem (4)

No 164

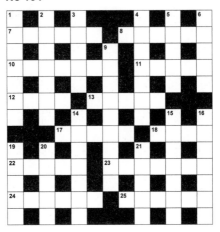

Across
7 - Place of refuge (6)
8 - Believable (6)
10 - Become husky (7)
11 - Mounds of loose sand (5)
12 - Leave out (4)
13 - Eg oxygen; nitrogen (5)
17 - Holding device (5)
18 - Soft mineral (4)
22 - Altar stone (5)
23 - Censure (7)
24 - Residents (6)
25 - Snow sport (6)

Down
1 - Male adult state (7)
2 - Polyhedron (7)
3 - Small fluid-filled sac (5)
4 - Inclination (4-3)
5 - Narrow leather strips (5)
6 - Rover (5)
9 - Brings into harm's way (9)
14 - Devotedly (7)
15 - Terse (7)
16 - Area of ground (7)
19 - Stroll (5)
20 - Bump (5)
21 - Talked audibly (5)

No 165

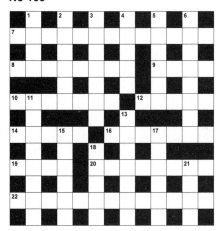

Across

7 - Crude but effective (5-3-5)
8 - Having a striking hue (8)
9 - Vocal solo (4)
10 - Small portable container (7)
12 - Guide (5)
14 - Cooking method (5)
16 - Farthest away (7)
19 - Dynasty in China (4)
20 - Educated (8)
22 - A transient occurrence (5,2,3,3)

Down

1 - Indifferent (2-2)
2 - Ancient or well established (3-3)
3 - Midpoint (7)
4 - Pastoral poem (5)
5 - Panted (anag) (6)
6 - Anxiety (8)
11 - Landing and take-off area (8)
13 - Help yourself meals (7)
15 - Take in (6)
17 - Place of trade (6)
18 - Songbird (5)
21 - Test (4)

No 166

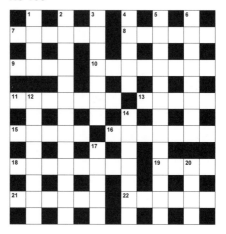

Across
7 - Rigid bars (6)
8 - Sections of garlic (6)
9 - Desert in central China (4)
10 - Faith; belief (8)
11 - Eg USA (7)
13 - Retaining strip (5)
15 - Entertain (5)
16 - Scrubber (7)
18 - Roman emperor (8)
19 - Nothing (4)
21 - Alter (6)
22 - Spread rumor (6)

Down
1 - Protest march (4)
2 - Partially awake (13)
3 - Fish hawks (7)
4 - Relative magnitude (5)
5 - Absent-mindedness (13)
6 - Embellish (8)
12 - Military unit (8)
14 - Scrawny (7)
17 - Songs by two people (5)
20 - Animal's den (4)

No 167

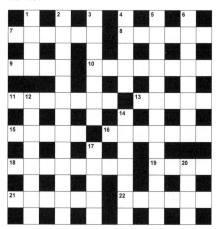

Across

7 - Seek (6)
8 - Mechanical devices (6)
9 - Crush food (4)
10 - Memento (8)
11 - Creamy chocolate candy (7)
13 - Paces (5)
15 - Gyrates (5)
16 - Performer of gymnastic feats (7)
18 - Fit together tightly (8)
19 - Chopped (4)
21 - Give in (6)
22 - Swallowed (6)

Down

1 - Volcano in Sicily (4)
2 - Prone to steal (5-8)
3 - Female reflexive pronoun (7)
4 - Arrogant (5)
5 - Causing disapproval (13)
6 - Republic in E Africa (8)
12 - Censure (8)
14 - Branch of biology (7)
17 - Mages (anag) (5)
20 - Supplements (4)

No 168

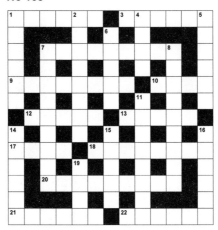

Across

1 - Plan of action (6)
3 - Put away (6)
7 - Give religious instruction to (9)
9 - Water based aircraft (8)
10 - Partly open (4)
12 - Norwegian (5)
13 - Wears (5)
17 - Plunder; take illegally (4)
18 - Liable to error (8)
20 - At an angle (9)
21 - Pressing keys (6)
22 - More gruesome (6)

Down

1 - Bear witness (6)
2 - Unaffected by time (8)
4 - Second of pair (4)
5 - Puts off (6)
6 - Small rounded cake (5)
7 - Offensively loud (9)
8 - Pleasurable (9)
11 - Making a hole (8)
14 - Dark wine (6)
15 - Excessively quick (5)
16 - Swordsman (6)
19 - Futile (4)

No 169

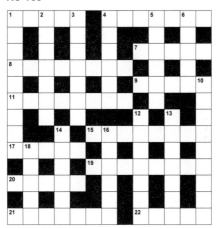

Across

1 - Proceeding from the pope (5)
4 - Compress (7)
7 - Dye (5)
8 - Rear door on a car (8)
9 - Attach to (5)
11 - Make hostile (8)
15 - Ballroom dance (8)
17 - Is enamored with (5)
19 - Make gradual inroads (8)
20 - Lukewarm (5)
21 - Aids (7)
22 - Move sideways (5)

Down

1 - Representation (9)
2 - Large ocean (7)
3 - Tree cutting (7)
4 - Group of six (6)
5 - Degree (6)
6 - Republic in central Africa (5)
10 - Percussion instrument (9)
12 - Have impact (7)
13 - Pledged to marry (7)
14 - Third sign of the zodiac (6)
16 - Wildcats (6)
18 - Baking appliances (5)

No 170

Across

1 - Water ice (6)
5 - Debars (anag) (6)
8 - Bend (4)
9 - Questioner (8)
10 - Extinct birds (5)
11 - Walk with difficulty (7)
14 - Relating to a geological era (13)
16 - Attains (7)
18 - Exhaust gases (5)
20 - Speak unfavorably about (8)
22 - Hoodwink (4)
23 - Liquid container (6)
24 - Small and slender wolf (6)

Down

2 - Place side by side (9)
3 - Conceited dandy (7)
4 - Supplements (4)
5 - Make more pleasing (8)
6 - Getting older (5)
7 - Female deer (3)
12 - Enthusiastic (9)
13 - Not safe (8)
15 - Approximately (7)
17 - Celestial body (5)
19 - Stylish (4)
21 - Ruction (3)

No 171

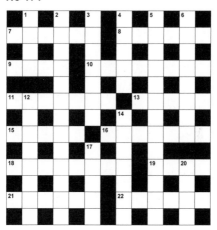

Across
7 - World's largest country (6)
8 - Compensate for (6)
9 - Fencing sword (4)
10 - Feud (8)
11 - Boorish (7)
13 - Motionless (5)
15 - Attach (5)
16 - Academic administrator (7)
18 - Historian (8)
19 - Fleet (4)
21 - Bullet (6)
22 - Set of prayers (6)

Down
1 - Aggregation (4)
2 - Capable of being found out (13)
3 - The gathering of crops (7)
4 - Determine the number of (5)
5 - Success (13)
6 - Cold-blooded vertebrates (8)
12 - Hurt; disrespected (8)
14 - Steep-sided depressions (7)
17 - NY shopping avenue (5)
20 - Extremely (4)

No 172

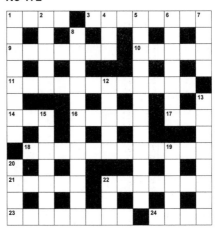

Across
1 - Jumps (4)
3 - Expressed disregard (8)
9 - Get back (7)
10 - Fates (5)
11 - Assembling (12)
14 - Level golf score (3)
16 - A large smoke (5)
17 - Two (3)
18 - Astonishing (3-9)
21 - Domestic dog (5)
22 - Welcomed (7)
23 - Having supreme skill (8)
24 - Bouquet (4)

Down
1 - Paper printout of data (4,4)
2 - Brown oval nut (5)
4 - Bustle (3)
5 - Not precisely established (12)
6 - Moaned (7)
7 - Flat circular plate (4)
8 - Skillfully prepared food (5,7)
12 - Proposes (5)
13 - Obstinately (8)
15 - Incentives (7)
19 - Start of something (abbrev) (5)
20 - Con (4)
22 - Leg (anag) (3)

No 173

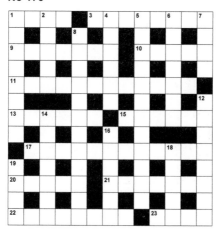

Across
1 - Utters (4)
3 - Vehicle with three wheels (8)
9 - Nonbeliever in God (7)
10 - Edges (5)
11 - Relation by marriage (7-2-3)
13 - Vulgarity (6)
15 - Walk (6)
17 - Religious group (12)
20 - Dimension (5)
21 - Sour in taste (7)
22 - Move out the way of (8)
23 - Hide (4)

Down
1 - Sheath for a sword (8)
2 - Loutish male (5)
4 - Go back (6)
5 - Woodworker (12)
6 - The Windy City (7)
7 - Relaxation (4)
8 - Garments worn in bed (12)
12 - Scientifically detached (8)
14 - Overturned (7)
16 - Vehement speech (6)
18 - Suffuse with color (5)
19 - Possesses (4)

No 174

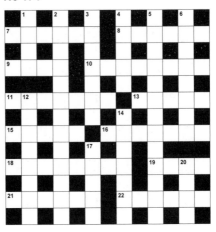

Across

7 - Lower (6)
8 - Republic in Central America (6)
9 - Wild swine (4)
10 - Fortress in Paris (8)
11 - Spoke solemnly (7)
13 - Type of plastic (5)
15 - In what place (5)
16 - Triumph (7)
18 - Sandal (4-4)
19 - Intellectual faculty (4)
21 - Positive features (6)
22 - Food storeroom (6)

Down

1 - Change again (4)
2 - Musical dance co-ordinator (13)
3 - Multiplied threefold (7)
4 - Involuntary muscle contraction (5)
5 - Type of medication (13)
6 - Boss (8)
12 - Anarchy (8)
14 - River in S Africa (7)
17 - Conflict (5)
20 - Emperor of Rome 54-68 (4)

No 175

Across
1 - Encircles (8)
5 - ___ facto: by the fact itself (4)
8 - Prophet (5)
9 - Very large (7)
10 - Gave out (7)
12 - Maxims (7)
14 - Lie scattered over (7)
16 - Capital of Indonesia (7)
18 - Reduction (3,4)
19 - Smashed (5)
20 - Rose (anag) (4)
21 - And so on (2,6)

Down
1 - Not strong (4)
2 - Fourscore (6)
3 - Torturer (9)
4 - Calls forth (6)
6 - Colorants (6)
7 - Create an account deficit (8)
11 - Irritable (9)
12 - Topics (8)
13 - Ice mover (6)
14 - Container (6)
15 - Take away (6)
17 - Second Greek letter (4)

No 176

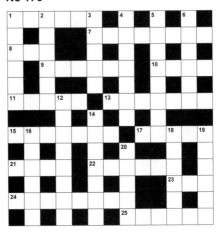

Across

1 - Adventurous expedition (6)
7 - Aware (8)
8 - Antelope (3)
9 - Very pleasing to the eye (6)
10 - Office table (4)
11 - Cloth (5)
13 - Word with the opposite meaning (7)
15 - Faint (4,3)
17 - Lane (5)
21 - Fine mineral powder (4)
22 - Division of a group (6)
23 - Slippery liquid (3)
24 - Native American game (8)
25 - Done in stages (6)

Down

1 - Devices for aiming (6)
2 - Regulator of liquid flow (6)
3 - Islands (5)
4 - Eternal (7)
5 - Game bird (8)
6 - Gaudy (6)
12 - Not safe (8)
14 - Remain alive (7)
16 - Graphical representation (6)
18 - Yellow citrus fruits (6)
19 - Shouted (6)
20 - Faint bird cry (5)

No 177

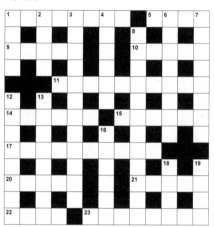

Across
1 - Rummage (8)
5 - Con (4)
9 - Receive the ball (5)
10 - Tells (5)
11 - Uneducated (10)
14 - Not these (6)
15 - Abroad (6)
17 - Pullover; jersey (10)
20 - Repeat an action (5)
21 - Mother-of-pearl (5)
22 - Natural fertilizer (4)
23 - Victim of social injustice (8)

Down
1 - Inner circle (4)
2 - Performs (4)
3 - Feeling of great joy (12)
4 - Strong flavor (6)
6 - Semi-rural dwellings (8)
7 - Wrongdoings (8)
8 - Disturbance (12)
12 - Leaning to one side (8)
13 - Endanger (8)
16 - Selected (6)
18 - Not an alkaline (4)
19 - Mass of floating ice (4)

No 178

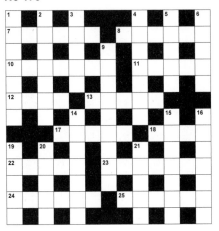

Across

7 - Number of Apostles (6)
8 - Dark blue dye (6)
10 - Split into pieces (5,2)
11 - Farm (5)
12 - Consumes (4)
13 - Stage items (5)
17 - Boldness (5)
18 - Brownish purple (4)
22 - Collection of maps (5)
23 - Stinging weeds (7)
24 - Face-to-face (4-2)
25 - Amorous relationship (6)

Down

1 - Buildings for horses (7)
2 - Hates (7)
3 - Cause; create (5)
4 - Encode (7)
5 - Very tall person (5)
6 - Scottish lakes (5)
9 - Authorizing (9)
14 - Variant (7)
15 - ___ power: power from uranium (⬚)
16 - Time off (7)
19 - Very masculine (5)
20 - Beam of light (5)
21 - Rigid (5)

No 179

Across

1 - Two pairs (8)
6 - Commit to memory (^)
8 - Rigid; stern (6)
9 - Religious writing (6)
10 - Liquid used for washing (3)
11 - Sharp bites (4)
12 - Least polite (6)
13 - Diminished in size (6)
15 - Climbing tool (6)
17 - Lump or blob (6)
20 - Stolen goods (4)
21 - Unwell (3)
22 - Married woman (6)
23 - Shelter (6)
24 - Change or deviate (4)
25 - Allergy to pollen (8)

Down

2 - Very large bird (7)
3 - Precipitates (5)
4 - Belief (7)
5 - Gardening tool (5)
6 - Domiciled (7)
7 - Levels; ranks (5)
14 - Hypersensitivity reaction (7)
15 - Simple song (7)
16 - Migrant (7)
18 - Barack ___ : US President (5)
19 - Compress sharply (5)
20 - Form of expression (5)

No 180

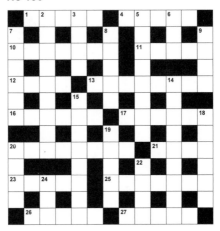

Across
1 - Away (5)
4 - Worship (5)
10 - Treatment (7)
11 - Irresistible belief (5)
12 - Young men (4)
13 - Comfy seat (8)
16 - Verse (6)
17 - Drumbeat (6)
20 - Humorous verse (8)
21 - Gape (4)
23 - Lead discussion (5)
25 - Aperture or hole (7)
26 - Supports (5)
27 - Item of value (5)

Down
2 - Pen name (9)
3 - Wander (4)
5 - Eg Hillary Clinton (8)
6 - Flee (3)
7 - Photos (6)
8 - Aromatic resin (5)
9 - Animal's den (4)
14 - Make real (9)
15 - Drop from the eye (8)
18 - Fish hawk (6)
19 - Performing artist (5)
20 - Deficiency (4)
22 - Depressions (4)
24 - Mock (3)

No 181

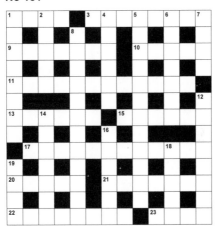

Across
1 - Exhausts (4)
3 - Trustworthy (8)
9 - Coward (7)
10 - Fizzy drinks (5)
11 - Pedigree (12)
13 - Hoarding bird (6)
15 - Chief journalist (6)
17 - Immutable (12)
20 - Make right (5)
21 - Snail-shaped tube (7)
22 - Musician (8)
23 - Having little hair (4)

Down
1 - Erstwhile (8)
2 - Infectious disease (5)
4 - Refute (6)
5 - Insubordination (12)
6 - Unrecoverable money owed (3,4)
7 - Relaxation (4)
8 - Amazement (12)
12 - Without mechanical aids (8)
14 - Venetian boat (7)
16 - Plays (6)
18 - Light wood (5)
19 - Child who has no home (4)

No 182

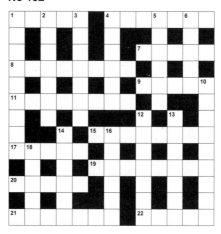

Across
1 - Mounds of loose sand (5)
4 - Sugar (7)
7 - Issue forth with force (5)
8 - Style of speech (8)
9 - Chats (5)
11 - Come together (8)
15 - Assimilate again (8)
17 - Adversary (5)
19 - Hot pepper (8)
20 - Expression; artistic style (5)
21 - Bans (7)
22 - Pertaining to sound (5)

Down
1 - Move out of position (9)
2 - Beginning to exist (7)
3 - Seats (7)
4 - Powerful (6)
5 - Happen again (6)
6 - Unable to move (5)
10 - Living together (9)
12 - Acquires (7)
13 - Supervisor (7)
14 - Raise in relief (6)
16 - Demands penalty (6)
18 - Prod with elbow (5)

No 183

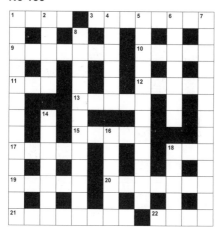

Across
1 - Person who will inherit (4)
3 - Engravings (8)
9 - Personal (7)
10 - Enthusiasm (5)
11 - Long-leaved lettuce (3)
12 - Damp (5)
13 - Musical times (5)
15 - Strayed (5)
17 - River formation (5)
18 - Inflated feeling of pride (3)
19 - Maladroit (5)
20 - Directories on a computer (7)
21 - Eg resident of Montreal (8)
22 - Linger (4)

Down
1 - Valetudinarian (13)
2 - Vines (5)
4 - Belief in one God (6)
5 - In a principled manner (4-8)
6 - Unpleasively (7)
7 - Impulsively (13)
8 - Timorous (5-7)
14 - Sailing ship (7)
16 - Fiber for making mats (6)
18 - Remove; expel (5)

No 184

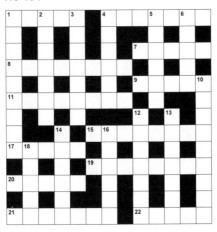

Across
1 - Electronic communication (1-4)
4 - Five singers (7)
7 - Government (5)
8 - Capsize (8)
9 - Trimmings of meat (5)
11 - Prevail over (8)
15 - Expression of gratitude (5,3)
17 - Spiced dish (5)
19 - Pasta (8)
20 - Channel filled with water (5)
21 - Eg anger or love (7)
22 - Threshold (5)

Down
1 - Efficient (9)
2 - Made irate (7)
3 - Framework (7)
4 - Number needed for a valid vote (6)
5 - Inform (6)
6 - Additional (5)
10 - Lush (9)
12 - Disentangle (7)
13 - Word having a similar meaning (7)
14 - Fleshy white poultry meat (6)
16 - Face-to-face (4-2)
18 - Disarm (5)

No 185

Across

1 - Gaming cubes (4)
3 - Tyrannic (8)
9 - John ___ : tennis player (7)
10 - Less common (5)
11 - Difficult to deal with (5-7)
14 - Bristlelike appendage (3)
16 - Small regular shapes (5)
17 - Belonging to us (3)
18 - Unsophisticated (12)
21 - Group of eight (5)
22 - Speaking (7)
23 - Removing contents (8)
24 - Hero (4)

Down

1 - Eg Al Gore (8)
2 - Doctrine (5)
4 - Supplement (3)
5 - Liberally (12)
6 - Underwater projectile (7)
7 - Rope (4)
8 - Long race (5,7)
12 - Machine (5)
13 - Extravagant (8)
15 - Without interruption (7)
19 - Reliable (5)
20 - Ripped; rote (anag) (4)
22 - Metal; can (3)

No 186

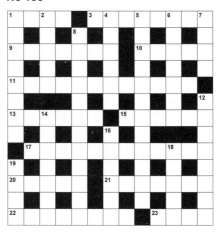

Across
1 - Waist band (4)
3 - Cause resentment (8)
9 - Spring back (7)
10 - Stop (5)
11 - Modestly (12)
13 - Irish capital (6)
15 - Hawk (6)
17 - Recognizable (12)
20 - Ascend (5)
21 - Combusted (7)
22 - All people (8)
23 - Smell (4)

Down
1 - Red table wine (8)
2 - Star sign (5)
4 - Title for a woman (6)
5 - Untimely (12)
6 - Followed (7)
7 - Ostrichlike bird (4)
8 - Doubtfully (12)
12 - Protector (8)
14 - Space alongside a bed (7)
16 - Minor official (6)
18 - Held in breath (5)
19 - Race (anag) (4)

No 187

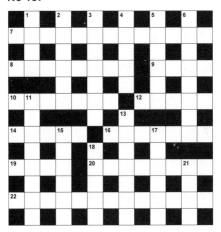

Across
7 - Markedly new (13)
8 - Act a part (8)
9 - Otherwise (4)
10 - Disdained (7)
12 - Piece of cloth (5)
14 - Fast (5)
16 - Birds eaten at Thanksgiving (7)
19 - Broken husks of seeds (4)
20 - Edges of roofs (8)
22 - A transient occurrence (5,2,3,3)

Down
1 - Presentation (4)
2 - Exhibitionist (6)
3 - Enclosure for prisoners (7)
4 - Plastic (5)
5 - Dream up (6)
6 - Playfully (8)
11 - Craven (8)
13 - Costing less than usual (3-4)
15 - Terminate (6)
17 - German astronomer (6)
18 - Kingdom in SW Europe (5)
21 - Melt (4)

No 188

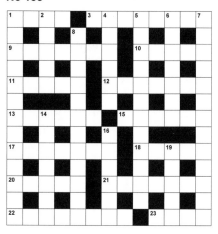

Across
1 - To pawn (4)
3 - Dishes of the day (8)
9 - Protective coverings (7)
10 - Lover of Juliet (5)
11 - Disarm (5)
12 - Noisiest (7)
13 - Starting data (6)
15 - Tropical fly (6)
17 - Appropriately (7)
18 - Renew (5)
20 - Declare (5)
21 - Shellfish (7)
22 - Class of small freeholders (8)
23 - Push (4)

Down
1 - Visionary (13)
2 - Latin American dance (5)
4 - Stone tool (6)
5 - Restrict (12)
6 - Part of a chair (7)
7 - Easily angered (5-8)
8 - Words that mimic sounds (12)
14 - Porch (7)
16 - Horse groom (6)
19 - Supply (5)

No 189

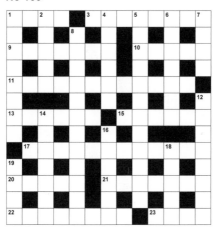

Across
1 - Furniture wood (4)
3 - Encircles (8)
9 - Finery (7)
10 - Odor releasing animal (5)
11 - Ate too much (12)
13 - Substitute (6)
15 - Dual audio (6)
17 - Identifiably (12)
20 - Soft fruit (5)
21 - Appearance (7)
22 - Reevaluate (8)
23 - Extremely (4)

Down
1 - Turtle (8)
2 - Tiny aquatic plants (5)
4 - Republic in central Africa (6)
5 - Lowest possible temperature (8,4)
6 - Haughtiness (7)
7 - Japanese beverage (4)
8 - Ordinary dress (5,7)
12 - Having many spouses (8)
14 - Japanese flower arranging (7)
16 - Sandpipers (6)
18 - Smashed into pieces (5)
19 - Goad on (4)

No 190

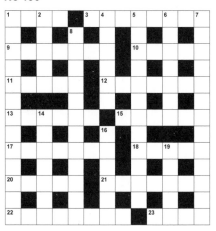

Across
1 - Skin disorder (4)
3 - Woolen clothing (8)
9 - Curdle (7)
10 - Coral reef (5)
11 - Wild dog of Australia (5)
12 - Not connected (3-4)
13 - Nuance (6)
15 - Symbolic (6)
17 - Not in a hurry (7)
18 - Republic in S Asia (5)
20 - Small Italian fruit (5)
21 - Acquire from someone else (7)
22 - Penultimate teenage year (8)
23 - Ale (4)

Down
1 - Liable to mishaps (8-5)
2 - Silk or thin fabric (5)
4 - Wrestling hold (6)
5 - Stop-go device (7,5)
6 - Eg anger or love (7)
7 - Amusement park ride (6,7)
8 - Disregarding the rules (5,3,4)
14 - Sarcastic (7)
16 - Walk with long steps (6)
19 - Funeral hymn (5)

No 191

Across
1 - Effusion (8)
6 - Aisle of a church (4)
8 - Needle (6)
9 - Eastern temple (6)
10 - Stimulus (3)
11 - Nobleman (4)
12 - Boldness (6)
13 - Weave (6)
15 - Pamper (6)
17 - Eagerly (6)
20 - Effervesce (4)
21 - Mature (3)
22 - Dig a hole (6)
23 - Opposing (6)
24 - Sic (4)
25 - Spatters with liquid (8)

Down
2 - Lie (7)
3 - Lump or bump (5)
4 - Revoke (7)
5 - Recorded (5)
6 - Made irate (7)
7 - Type of car (5)
14 - Withstands (7)
15 - Cautious (7)
16 - Medicated tablet (7)
18 - Pledge (5)
19 - Shows tiredness (5)
20 - Accurate pieces of information (5)

No 192

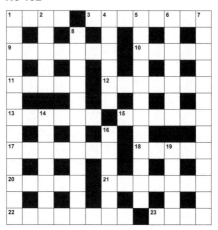

Across
1 - Entering (4)
3 - Resisting (8)
9 - First performance (7)
10 - Capital of Bulgaria (5)
11 - Aircraft detection system (5)
12 - Huge wave (7)
13 - Unless (6)
15 - Heavy mineral (6)
17 - Table support (7)
18 - Musical times (5)
20 - Promotional wording (5)
21 - Eg from Moscow (7)
22 - Writer (8)
23 - Fixing; make tight (4)

Down
1 - Subtle (13)
2 - Thick woolen fabric (5)
4 - Buccaneer (6)
5 - Obfuscation (12)
6 - Catch fire (7)
7 - Relating to an attractive force (13)
8 - Disgracefully (12)
14 - Infants; angels (7)
16 - Playing cards suit (6)
19 - Cereal grass (5)

No 193

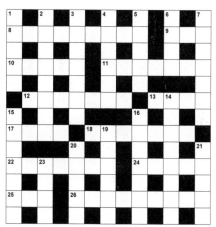

Across

8 - Sailboat (9)
9 - Expert (3)
10 - Talent (5)
11 - Highly original (7)
12 - Eternal (7)
13 - Reflection (4)
17 - Part of foot (4)
18 - Causes (7)
22 - Inert substance (7)
24 - Light blue (5)
25 - Deer (3)
26 - Make insensitive (9)

Down

1 - Eat quickly (5)
2 - Ramble (8)
3 - Cleverly (7)
4 - Plants (6)
5 - Antagonist (5)
6 - Puns (anag) (4)
7 - Chest for implements (7)
14 - Having a sweet nature (8)
15 - Small slender dog (7)
16 - Widens (7)
19 - Exaggerate (4,2)
20 - Freshwater food fish (5)
21 - Unit of length (5)
23 - Seabirds (4)

No 194

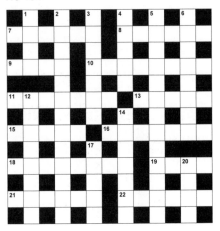

Across

7 - Pollute (6)
8 - Sufficient (6)
9 - Female child (4)
10 - Imitations (8)
11 - Icy statue (7)
13 - Plait (5)
15 - Soft and comfortable (5)
16 - The Windy City (7)
18 - Belief in pleasure (8)
19 - Separate (4)
21 - Created (6)
22 - Chairs (6)

Down

1 - Penultimate round (4)
2 - Continue a stroke (6,7)
3 - Boat launcher (7)
4 - Style (5)
5 - Computerized typewriter (4,9)
6 - According (8)
12 - Feel sick (8)
14 - Scientist (7)
17 - Types (5)
20 - Satiate (4)

No 195

Across

7 - Campaigner (8)
8 - Lazy (4)
9 - Domesticated ox (4)
10 - Adorn (8)
11 - Pasted up artistic image (7)
12 - Express in speech (5)
15 - Engages in (5)
17 - Skipped about (7)
20 - Developing (8)
22 - Current (4)
23 - Cover (4)
24 - Maintain (8)

Down

1 - Precede (6)
2 - Suddenly (8)
3 - Ancestry (7)
4 - Wounds (5)
5 - Permit to enter (4)
6 - Nearly (6)
13 - Observant (4-4)
14 - Interlaced (7)
16 - Active (6)
18 - Salad plant (6)
19 - Lively (5)
21 - Woman (4)

No 196

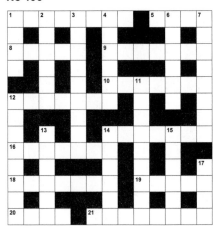

Across
1 - Applying a remedy (8)
5 - Cattle; meat (4)
8 - Maladroit (5)
9 - Bar rooms (7)
10 - Stimulate (7)
12 - Combusted (7)
14 - Lectures (7)
16 - Encroach (7)
18 - Slanted characters (7)
19 - Egg-shaped (5)
20 - Egypt's river (4)
21 - Pushing (8)

Down
1 - Small branch (4)
2 - Ten plus one (6)
3 - Technique used in chemistry (9)
4 - Implanted (6)
6 - Change gradually (6)
7 - Rapidity (8)
11 - Places (9)
12 - Act of setting on fire (8)
13 - Spread out awkwardly (6)
14 - Tricky puzzle (6)
15 - American state (6)
17 - Austrian composer (4)

No 197

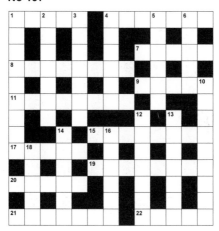

Across
1 - Effluent system (5)
4 - Burdens (7)
7 - Obnoxiously forward (5)
8 - Pattern of circular spots (5,3)
9 - Farm (5)
11 - Edible crustaceans (8)
15 - Short heavy club (8)
17 - Play a guitar (5)
19 - Ahead of the times (8)
20 - Card game (5)
21 - Edible mollusk (7)
22 - Avoid (5)

Down
1 - Formless (9)
2 - Aspiring (5-2)
3 - Remolds (7)
4 - Not outside (6)
5 - Of the eye (6)
6 - Principle of morality (5)
10 - Mesmerize (9)
12 - Declare to be (7)
13 - Diacritical mark (7)
14 - Beat with the fists (6)
16 - Living room (6)
18 - Pollex (5)

No 198

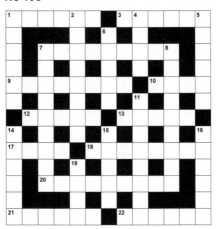

Across
1 - Grouchy (6)
3 - Declare (6)
7 - Self-centered person (9)
9 - Surname of Judas (8)
10 - Large wading bird (4)
12 - Unwanted plants (5)
13 - Livid (5)
17 - Race along (4)
18 - Insistent person (8)
20 - Repeated (9)
21 - Second of two (6)
22 - Foolish (6)

Down
1 - Evil-tempered spirit (6)
2 - Thrust forward (8)
4 - Just (4)
5 - Chilled dessert (6)
6 - Cut of pork (5)
7 - Treasury (9)
8 - One-horse carriage (9)
11 - Formal meal (8)
14 - Assault (6)
15 - Grim (5)
16 - Tramp (6)
19 - Spots (4)

No 199

Across
1 - Metal (4)
3 - Ritual washing (8)
9 - US currency (plural) (7)
10 - Pretend (5)
11 - Small drink (3)
12 - Dole out (5)
13 - Disturb (5)
15 - Suffuse with color (5)
17 - Relay device (5)
18 - Dishonorable person (3)
19 - To come with (5)
20 - Mental strain (7)
21 - Longing (8)
22 - Accurate (4)

Down
1 - Ineffably (13)
2 - Spring flower (5)
4 - Work chiefs (6)
5 - Uncomplimentary (12)
6 - Frozen water spears (7)
7 - Absence (13)
8 - Trip-inducing drug (12)
14 - Greek wine (7)
16 - Secure with wooden strips (6)
18 - Announcer (5)

No 200

Across

7 - Blankly (8)
8 - Curse; solemn promise (4)
9 - Having pains (4)
10 - Woman working in a dairy (8)
11 - Use (7)
12 - Stallion (5)
15 - Accept (5)
17 - Explain again (7)
20 - Capital of Finland (8)
22 - Highest male voice (4)
23 - Greek cheese (4)
24 - Sinfully (8)

Down

1 - Regulator of liquid flow (6)
2 - Dark color that is virtually black (4,4)
3 - Spray very finely (7)
4 - Go through (5)
5 - Configuration (4)
6 - Flight of steps (6)
13 - Outmoded (8)
14 - Charm (7)
16 - Diving birds (6)
18 - Gossip (6)
19 - Understands (5)
21 - Fraud (4)

No 201

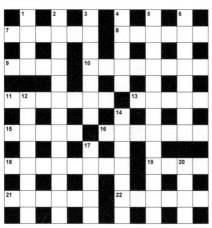

Across
7 - Reprimand (6)
8 - Leads (6)
9 - Helper (4)
10 - Part of male Tudor dress (8)
11 - Seats for two or more people (7)
13 - Religious writing (5)
15 - Remove facial hair (5)
16 - Lower in quality (7)
18 - Majesty (8)
19 - Italian acknowledgment (4)
21 - Passes by degrees (6)
22 - Smiles contemptuously (6)

Down
1 - Republic in W Africa (4)
2 - Success (13)
3 - Impeded (7)
4 - Darts very quickly (5)
5 - Scared (5-8)
6 - Having small brown spots (8)
12 - Delicate (8)
14 - Closest (7)
17 - Party (5)
20 - Twisted toward one side (4)

No 202

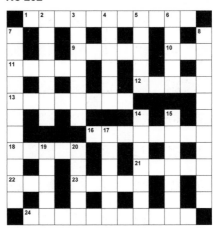

Across
1 - Peculiarity (11)
9 - Seeped (5)
10 - Unwell (3)
11 - Overclothes (5)
12 - Symbols of oppression (5)
13 - Soldiers (8)
16 - Driven to (8)
18 - Indian social class (5)
21 - Awaken (5)
22 - Sheep (3)
23 - Extreme (5)
24 - Evolutionary changes (11)

Down
2 - Floating mass of frozen water (7)
3 - Costing (anag) (7)
4 - Less motivated to act (6)
5 - Reddish (5)
6 - Having many layers (5)
7 - Ornithologist (4,7)
8 - State of supreme happiness (11)
14 - Italian fast racing car (7)
15 - Egg white protein (7)
17 - Sacred writing (6)
19 - Role; office (5)
20 - Supply (5)

No 203

Across

7 - Flower arrangement (6)
8 - Threaten (6)
9 - Ruin (4)
10 - Muscle therapists (8)
11 - Acute food shortages (7)
13 - Muscular (5)
15 - Nimble (5)
16 - Coal bucket (7)
18 - Taxi rank (8)
19 - Narrow strip of land (4)
21 - Performing (6)
22 - Succeed (6)

Down

1 - Killer whale (4)
2 - Desiring worldly possessions (13)
3 - Glisten (7)
4 - Bump (5)
5 - Compellingly (13)
6 - Derisive (8)
12 - Debatably (8)
14 - Make sour (7)
17 - Extent or limit (5)
20 - Cut (4)

No 204

Across

7 - Close friend (8)
8 - Compass point (4)
9 - Spanish surrealist painter (4)
10 - Ways of life (8)
11 - Treat cruelly (7)
12 - Indistinct (5)
15 - Song (5)
17 - Intoxicants (7)
20 - Projectile rebound (8)
22 - Throw away as refuse (4)
23 - Indication (4)
24 - Moderately rich (4-2-2)

Down

1 - Emanating from God (6)
2 - Witness (8)
3 - Cookie (7)
4 - Ability (5)
5 - Republic in W South America (4)
6 - Feature (6)
13 - Deluge (8)
14 - Horizontal beams (7)
16 - Water ice (6)
18 - Put right (6)
19 - Ostentatious (5)
21 - Unwrap present (4)

No 205

Across
7 - Showered (6)
8 - Free from discord (6)
10 - Speak quietly (7)
11 - Extent (5)
12 - Real (anag) (4)
13 - Army rank (5)
17 - Succulent (5)
18 - Couple (4)
22 - Correct (5)
23 - Attendant (7)
24 - Frozen plain (6)
25 - Declares invalid (6)

Down
1 - Obsequious person (7)
2 - Imitation (7)
3 - Jumps (5)
4 - Six sided shape (7)
5 - Bludgeons (5)
6 - Hits swiftly (5)
9 - Transmit (9)
14 - Dairy products (7)
15 - Capital of Nicaragua (7)
16 - From the United Kingdom (7)
19 - Fact (5)
20 - Representative (5)
21 - Ownership mark (5)

No 206

Across
1 - Particles around a comet (4)
3 - Church rules (5,3)
9 - Increased (7)
10 - Ornament (5)
11 - Ethos (anag) (5)
12 - Make a big profit (5,2)
13 - Threaten (6)
15 - Plaster decoration (6)
17 - Interstellar gas clouds (7)
18 - Gnat (5)
20 - Greeting (5)
21 - Wrongdoers (7)
22 - Sunshades (8)
23 - Smell (4)

Down
1 - Skill in a trade (13)
2 - Extremely small (5)
4 - Advance evidence for (6)
5 - First part of the Bible (3,9)
6 - Terse (7)
7 - Computerized typewriter (4,9)
8 - Conceited (12)
14 - Biter (7)
16 - Small carnivorous mammal (6)
19 - Fear (5)

No 207

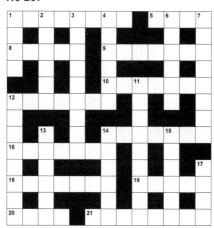

Across
1 - Similarity (8)
5 - Spots (4)
8 - Group of singers (5)
9 - Base (7)
10 - Helps to happen (7)
12 - Guaranteed (7)
14 - Disputing (7)
16 - Against (7)
18 - Place out of sight (7)
19 - Receded (5)
20 - Run quickly (4)
21 - Gesticulates (8)

Down
1 - Fine and delicate (4)
2 - Hills (6)
3 - Rooms for young children (9)
4 - Chopped (6)
6 - Pave (6)
7 - Evening prayer (8)
11 - State of being lined up (9)
12 - Sanctioned (8)
13 - Flecks (6)
14 - Stick to (6)
15 - Line of equal pressure (6)
17 - Probability (4)

No 208

Across
1 - Not difficult (4)
3 - Forward movement (8)
9 - Chase (7)
10 - Protective garment (5)
11 - Statistical data of a population (12)
14 - Double (3)
16 - Coral reef (5)
17 - Adam's mate (3)
18 - Mentally acute (5-7)
21 - Last Greek letter (5)
22 - Carry on (7)
23 - Dregs (8)
24 - Antelopes (4)

Down
1 - Speed up (8)
2 - Play a guitar (5)
4 - Mud channel (3)
5 - Handwriting analyst (12)
6 - Annoying pain (7)
7 - Dispatched (4)
8 - Loud security device (7,5)
12 - Microscopic structures (5)
13 - Titles (8)
15 - Plant species like flax (7)
19 - Two (5)
20 - Canines (4)
22 - Male offspring (3)

No 209

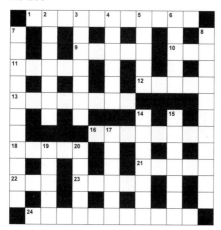

Across
1 - Teasing (11)
9 - Watch (5)
10 - Teacher (3)
11 - Lines in circle (5)
12 - Fifty two of these yearly (5)
13 - Awkward (8)
16 - Oil and water mix (8)
18 - Household garbage (5)
21 - Musical times (5)
22 - Steal (3)
23 - Get up (5)
24 - Energetically (11)

Down
2 - Information (7)
3 - Rewrites (7)
4 - Rowed (6)
5 - Relative by marriage (2-3)
6 - Unwarranted (5)
7 - Hasty (11)
8 - Unnecessary (11)
14 - Flat highland (7)
15 - Postal service (7)
17 - Environment (6)
19 - Monastery superior (5)
20 - Lift; elevate (5)

No 210

Across

1 - Bird sound (6)
5 - Stimulus (3)
7 - Solid filling (5)
8 - Strife (7)
9 - Egg centers (5)
10 - Shape guides (8)
12 - Song words (6)
14 - Case (6)
17 - Fondly (8)
18 - Tiny crustaceans (5)
20 - Progress; forward motion (7)
21 - Sisters of one's parents (5)
22 - Come together (3)
23 - Sporting dog (6)

Down

2 - Softly (7)
3 - Game bird (8)
4 - Criticize strongly (4)
5 - Tornado (7)
6 - Letter (7)
7 - Pastoral poem (5)
11 - Last (8)
12 - Viewing (7)
13 - Musical entertainment (7)
15 - Common (7)
16 - Scottish lakes (5)
19 - Solitary (4)

No 211

Across
1 - Recollect (8)
6 - Tabs (anag) (4)
8 - Ear bone (6)
9 - Pain in the side (6)
10 - Cool down (3)
11 - Hunted animal (4)
12 - Not tea (anag) (6)
13 - Promotional material (6)
15 - Thick innermost digits (6)
17 - Multiply by two (6)
20 - Heavy hammer (4)
21 - Small drink (3)
22 - Takes the place of (6)
23 - Written agreement (6)
24 - Requests (4)
25 - Guards (8)

Down
2 - Went in (7)
3 - Make void (5)
4 - Most active (7)
5 - Ascended (5)
6 - Japanese massage technique (7)
7 - Famous English racetrack (5)
14 - Sets out (7)
15 - Submarine weapon (7)
16 - Bedroom (7)
18 - Fertile area in a desert (5)
19 - Try (5)
20 - Variety of coffee (5)

No 212

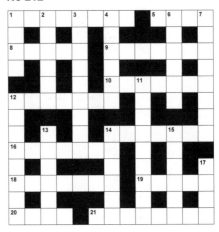

Across

1 - Very successful businessmen (8)
5 - Musical staff sign (4)
8 - Revel (anag) (5)
9 - Disturbance; commotion (7)
10 - Innocently (7)
12 - Indicated (7)
14 - Widen (7)
16 - Small detail (7)
18 - Shine (7)
19 - Metal spikes (5)
20 - Ooze (4)
21 - Power to float (8)

Down

1 - Temperate (4)
2 - Providing (6)
3 - West Indian plant (9)
4 - Trip (6)
6 - Linger aimlessly (6)
7 - Comedian (8)
11 - Powerlessness (9)
12 - Gives life to (8)
13 - Tempt (6)
14 - Flat-bottomed rowboat (6)
15 - Creative act (6)
17 - Catch sight of (4)

No 213

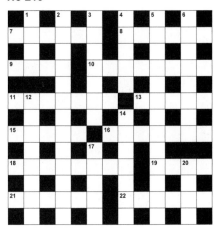

Across
7 - Make beloved (6)
8 - Factory siren (6)
9 - Unable to hear (4)
10 - Washed thoroughly (8)
11 - Elongated rectangles (7)
13 - Aromatic plants (5)
15 - Enlighten (5)
16 - Carriers (7)
18 - Feud (8)
19 - Box lightly (4)
21 - Inclined at an angle (6)
22 - Treatise (6)

Down
1 - Hinge joint (4)
2 - Assured of one's abilities (4-9)
3 - Foreboding (7)
4 - Not here (5)
5 - Betrayed (6-7)
6 - 12th month of the year (8)
12 - Persuaded constantly (8)
14 - Lease holders (7)
17 - Musical study piece (5)
20 - Very keen (4)

No 214

Across
1 - Barbed (6)
5 - Duplicity (6)
8 - Flat region (4)
9 - Fuel generating sites (8)
10 - Growing old (5)
11 - Depraved (7)
14 - Impermeable coating (13)
16 - Big cat (7)
18 - Blunt (5)
20 - Journeyed (8)
22 - Soot particle (4)
23 - Familiarized (6)
24 - Sycophant (3-3)

Down
2 - Handwritten document (9)
3 - Group of servants (7)
4 - System of contemplation (4)
5 - Fade (8)
6 - Group of singers (5)
7 - Variety (3)
12 - Land nearly surrounded by water (9)
13 - Spread out (8)
15 - Woods (7)
17 - ___ Presley: king of rock and roll (5)
19 - Nervy (4)
21 - Cereal grass (3)

216

No 215

Across
1 - Cause to become (6)
5 - Tavern (3)
7 - Humped ruminant (5)
8 - Unpleasant person (7)
9 - Plant fiber (5)
10 - Openers (8)
12 - Dangerous snake (6)
14 - Irregular (6)
17 - Bivalve mollusks (8)
18 - Venomous snake (5)
20 - Deterioration (4-3)
21 - Precipitates (5)
22 - Belonging to him (3)
23 - Causes to act (6)

Down
2 - Precisely (7)
3 - Voting process (8)
4 - Flightless birds (4)
5 - Easily shaped (7)
6 - Hotel page (7)
7 - Spiced dish (5)
11 - Room for dancing (8)
12 - Irritated (7)
13 - Fiddles with (7)
15 - Aspirant (7)
16 - Sour substances (5)
19 - Attack (4)

No 216

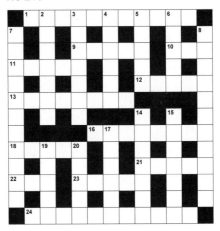

Across
1 - Dissolution (11)
9 - Exhaust gases (5)
10 - Hotel (3)
11 - Insects related to butterfly (5)
12 - Furnish (5)
13 - Deceiving (8)
16 - Printmaker (8)
18 - Come to a point (5)
21 - Nook (5)
22 - Liquid used for washing (3)
23 - Ancient stringed instruments (5)
24 - Dryness (11)

Down
2 - In an annoyed manner (7)
3 - Illegally in advance of the ball (7)
4 - Enticement (4-2)
5 - Untidy (5)
6 - Ingenuous (5)
7 - At once (11)
8 - Heedless (11)
14 - Pass across (7)
15 - Edible fruit (7)
17 - Fruit juice (6)
19 - Part of (5)
20 - Inspire anew (5)

No 217

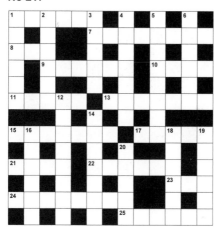

Across
1 - Vegetable with a strong odor (6)
7 - Equipment (8)
8 - Eg oxygen (3)
9 - Graphs (6)
10 - Shaft (4)
11 - Poem (5)
13 - Most active (7)
15 - Drop sharply (7)
17 - Suffering (5)
21 - Elegance (4)
22 - Bribe (6)
23 - Not well (3)
24 - Capital of Finland (8)
25 - Type of edible nut (6)

Down
1 - Stare (6)
2 - Free from danger (6)
3 - Stir milk (5)
4 - Arm exercise (5-2)
5 - Pinching (8)
6 - Mythical monsters (6)
12 - Lameness (8)
14 - Tearful (7)
16 - Quietened (6)
18 - Aloof (6)
19 - Spectral color (6)
20 - Verse form (5)

No 218

Across
1 - An archer (6)
5 - Exhaust (3)
7 - Simpleton (5)
8 - Stopping place (7)
9 - Arrives (5)
10 - Shabby (3-5)
12 - Oblique (6)
14 - Rarely encountered (6)
17 - Inhumane act (8)
18 - Scraped at (5)
20 - Capital of Thailand (7)
21 - Faith groups (5)
22 - Exclamation of surprise (3)
23 - Bush hedge (6)

Down
2 - Defensive structure (7)
3 - Excited (8)
4 - Metallic element (4)
5 - Speak haltingly (7)
6 - Officiate (7)
7 - Interior (5)
11 - Sailing vessel (8)
12 - Shoulder bone (7)
13 - Rinsing fluid (7)
15 - Negative electrode (7)
16 - Remains (5)
19 - Passage (4)

No 219

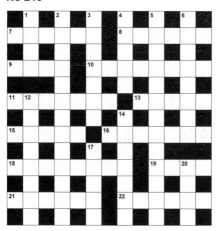

Across

7 - Small stones (6)
8 - Fraud (3-3)
9 - Sneer (4)
10 - Spring of water (8)
11 - Set down on paper (7)
13 - More recent (5)
15 - Narrow openings (5)
16 - Most active (7)
18 - Grated Italian cheese (8)
19 - Tuna (anag) (4)
21 - Flat (6)
22 - Ruler's house (6)

Down

1 - Woody plant (4)
2 - Exaggeration (13)
3 - Person who tries to deceive (7)
4 - Assembly (5)
5 - Uninterestedly (13)
6 - Policemen (8)
12 - Trustworthily (8)
14 - Root vegetables (7)
17 - Exorbitant interest rate (5)
20 - Pleasant (4)

No 220

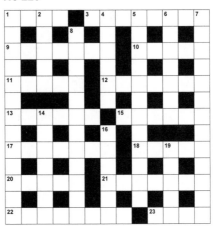

Across
1 - Ire (4)
3 - Abnormal (8)
9 - Parachute opener (7)
10 - White water bird (5)
11 - Maladroit (5)
12 - Unconscious (7)
13 - Place inside (6)
15 - Repressed (4-2)
17 - Mercury alloy (7)
18 - Lowest point (5)
20 - River cove; bay (5)
21 - Capture (7)
22 - Recently married (8)
23 - For fear that (4)

Down
1 - Defensive structure (13)
2 - Sri Lankan monetary unit (5)
4 - Boredom (6)
5 - Readiness (12)
6 - Edible berry (7)
7 - Correct to the last detail (6-7)
8 - Honestly (12)
14 - Devour (7)
16 - Measure of electrical current (6)
19 - Male duck (5)

No 221

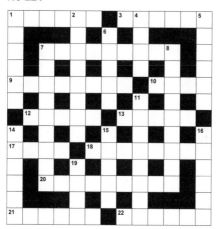

Across
1 - Land surrounded by water (6)
3 - Fissures (6)
7 - Related to classification (9)
9 - Conduit (8)
10 - Computer virus (4)
12 - Benefactor (5)
13 - Redden (5)
17 - Public disturbance (4)
18 - Sharply discordant (8)
20 - Criterion (9)
21 - Small birds (6)
22 - Sticky sugars (6)

Down
1 - Eg from New Delhi (6)
2 - In the adjacent residence (4,4)
4 - Green citrus fruit (4)
5 - Takes by force (6)
6 - Play (5)
7 - Needless repetition of words (9)
8 - Tapered eating device (9)
11 - Ostentatiously (8)
14 - Cover (4,2)
15 - Burst of light (5)
16 - Representatives (6)
19 - Exclamation of frustration (4)

No 222

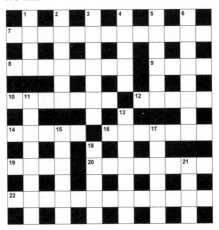

Across
7 - Circulation (13)
8 - Thawed (8)
9 - Left side of a ship (4)
10 - Moving back and forth (7)
12 - Investigate (5)
14 - Up and about (5)
16 - Folds (7)
19 - Sell (4)
20 - Positive disposition (8)
22 - Inferiority (13)

Down
1 - Right to hold property (4)
2 - Small hawk (6)
3 - Incredible (7)
4 - Senseless (5)
5 - Strong lethargy (6)
6 - Atrocious (8)
11 - Prodigal (8)
13 - Strident (7)
15 - Not outside (6)
17 - Allows (6)
18 - Verbose (5)
21 - Mark or blemish (4)

No 223

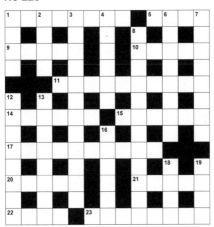

Across
1 - Approximate (8)
5 - Gape (4)
9 - Adult (5)
10 - Strangely (5)
11 - Detain in conversation (10)
14 - Acquired (6)
15 - Among (6)
17 - Sociable (10)
20 - Model; perfect (5)
21 - Sardonic humor (5)
22 - The Orient (4)
23 - Smear (8)

Down
1 - Nervy (4)
2 - Blast of a horn (4)
3 - Manageable (12)
4 - Hosiery (6)
6 - Automatons (8)
7 - Remittances (8)
8 - Sleepwalking (12)
12 - Light again (8)
13 - Cooling devices (8)
16 - Mist (6)
18 - Disagreeable person (4)
19 - Story (4)

No 224

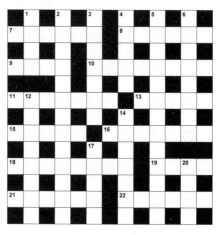

Across
7 - Dangerous snake (6)
8 - Undid (6)
9 - At another time (4)
10 - Confine (8)
11 - Additions to document (7)
13 - Softly radiant (5)
15 - Hiding place (5)
16 - Move (7)
18 - Derisive (8)
19 - Hired form of transport (4)
21 - Mexican cloak (6)
22 - Without ethics (6)

Down
1 - Church song (4)
2 - Astonished (13)
3 - Trespass (7)
4 - Small woodland (5)
5 - Cooling (13)
6 - Airport for choppers (8)
12 - Electronic device (8)
14 - Delude (7)
17 - Currently in progress (5)
20 - Type of high-energy radiation (1-3)

No 225

Across
1 - Resistance units (4)
3 - Diminishes (8)
9 - Tries hard (7)
10 - Chocolate drink (5)
11 - Altruism (12)
14 - Adam's mate (3)
16 - Armistice (5)
17 - Health resort (3)
18 - Determined (6-6)
21 - Black and white animal (5)
22 - Legislator (7)
23 - Quotidian (8)
24 - Layabout (4)

Down
1 - Overwhelmed with concern (8)
2 - Ethical (5)
4 - Possesses (3)
5 - Untimely (12)
6 - Explanations (7)
7 - Break (4)
8 - Developmental (12)
12 - Smarted (5)
13 - Chinese language (8)
15 - Friendly understanding (7)
19 - Game of luck (5)
20 - Aisle of a church (4)
22 - Salt water (3)

No 226

Across
1 - Profundity (8)
6 - Web site visits (4)
8 - Moonstruck (6)
9 - Resembling a horse (6)
10 - Mythical monster (3)
11 - ___ Minnelli: US actress (4)
12 - Chess piece (6)
13 - Spurn (6)
15 - Wrote one's signature (6)
17 - Laborer who cuts wood (6)
20 - Brood (4)
21 - Deciduous tree (3)
22 - Marksman (6)
23 - Prototype (4-2)
24 - Sight organs (4)
25 - Reads out (8)

Down
2 - Meriting (7)
3 - Italian open pie (5)
4 - Approve or support (7)
5 - Small spot (5)
6 - Accommodation (7)
7 - Freshwater food fish (5)
14 - Mountain in NE Greece (7)
15 - Glisten (7)
16 - Choose and follow (7)
18 - Harass (5)
19 - Repeat (5)
20 - Variety of coffee (5)

No 227

Across

1 - Foamy (6)
5 - Battered (6)
8 - Hit with legs (4)
9 - Moves forward (8)
10 - Currently in progress (5)
11 - Respire (7)
14 - Skill in a trade (13)
16 - Official sitting (7)
18 - Steer an airplane (5)
20 - Thick dark syrup (8)
22 - Depend (4)
23 - Without ethics (6)
24 - ___ Loren: famous actress (6)

Down

2 - Strengthen (9)
3 - Imitate (4,3)
4 - Chinese monetary unit (4)
5 - About-face (8)
6 - Ray (5)
7 - Female sheep (3)
12 - The masses (3,6)
13 - Marriage ceremony (8)
15 - Foot support (7)
17 - Step (5)
19 - Purposes (4)
21 - Unit of electrical resistance (3)

No 228

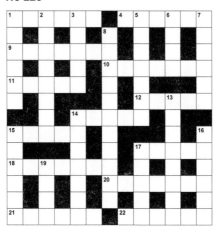

Across
1 - Bear witness (6)
4 - Take up (6)
9 - Conceited dandy (7)
10 - Look after children (4-3)
11 - Pertaining to the Netherlands (5)
12 - Twisted to one side (5)
14 - Intimate companion (5)
15 - Magical spirits (5)
17 - Tool for boring holes (5)
18 - Agitate (7)
20 - Encourages (7)
21 - Yodel (6)
22 - Classify (6)

Down
1 - Give in (6)
2 - Act of imposing levies (8)
3 - Apathy (5)
5 - Persistent problem (7)
6 - Spheres (4)
7 - Confer (6)
8 - Shortened (11)
13 - Pouched mammal (8)
14 - Free thinker (7)
15 - Laugh boisterously (6)
16 - Adjust in advance (6)
17 - Fire remains (5)
19 - Raise (4)

No 229

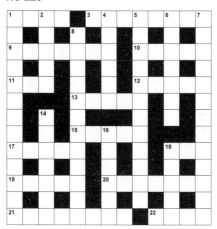

Across

1 - Unattractive (4)
3 - Staff officer (8)
9 - Capture (7)
10 - Substances burnt for energy (5)
11 - Large cup for hot liquids (3)
12 - Isolated (5)
13 - River cove; bay (5)
15 - Alert (5)
17 - Established custom (5)
18 - Long-leaved lettuce (3)
19 - Teacher (5)
20 - Trust (7)
21 - Having no wire (8)
22 - Imitates (4)

Down

1 - Uncaring (13)
2 - Misrepresenting (5)
4 - Type of engine (6)
5 - Uncomplimentary (12)
6 - Absolutely incredible (7)
7 - Blandness (13)
8 - Having many sides (12)
14 - Judge (7)
16 - Calculating machine (6)
18 - Overcook (5)

No 230

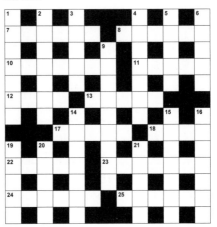

Across
7 - Child's toy (6)
8 - Apartment (6)
10 - Leafage (7)
11 - Delete (5)
12 - Destroy (4)
13 - Bony structure in the head (5)
17 - Departing (5)
18 - Company symbol (4)
22 - Let go of (5)
23 - Person in general (7)
24 - Ticket (6)
25 - Mountain chain (6)

Down
1 - Courage (7)
2 - Foot support (7)
3 - Collection of songs (5)
4 - Tower (7)
5 - Thoughts (5)
6 - Individualist (5)
9 - Cheerfulness (9)
14 - In an unspecified manner (7)
15 - Temporary stay (7)
16 - Weasel-like animal (7)
19 - Bird sound (5)
20 - Bunkum (5)
21 - Electronic communication (1-4)

No 231

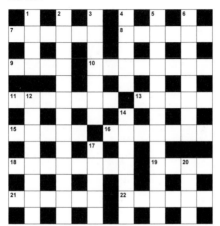

Across

7 - Finch (6)
8 - Sticky sugars (6)
9 - Child who has no home (4)
10 - Rushing (2,1,5)
11 - In an opposing direction (7)
13 - Kentucky ___ : annual horse race (5)
15 - One more than fifth (5)
16 - Talk (7)
18 - Building examiner (8)
19 - Confine (4)
21 - Metal screen or grating (6)
22 - Fair-haired people (6)

Down

1 - Capital of Peru (4)
2 - Unsuccessfully (13)
3 - Extremely desirous (7)
4 - Motion picture award (5)
5 - Disputation (13)
6 - Performable (8)
12 - Cocktail (8)
14 - Thus (7)
17 - Sorts (5)
20 - Increases (4)

No 232

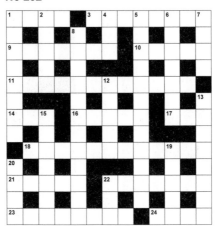

Across
1 - Long for (4)
3 - Increase (8)
9 - Absconder (3,4)
10 - Hard (5)
11 - Fast food dish (12)
14 - Twitch (3)
16 - Common tree (5)
17 - Salt water (3)
18 - In a notional manner (12)
21 - Ring (5)
22 - Musical movements (7)
23 - Separate (8)
24 - Footwear (4)

Down
1 - Juicy fruits (8)
2 - Door hanger (5)
4 - Socially inept (3)
5 - Reconsideration (12)
6 - Charms (7)
7 - Reflection (4)
8 - Flamboyant adventurer (12)
12 - Short high tone (5)
13 - Genteel (8)
15 - Cask makers (7)
19 - Ungainly walk (5)
20 - Slide (4)
22 - Posed (3)

No 233

Across
1 - Ascends (6)
4 - Lessens (6)
9 - Quick musical tempo (7)
10 - Surrounding environments (7)
11 - Gives out (5)
12 - Boxing contests (5)
14 - Air current (5)
15 - Strong eagerness (5)
17 - Incites (5)
18 - Branch of maths (7)
20 - Inert (7)
21 - Abrupt (6)
22 - Game participant (6)

Down
1 - Place of worship (6)
2 - Inopportune (3-5)
3 - Counterfeit (5)
5 - Unrecoverable money owed (3,4)
6 - Bean curd (4)
7 - Notices (6)
8 - Plaintiff (11)
13 - Unjustly (8)
14 - Trickle (7)
15 - Prizes (6)
16 - Stableman (6)
17 - Oatmeal dish (5)
19 - Surround (4)

No 234

Across
1 - Moving wings quickly (8)
5 - Goad on (4)
9 - Ballroom dance (5)
10 - Possessed (5)
11 - To be dismissed from work (3,3,4)
14 - Wiped out (6)
15 - Rough shelter (4-2)
17 - Reevaluate (10)
20 - Apprehended with certainty (5)
21 - Alters (5)
22 - Less than average tide (4)
23 - Gremlins (8)

Down
1 - True information (4)
2 - Female relation (4)
3 - Maintenance of a truce (12)
4 - Invalidate (6)
6 - Strong inclination (8)
7 - Reassign (8)
8 - Vagrancy (12)
12 - Tall hat (8)
13 - Baseless distrust of others (8)
16 - Small summerhouse (6)
18 - Gaming cubes (4)
19 - Cobras (4)

No 235

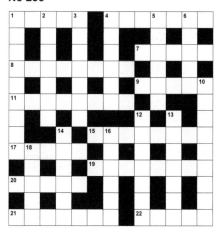

Across

1 - Gossip (5)
4 - Depository (7)
7 - Relative by marriage (2-3)
8 - Outmoded (8)
9 - Creases (5)
11 - Type of employment (4-4)
15 - Elementary particle (8)
17 - Vine (5)
19 - Capital of Liberia (8)
20 - Receded (5)
21 - Unpowered airplanes (7)
22 - Chasm (5)

Down

1 - Regaining (9)
2 - Spice with a pungent flavor (7)
3 - Remolds (7)
4 - Body of running water (6)
5 - Ill will (6)
6 - Secreting organ (5)
10 - Norms of requirement (9)
12 - Musical wind instrument (7)
13 - Seriousness (7)
14 - Supported (6)
16 - Lets go of (6)
18 - Insurgent (5)

No 236

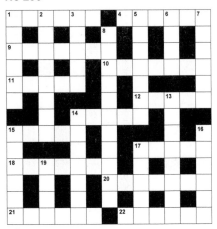

Across
1 - Deadly (6)
4 - Soul (6)
9 - Controversial (7)
10 - Relating to sight (7)
11 - Possessed (5)
12 - Relaxed; not tense (5)
14 - Axiom (5)
15 - Hard to please (5)
17 - Wedding assistant (5)
18 - Traveler (7)
20 - Obligate (7)
21 - Say again (6)
22 - Stagnation or inactivity (6)

Down
1 - Elementary particle (6)
2 - Loftiness (8)
3 - Equipped (5)
5 - Kitchen implement (7)
6 - Stylish (4)
7 - Change gradually (6)
8 - Troop leader (11)
13 - Fruit gardens (8)
14 - Expressive (7)
15 - Male parent (6)
16 - Moves very slowly (6)
17 - Unsuitable (5)
19 - Undivided whole (4)

No 237

Across

1 - Wash with water (5)
4 - Announcement (5)
10 - Plumbing fixture (7)
11 - Plentiful (5)
12 - Shaft (4)
13 - Unlearned (8)
16 - Martial art (4,2)
17 - Promotional material (6)
20 - Go beyond a limit (8)
21 - High-quality audio format (2-2)
23 - Group of shots (5)
25 - Shows (7)
26 - Festivities (5)
27 - Grains (5)

Down

2 - Laziness (9)
3 - Move back and forth (4)
5 - Very hard carbon gems (8)
6 - Policeman (3)
7 - Diminished in size (6)
8 - Period (5)
9 - Reduce with heat (4)
14 - Natives of the USA (9)
15 - Away from land (8)
18 - Desire for water (6)
19 - British nobles (5)
20 - Remove (4)
22 - At any time (4)
24 - False statement (3)

No 238

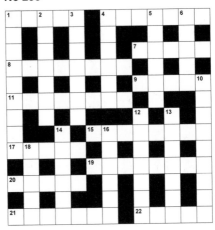

Across

1 - Component parts (5)
4 - False argument (7)
7 - Genuflect (5)
8 - Outbreak (8)
9 - Flowering tree; syrup (5)
11 - Cruel (8)
15 - Remove as if by suction (8)
17 - Wood pin (5)
19 - Solidity (8)
20 - Infectious agent (5)
21 - Enlarge (7)
22 - Ridge (5)

Down

1 - Not clear (9)
2 - Visible (7)
3 - Emits loud sound (7)
4 - Monkey (6)
5 - Aircraft housing (6)
6 - What a magician might cast (5)
10 - Wide ranging (9)
12 - Postal service (7)
13 - Narrowing (7)
14 - Consequence (6)
16 - Ragtime dance (6)
18 - Abhorrence (5)

No 239

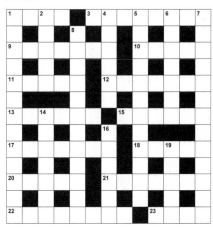

Across
1 - Wharf (4)
3 - Overwhelmed with concern (8)
9 - Efficiency (7)
10 - Golf shots (5)
11 - Unit of heat (5)
12 - Not either (7)
13 - Supernatural forces (6)
15 - Shade of purple (6)
17 - Child's room (7)
18 - Tortilla topped with cheese (5)
20 - Republic in S Europe (5)
21 - Republic in central Europe (7)
22 - First principles (8)
23 - Frolic (4)

Down
1 - Survey form (13)
2 - Got up (5)
4 - Barking (6)
5 - Clarity (12)
6 - School bag (7)
7 - Optional (13)
8 - Preservative (12)
14 - Heart-shaped (7)
16 - Dictator (6)
19 - Joyful religious song (5)

No 240

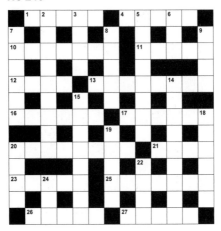

Across
1 - Trample heavily (5)
4 - Ascending ledges (5)
10 - Obsequious person (7)
11 - Verse form (5)
12 - Rodents (4)
13 - Reversed; changed order (8)
16 - Residential area (6)
17 - Street (6)
20 - Commoner (8)
21 - Prefix for small (4)
23 - Spanish friend (5)
25 - Identifying outfit (7)
26 - Of Wales (5)
27 - Vapor from a fire (5)

Down
2 - Yielding (9)
3 - Dairy product (4)
5 - Grammatical case (8)
6 - For each (3)
7 - Disrespects (6)
8 - Boatsmen (5)
9 - Dice (anag) (4)
14 - Artisanship (9)
15 - Causing grief (8)
18 - Mystery; riddle (6)
19 - Not clearly stated (5)
20 - Address a deity (4)
22 - Solid and secure (4)
24 - Anger (3)

No 241

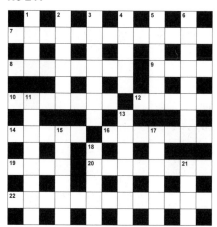

Across

7 - State of supreme happiness (13)
8 - Traveler (8)
9 - Tiny amount (4)
10 - More than two (7)
12 - Hurt (5)
14 - Date (5)
16 - Wave riders (7)
19 - Trademark (4)
20 - 11th month of the year (8)
22 - Consideration (13)

Down

1 - Second Greek letter (4)
2 - Suppress (6)
3 - Away from the highway (3-4)
4 - Steep slope (5)
5 - Entrance hall (6)
6 - Idler (8)
11 - Boss (8)
13 - Continue to live (7)
15 - Select (6)
17 - Give off smoke (6)
18 - Stang (anag) (5)
21 - Relaxation (4)

No 242

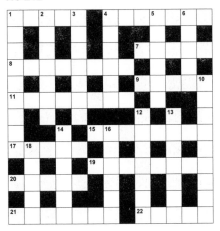

Across
1 - Oak tree nut (5)
4 - Heavy rain (7)
7 - Hiding place (5)
8 - Voting process (8)
9 - Remains (5)
11 - Uncertainty (8)
15 - Stone of great size (8)
17 - Snare (5)
19 - Against the current (8)
20 - Lure (5)
21 - Official; umpire (7)
22 - Diacritical mark (5)

Down
1 - Rise (9)
2 - Front of a coin (7)
3 - Not this or that (7)
4 - Pulsates (6)
5 - Revolve (6)
6 - Beastly (5)
10 - Second-year undergraduate (9)
12 - Speediest (7)
13 - Having two feet (7)
14 - On the beach; on land (6)
16 - Domain (6)
18 - Corpulent (5)

No 243

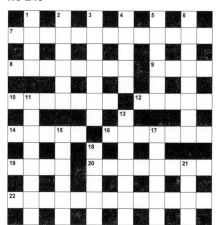

Across

7 - Updating (13)
8 - Ridicule (8)
9 - Wildcat (4)
10 - Not solid or liquid (7)
12 - Worship (5)
14 - Loft (5)
16 - Ate in small pieces (7)
19 - Top tennis serves (4)
20 - Work clothes (8)
22 - Paid announcement (13)

Down

1 - Seep; exude (4)
2 - Seaport in NE Italy (6)
3 - Full of jealousy (7)
4 - Layer above the earth (5)
5 - Simple (6)
6 - Trade (8)
11 - Precede (8)
13 - Dullness (7)
15 - Contents (6)
17 - German composer (6)
18 - Modifies (5)
21 - Geologic times (4)

No 244

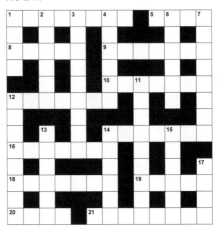

Across

1 - Writers of Internet weblogs (8)
5 - Ammunition (abbrev) (4)
8 - Sloping edge (5)
9 - Prayers for nine days (7)
10 - Consumes fully (7)
12 - Go back (7)
14 - Bulrush (7)
16 - Wader (7)
18 - Mischievous (7)
19 - Follows orders (5)
20 - Realizes (4)
21 - Physiologically dependent (8)

Down

1 - Protective napkins (4)
2 - Flowing gently (6)
3 - Award for first place (4,5)
4 - Styles and collections (6)
6 - Extracting ores (6)
7 - Preoccupies (8)
11 - Pork and beef sausage (9)
12 - Replies (8)
13 - Advance evidence for (6)
14 - Entreated; beseeched (6)
15 - Return to a former condition (6)
17 - Employed (4)

No 245

Across
1 - Thrive (8)
6 - Blunder (4)
8 - Secure with wooden strips (6)
9 - Beat soundly (6)
10 - Frozen water (3)
11 - Continent (4)
12 - Wheel (6)
13 - Bumps into (6)
15 - Catchphrase (6)
17 - Sacred writing (6)
20 - Appear (4)
21 - Intentionally so written (3)
22 - Accident (6)
23 - Assert (6)
24 - Cut (4)
25 - Pest controlling worm (8)

Down
2 - Secret affair (7)
3 - Extreme (5)
4 - Burns (7)
5 - Lumberjack (5)
6 - U.S. space probe to Jupiter (7)
7 - Layer above earth (5)
14 - Learn belatedly (5,2)
15 - Type of humor (7)
16 - Exacted retribution (7)
18 - Negative ion (5)
19 - Trembling poplar (5)
20 - Break up (5)

No 246

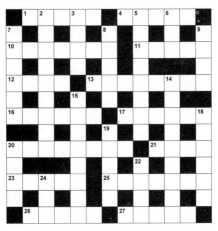

Across
1 - Put into service (5)
4 - Stroll (5)
10 - Musical instrument (7)
11 - Male duck (5)
12 - Liquid food (4)
13 - Internal conflict (5,3)
16 - Underpass (6)
17 - Full of trivial conversation (6)
20 - Unyielding (8)
21 - Journey (4)
23 - Obscurity (5)
25 - Radio pioneer (7)
26 - Raise (5)
27 - Loathe (5)

Down
2 - Anxious (9)
3 - Capital of Peru (4)
5 - 00:00 on a 24-hour clock (8)
6 - Grassland (3)
7 - Entertains (6)
8 - Herb (5)
9 - Animal (4)
14 - Sport played in a pool (5,4)
15 - Fighters (8)
18 - Well-paid young professional (6)
19 - Plant supports (5)
20 - Solely (4)
22 - Snatch (4)
24 - Sound of a cow (3)

No 247

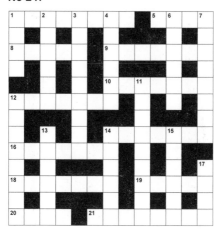

Across
1 - Ornamental climbing plant (8)
5 - Russian sovereign (4)
8 - Irritates (5)
9 - Long-bodied reptiles (7)
10 - Tenth month of the year (7)
12 - Informs on (7)
14 - Fragment (7)
16 - Alongside each other (7)
18 - Of plant or animal origin (7)
19 - Come in (5)
20 - Skirt worn by ballerinas (4)
21 - Interpret (8)

Down
1 - Animal enclosure (4)
2 - Procure (6)
3 - Continent SE of Asia (9)
4 - Ice buildings (6)
6 - Flashing light (6)
7 - Confine (8)
11 - Fear (9)
12 - Escape suddenly (5,3)
13 - Sudden fear (6)
14 - Plaster decoration (6)
15 - Malleable metal alloy (6)
17 - Insist (4)

No 248

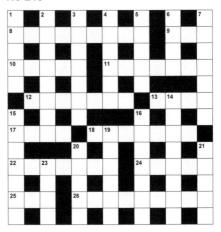

Across
8 - Ballet pose (9)
9 - Solid water (3)
10 - From that time (5)
11 - Escaping (7)
12 - Competent (7)
13 - Adjoin (4)
17 - Flows (4)
18 - Athletics field event (7)
22 - The act of accumulating (7)
24 - Civilian dress (5)
25 - Antelope (3)
26 - Abbreviated (9)

Down
1 - Stern (5)
2 - Preserve (8)
3 - Experienced serviceman (7)
4 - Sharp shrill cry (6)
5 - Food offerings (5)
6 - Prefix for small (4)
7 - Burdens (7)
14 - Instructions (8)
15 - Accuse of a wrong (7)
16 - Alter (7)
19 - Bursting into flower (6)
20 - Sharp transient wave (5)
21 - Diacritic symbol (5)
23 - Sports group (4)

No 249

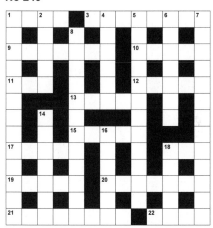

Across

1 - Dither (4)
3 - Questionable (8)
9 - Musical wind instrument (7)
10 - Fasten (5)
11 - Leap on one foot (3)
12 - Roamer (5)
13 - Travels (5)
15 - Urged (5)
17 - Maladroit (5)
18 - How (anag) (3)
19 - Fill with high spirits (5)
20 - Clergymen (7)
21 - Photograph (8)
22 - Dairy product (4)

Down

1 - Recklessness (13)
2 - Pointed; acute (5)
4 - Brought up (6)
5 - Unappreciated (12)
6 - Ship workers (7)
7 - Efficiently (13)
8 - Unobtrusiveness (12)
14 - Japanese flower arranging (7)
16 - South American cowboy (6)
18 - Measure heaviness (5)

No 250

Across
1 - Antique (8)
5 - Cover (4)
8 - Gives out (5)
9 - Baltic country (7)
10 - Engraving (7)
12 - Treachery (7)
14 - Opens (7)
16 - Blushes (7)
18 - Upmarket (7)
19 - Concur (5)
20 - Ice (4)
21 - Gathering (8)

Down
1 - Unwrap (4)
2 - Steal (6)
3 - Addicted to (9)
4 - Number in a soccer team (6)
6 - Legume (6)
7 - Game of checkers (8)
11 - Place side by side (9)
12 - Exhaustive (8)
13 - Ukrainian port (6)
14 - Cinema guides (6)
15 - Winged child (6)
17 - Extremely (4)

No 251

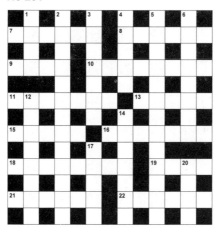

Across

7 - Scarcity (6)
8 - Fiber from the Angora goat (6)
9 - Ron Howard comedy movie (2,2)
10 - Overcome (8)
11 - Scary things (7)
13 - Sulks (5)
15 - Make unclear (5)
16 - Cracked a secret message (7)
18 - Extraordinary (8)
19 - Symbol (4)
21 - Accepted (6)
22 - Flashy (6)

Down

1 - Music group (4)
2 - Eloquent (6-7)
3 - Ugly thing (7)
4 - Rulers (5)
5 - Arranged in temporal order (13)
6 - Small illustrative sketch (8)
12 - Latter part of days (8)
14 - Noblewoman (7)
17 - Break loose (5)
20 - Exuding moisture (4)

No 252

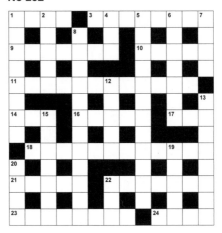

Across
1 - Blatant promotion (4)
3 - Insect trap (8)
9 - Heartily (7)
10 - Fright (5)
11 - Pictorial (12)
14 - Tuber (3)
16 - Aircraft detection system (5)
17 - Saw (anag) (3)
18 - Building design (12)
21 - Monetary unit (5)
22 - Tiny amounts (7)
23 - Agrees (8)
24 - Goad on (4)

Down
1 - Vacations (8)
2 - Staple food (5)
4 - Put down (3)
5 - Specialist in baby care (12)
6 - Trailer (7)
7 - Travel by horse (4)
8 - Classified by rank (12)
12 - In the middle of (5)
13 - Evaluator (8)
15 - Human beings (7)
19 - Supplant (5)
20 - From a distance (4)
22 - Eg steak and kidney (3)

No 253

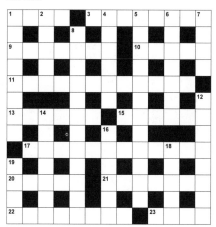

Across

1 - Support (4)
3 - Sanctions (8)
9 - Backtrack (7)
10 - Exhaust (5)
11 - Now and then (12)
13 - Outcast (6)
15 - Stop talking (4,2)
17 - Extremely harmful (12)
20 - Reason for innocence (5)
21 - Skilled artist; master (7)
22 - Type of sweater (4-4)
23 - Sic (4)

Down

1 - Acts (8)
2 - Nerve in the eye (5)
4 - Country (6)
5 - Antique (3,9)
6 - Young promising actress (7)
7 - Produced tones (4)
8 - Sweat (12)
12 - Roomy (8)
14 - Sporting dog (7)
16 - Infinitesimally small (6)
18 - Small cabin (5)
19 - Moist (4)

No 254

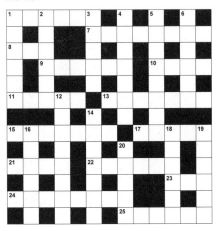

Across
- 1 - Disagreeable woman (6)
- 7 - Having considerable worth (8)
- 8 - Steel bar (3)
- 9 - Lessens (6)
- 10 - Greek god of war (4)
- 11 - Sticky tree sap (5)
- 13 - Turn aside (7)
- 15 - Disperse (7)
- 17 - Start of (5)
- 21 - Stolen goods (4)
- 22 - Mock (6)
- 23 - Pen point (3)
- 24 - Rolling grasslands (8)
- 25 - Boat crews (6)

Down
- 1 - Church official (6)
- 2 - Measuring devices (6)
- 3 - Egg-shaped (5)
- 4 - School groups (7)
- 5 - The act of swimming (8)
- 6 - Oldest (6)
- 12 - Printmaking technique (8)
- 14 - Slender stemlike appendage (7)
- 16 - Scared person (6)
- 18 - Stink (6)
- 19 - Social groups of people (6)
- 20 - Open up (5)

No 255

Across

1 - Surrounded (8)
5 - Imitates (4)
8 - Spirit (5)
9 - Provider of financial cover (7)
10 - Eliminate from the body (7)
12 - Ate a midday meal (7)
14 - Nonbeliever (7)
16 - Small persons (7)
18 - Earthquake scale (7)
19 - Hirsute (5)
20 - Run quickly (4)
21 - Maple tree (8)

Down

1 - Nervy (4)
2 - High-kicking dance (3,3)
3 - Overcome (9)
4 - Left (6)
6 - Money pouches (6)
7 - Army officer (8)
11 - Small dog (9)
12 - Unhurried (8)
13 - Manners (6)
14 - Far from the intended target (6)
15 - Deep blue color (6)
17 - Variety; sort (4)

No 256

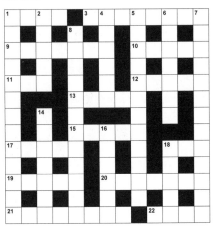

Across

1 - Move toward (4)
3 - Learned persons (8)
9 - Handbooks (7)
10 - Fragile (5)
11 - North American nation (1,1,1)
12 - Dog like mammal (5)
13 - Strange and mysterious (5)
15 - Severe (5)
17 - Protective garment (5)
18 - A knight (3)
19 - Visual representation (5)
20 - Boatman (7)
21 - Called the same (8)
22 - Movable barrier (4)

Down

1 - Method of conveying meaning (13)
2 - Ray (5)
4 - American general (6)
5 - Unofficially (3,3,6)
6 - Rhododendrons (7)
7 - Confidence (4-9)
8 - Accepted behavior whilst dining (5)
14 - Type of humor (7)
16 - Open up (6)
18 - Brazilian dance (5)

No 257

Across
1 - Type of book cover (8)
6 - Foolish (4)
8 - Confuse (6)
9 - Symbol (6)
10 - Quick sleep (3)
11 - Watchful (4)
12 - Tall structures (6)
13 - Resided (6)
15 - Fuss; harass (6)
17 - Natural elevations (6)
20 - Trigonometric function (4)
21 - Anger (3)
22 - Composite (6)
23 - Mythical monsters (6)
24 - Charities (4)
25 - Avoiding (8)

Down
2 - Inflexible (7)
3 - Silly (5)
4 - Exacted retribution (7)
5 - Tidily kept (5)
6 - Refuses to acknowledge (7)
7 - Surface upon which one walks (5)
14 - Dairy foods (7)
15 - Nonconformist (7)
16 - Animal oil (7)
18 - Pastoral poem (5)
19 - Move sideways (5)
20 - Sailing vessel (5)

No 258

Across
1 - Lacking consistency (6)
5 - Forms of identification (6)
8 - Boyfriend (4)
9 - Changing a title (8)
10 - Water vapor (5)
11 - Deposit (anag) (7)
14 - Constructively (13)
16 - Feathers (7)
18 - Strain (5)
20 - Rear curtain of a stage (8)
22 - Belonging to us (4)
23 - Stagnation or inactivity (6)
24 - Nation in N North America (6)

Down
2 - Existing in abundance (9)
3 - Tidal wave (7)
4 - Three feet length (4)
5 - Friendliness (8)
6 - Honored ladies (5)
7 - Geologic time (3)
12 - Brought to a destination (9)
13 - Do-nothings (8)
15 - Imaginary creature (7)
17 - Creates (5)
19 - Heroic poem (4)
21 - Toward the stern (3)

No 259

Across

1 - Cord (4)
3 - Soup (8)
9 - Move apart (7)
10 - Requirements (5)
11 - Growing stronger (12)
13 - Free (6)
15 - Force away (6)
17 - Memory (12)
20 - Ancient (5)
21 - Small explosive bomb (7)
22 - Out-of-date (8)
23 - Capital of Norway (4)

Down

1 - Marriages (8)
2 - Crave (5)
4 - Lacking energy (6)
5 - Miser (5,7)
6 - Make a big profit (5,2)
7 - Supersede (4)
8 - Intermediate (12)
12 - Alternate personality (5,3)
14 - Plans (7)
16 - Miniature (6)
18 - Approaches (5)
19 - Extinct bird (4)

No 260

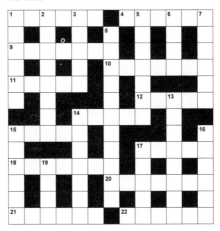

Across
1 - Up-to-date (6)
4 - Grades (6)
9 - Dutch port (7)
10 - Fundamental substance (7)
11 - Not odds (5)
12 - Dentition (5)
14 - Very small (5)
15 - Dizzy (5)
17 - Musical group of eight (5)
18 - Humorous drawing (7)
20 - Confident (7)
21 - Believer in God (6)
22 - Plaster decoration (6)

Down
1 - Taunter (6)
2 - Prestigious (8)
3 - Songs by two people (5)
5 - Brutality (7)
6 - Cereal grass (4)
7 - Grab (6)
8 - Functioning (11)
13 - Suitable for the public (8)
14 - Past events (7)
15 - Small racing car (2-4)
16 - Workplace (6)
17 - Start of (5)
19 - Method of learning (4)

No 261

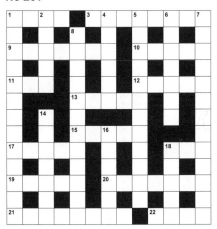

Across

1 - From a distance (4)
3 - Approximate (8)
9 - Chemical bond forming (7)
10 - Crushed malt (5)
11 - Point of pen (3)
12 - Olfactory perception (5)
13 - Discharge (5)
15 - Shadow (5)
17 - Having a specified border (5)
18 - Hip (anag) (3)
19 - Nerve in the eye (5)
20 - Variety of rummy (7)
21 - Speed up (8)
22 - Cautious of danger (4)

Down

1 - Daring (13)
2 - An unplanned speech (2-3)
4 - Hay cutting tool (6)
5 - Flattering (12)
6 - State in SW United States (7)
7 - Noteworthy (13)
8 - Unbiased (12)
14 - Illuminate (5,2)
16 - Lynx (6)
18 - Staple food (5)

No 262

Across
1 - Steps on stage (6)
4 - Black Sea peninsular (6)
9 - Found in cigarettes (7)
10 - Rushing (7)
11 - Sturdy (5)
12 - Decay (5)
14 - Long ___ owl: bird of prey (5)
15 - Seasons (5)
17 - Medication amounts (5)
18 - Soldier's hut (7)
20 - Conceited person (7)
21 - Account book (6)
22 - Cold symptom (6)

Down
1 - Irritable (6)
2 - Set out (8)
3 - Demesne (5)
5 - Cooked in oven (7)
6 - Region in South of France (4)
7 - Point furthest from Earth (6)
8 - Dismal (11)
13 - Surpass (8)
14 - Fugitive (7)
15 - Relating to a leg bone (6)
16 - African fly (6)
17 - Destroy by immersion (5)
19 - Attack (4)

No 263

Across

1 - Upper surfaces of rooms (8)
6 - Method of learning (4)
8 - Vent (6)
9 - Empty (6)
10 - Extremity of foot (3)
11 - Skillfully (4)
12 - Flour and water mixes (6)
13 - Extravagant meals (6)
15 - Cunningly defeat (6)
17 - Safety restraint (3,3)
20 - Forcible impact (4)
21 - Edge (3)
22 - Greek goddess of wisdom (6)
23 - Implant deeply (6)
24 - Legal document (4)
25 - Vacations (8)

Down

2 - Uniform (7)
3 - Frozen fruit juice on a stick (5)
4 - Chats (7)
5 - Rescued (5)
6 - Relate (7)
7 - Freshwater food fish (5)
14 - Implicit meaning (7)
15 - Porridge ingredient (7)
16 - Art of public speaking (7)
18 - Bury (5)
19 - Chart (5)
20 - Fitted out with cables (5)

No 264

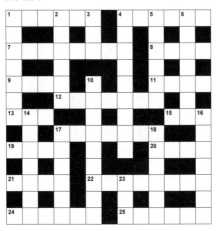

Across
1 - Season (6)
4 - Robust (6)
7 - Informant (8)
8 - Jump (4)
9 - Republic in W Africa (4)
11 - Yearn for (4)
12 - Altered (7)
13 - Piece of cloth (3)
15 - Raw (anag) (3)
17 - Ancient elephant (7)
19 - Sea eagle (4)
20 - Musical work (4)
21 - Reflection of sound (4)
22 - Opposites (8)
24 - Biochemical catalyst (6)
25 - Manipulates (6)

Down
1 - Pool based athlete (7)
2 - Nearsighted (6)
3 - Strong drink (3)
4 - Safe (9)
5 - Empty (6)
6 - Monetary unit (7)
10 - Having a soothing effect (9)
14 - Eg from Ethiopia (7)
16 - Withstands (7)
17 - Aria (6)
18 - Gruff (6)
23 - Pledge (3)

No 265

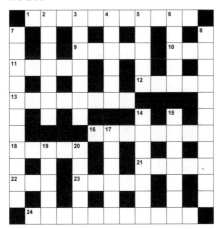

Across

1 - Inhalation (11)
9 - Elevators (5)
10 - Pasture (3)
11 - Midpoint (5)
12 - Soft drinks (5)
13 - Planned (8)
16 - Back and forth (2,3,3)
18 - Area shaded by trees (5)
21 - Rice dish (5)
22 - Piece of wood (3)
23 - Garden flower (5)
24 - Thanklessness (11)

Down

2 - Innocence (7)
3 - Moving in a certain direction (7)
4 - Shuffle (6)
5 - Duties (5)
6 - Lubricated (5)
7 - In a sociable manner (11)
8 - Create in bulk (4-7)
14 - Fragment (7)
15 - Transfer (7)
17 - Central American cat (6)
19 - Started (5)
20 - Armature (5)

No 266

Across
1 - Agricultural implement (4)
3 - Surrender (8)
9 - Not attached (7)
10 - Palpitate (5)
11 - Accounting entry (5)
12 - Larval salamander (7)
13 - Capital of Zimbabwe (6)
15 - Third sign of the zodiac (6)
17 - English poet (7)
18 - Spill (5)
20 - Musical group of eight (5)
21 - Spray very finely (7)
22 - Square scarf (8)
23 - Rapscallion (4)

Down
1 - Without stopping (5,3,5)
2 - Meat on a skewer (5)
4 - Extreme confusion (6)
5 - Outgoing disposition (12)
6 - Established in advance (1,6)
7 - Ornamentation (13)
8 - Brittle taffy (12)
14 - Creator (anag) (7)
16 - Hidden or secret (6)
19 - Willow twig (5)

No 267

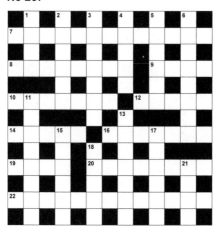

Across

7 - Surreptitiousness (13)
8 - Presumptuous (8)
9 - Matured (4)
10 - Ledges for books (7)
12 - Verse form (5)
14 - Bring about (5)
16 - Portable rocket launcher (7)
19 - Smudge (4)
20 - Least dear (8)
22 - Not fully valued (13)

Down

1 - Antelopes (4)
2 - Optical (6)
3 - Figures of speech (7)
4 - Steps of a ladder (5)
5 - Dishonor (6)
6 - Starlike symbol (8)
11 - Promontory (8)
13 - Musical ending (7)
15 - Fastenings (6)
17 - Parentless child (6)
18 - Neck warmer (5)
21 - Garden outbuilding (4)

No 268

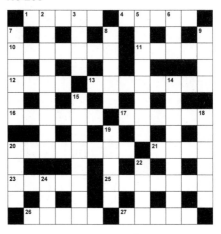

Across
1 - Eg heart or liver (5)
4 - Skin on top of head (5)
10 - Going away (7)
11 - Republic in S Asia (5)
12 - Wire (anag) (4)
13 - Innate ability (8)
16 - Perforate (6)
17 - End of daylight (6)
20 - Find (8)
21 - Look at amorously (4)
23 - Ray (5)
25 - Evidence of disease (7)
26 - Embarrass (5)
27 - Shallow carrying containers (5)

Down
2 - Cheerful consent (9)
3 - Among (4)
5 - Review (8)
6 - Boy (3)
7 - Inflate (4,2)
8 - Country in NE Africa (5)
9 - Stride (4)
14 - Unattractive (9)
15 - Learned persons (8)
18 - Heat energy units (6)
19 - Compact (5)
20 - Protest march (4)
22 - Arab ruler (4)
24 - Arrest (3)

No 269

Across
1 - Transporting (8)
6 - A great deal (4)
8 - Screams (6)
9 - Supplanted (6)
10 - For each (3)
11 - Push (4)
12 - Dairy product (6)
13 - Limit (6)
15 - The abode of God (6)
17 - Tricky (6)
20 - Small rodents (4)
21 - Donkey (3)
22 - Dormant state (6)
23 - Background actors (6)
24 - Ceases (4)
25 - Functional period (8)

Down
2 - Extremely desirous (7)
3 - Circular in shape (5)
4 - Look over carefully (7)
5 - Renown (5)
6 - Baked pasta dish (7)
7 - Belonging to them (5)
14 - Balances (7)
15 - Flesher (anag) (7)
16 - Cry out (7)
18 - Ascended (5)
19 - Folded back part of a coat (5)
20 - Short choral composition (5)

No 270

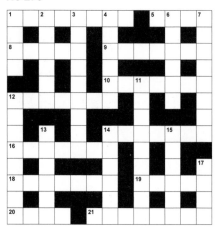

Across
1 - Quiescence (8)
5 - Developed (4)
8 - Gloomy (5)
9 - Speakers (7)
10 - Obliterate (7)
12 - Disobedient (7)
14 - Old Portuguese currency (7)
16 - Relished (7)
18 - Encroachments (7)
19 - Data received (5)
20 - Wound (4)
21 - Victim of social injustice (8)

Down
1 - Made (anag) (4)
2 - Scarcity (6)
3 - In a terrible manner (9)
4 - Bragged (6)
6 - The land (6)
7 - Sweet food courses (8)
11 - Period without war (9)
12 - Broadening (8)
13 - Walled inlets (6)
14 - American inventor (6)
15 - Clothed (6)
17 - Male deer (4)

No 271

Across

1 - Unstable (8)
6 - Opposite of front (4)
8 - Skiing race (6)
9 - Sounds like (6)
10 - Auction offer (3)
11 - Depressions (4)
12 - Slushy (6)
13 - Side road (6)
15 - Going out with (6)
17 - Image (6)
20 - Attack (4)
21 - Current unit (3)
22 - American general (6)
23 - Not outside (6)
24 - Having little hair (4)
25 - Explicit (8)

Down

2 - Nothingness (7)
3 - Leans (5)
4 - Material worn around the sleeve (7)
5 - Linear units (5)
6 - Refuse to sponsor (7)
7 - Crawl (5)
14 - Overlooked (7)
15 - Scorn (7)
16 - Capital of Kenya (7)
18 - All animal life (5)
19 - Stories (5)
20 - Lines in circle (5)

No 272

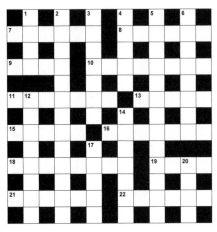

Across

7 - Exaggerate (6)
8 - Reveal (6)
9 - Ill-behaved child (4)
10 - Watchmen (8)
11 - Stuns with noise (7)
13 - Inquire into (5)
15 - Seasoning (5)
16 - Aridity (7)
18 - Emotional outburst (8)
19 - Part of the eye (4)
21 - Most intimate (6)
22 - Dissimilar (6)

Down

1 - Affirm with confidence (4)
2 - Pleasure (13)
3 - Blessing (7)
4 - Those aged 13 - 19 (5)
5 - Capable of being understood (13)
6 - Fragrant toiletries (8)
12 - Removing contents (8)
14 - Come to an end (5,2)
17 - Slatted wooden box (5)
20 - Writing fluids (4)

274

No 273

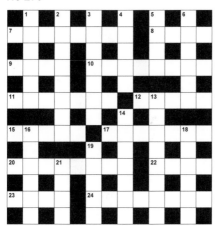

Across

7 - Scatter upon impact (8)
8 - Kitchen appliance (4)
9 - Linear unit (4)
10 - Hampered (8)
11 - Urgent (7)
12 - Big (5)
15 - Yellow color (5)
17 - Impromptu public singing (7)
20 - Greek hero of the Trojan War (8)
22 - Utters (4)
23 - Frame of a ship (4)
24 - Taking along (8)

Down

1 - Inscrutable person (6)
2 - Address forcefully (8)
3 - Skin sensation (7)
4 - Thin out (5)
5 - Bird of peace (4)
6 - Swiss city (6)
13 - Redeploy (8)
14 - Legal proceedings (7)
16 - Prototype (4-2)
18 - Entering data (6)
19 - Soil or farm land (5)
21 - Lazy (4)

No 274

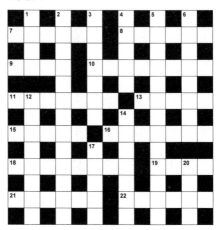

Across

7 - Spiritual head of a diocese (6)
8 - Upper classes (6)
9 - Ammunition (abbrev) (4)
10 - Use cautiously and frugally (8)
11 - Addresses; solicits (7)
13 - Motionless (5)
15 - Spy (5)
16 - Increases a deadline (7)
18 - Relating to the Middle Ages (8)
19 - Curved shapes (4)
21 - Spread out awkwardly (6)
22 - Refill (6)

Down

1 - Strict (4)
2 - Arranged in temporal order (13)
3 - Cloudiness (7)
4 - Cause (5)
5 - Secretly (5-3-5)
6 - Journeyed (8)
12 - Discourtesy (8)
14 - Look into (7)
17 - Ellipses (5)
20 - Steep and rugged rock (4)

No 275

Across

1 - Enclosed (6)
5 - Surprise attack (6)
8 - Den (4)
9 - Card game (8)
10 - Satellites (5)
11 - Violent act (7)
14 - Pious (13)
16 - Type of precision surgery (7)
18 - High up (5)
20 - Concluding section (8)
22 - Merriment (4)
23 - Anxiety (6)
24 - Enjoy greatly (6)

Down

2 - Ornate (9)
3 - Long-lasting and recurrent (7)
4 - Man made basin (4)
5 - Cartoon artist (8)
6 - Jazz (5)
7 - Droop (3)
12 - Rudeness; harshness (9)
13 - Settlements (8)
15 - Forbidden by law (7)
17 - Divide in two (5)
19 - A nobleman (4)
21 - Place (3)

No 276

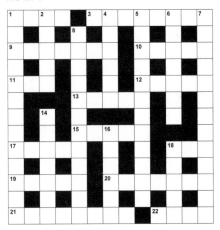

Across

1 - True information (4)
3 - Complete (8)
9 - Thieves (7)
10 - Hungarian composer (5)
11 - Mug (3)
12 - Palpitate (5)
13 - Loosen (5)
15 - Church administration (5)
17 - Abstraction (5)
18 - Tree (3)
19 - Call forth or cause (5)
20 - Process of proving a will (7)
21 - Social isolation (8)
22 - Let it stand (4)

Down

1 - Fierceness (13)
2 - Overcook (5)
4 - Breed of hound (6)
5 - Destruction (12)
6 - Increase (7)
7 - Institution (13)
8 - Denial (12)
14 - Type of pheasant (7)
16 - Tore (6)
18 - Look for; expect (5)

No 277

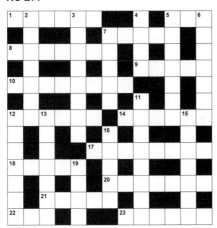

Across

1 - Dirty (6)
5 - Male sheep (3)
7 - Suffuse with color (5)
8 - Gave the letters of a word (7)
9 - Render (5)
10 - Predict (8)
12 - Photos (6)
14 - As compared to (6)
17 - Weapon firing darts (8)
18 - Disarm (5)
20 - Collections (7)
21 - Ticks over (5)
22 - Creative activity (3)
23 - Trip (6)

Down

2 - Harmonious relation (7)
3 - Refuge for an animal (4-4)
4 - Comply (4)
5 - Changes (7)
6 - Centers (7)
7 - Thoughts (5)
11 - Ocean contents (8)
12 - Redwood tree (7)
13 - Live in (7)
15 - Many (7)
16 - Thick slices (5)
19 - Republic in W Africa (4)

No 278

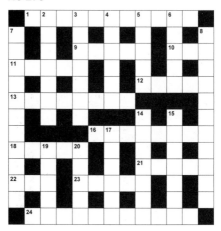

Across
- 1 - Past performances (5,6)
- 9 - Chocolate drink (5)
- 10 - Playing card (3)
- 11 - Medical worm (5)
- 12 - Symbolic figure or shape (5)
- 13 - Segment of the spinal column (8)
- 16 - Put into long-term storage (8)
- 18 - Develop (5)
- 21 - Supplementary component (3-2)
- 22 - Young mammal (3)
- 23 - Circumstance (5)
- 24 - Bizarrely (11)

Down
- 2 - Jollification (7)
- 3 - Snail-shaped tube (7)
- 4 - Better off (6)
- 5 - Loud resonant noise (5)
- 6 - Not hesitant (5)
- 7 - Ill will (11)
- 8 - Holland (11)
- 14 - Japanese massage technique (7)
- 15 - Small amount (7)
- 17 - Female giant (6)
- 19 - Brown earth pigment (5)
- 20 - Turn inside out (5)

No 279

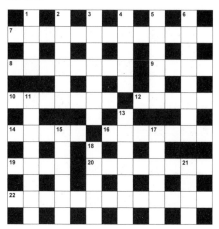

Across

7 - Harmlessly (13)
8 - Speed up (8)
9 - Touches (4)
10 - Freely (7)
12 - Harps (5)
14 - Steep slope (5)
16 - Utilizes (7)
19 - ___ facto: by the fact itself (4)
20 - Judgment Day; fate (8)
22 - Untrustworthiness (13)

Down

1 - Chalcedony (4)
2 - Makes available (6)
3 - Readable (7)
4 - Anemic looking (5)
5 - Eagerly (6)
6 - Swollen with fat (8)
11 - Resident (8)
13 - Enclosed fortification (7)
15 - Relaunch (6)
17 - Finally (6)
18 - Spontaneous remark (2-3)
21 - Skills (4)

No 280

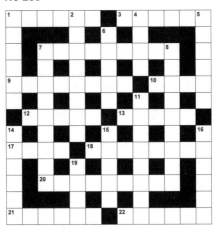

Across
1 - Large sticks (6)
3 - Boards (anag) (6)
7 - Eg natives of France of Germany (9)
9 - Emergency precaution (8)
10 - Verge (4)
12 - Watch over (5)
13 - Wash (5)
17 - Change (4)
18 - Vanquishment (8)
20 - Iniquitous (9)
21 - Creators (6)
22 - Former currency of Spain (6)

Down
1 - Flashing light (6)
2 - Management of growing timber (8)
4 - Academic administrator (4)
5 - Acrimonious; sour tasting (6)
6 - Set of tracks (5)
7 - Act of omitting (9)
8 - Dodges (9)
11 - Misrepresent (8)
14 - Inert gaseous element (6)
15 - Accumulate (5)
16 - Greek goddess of wisdom (6)
19 - From a distance (4)

No 281

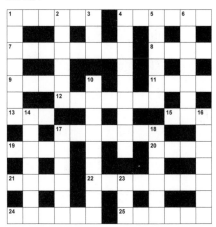

Across

1 - Spiritual head of a diocese (6)
4 - Related to blossom (6)
7 - Court of justice (8)
8 - Cereal (4)
9 - Function (4)
11 - Ruse (4)
12 - In a cheeky manner (7)
13 - Correlation coefficient (3)
15 - Belonging to him (3)
17 - Absolutely incredible (7)
19 - Soup (anag) (4)
20 - Move by rotating (4)
21 - Lattice (4)
22 - Read out loud (8)
24 - Eg Australia (6)
25 - Snuggle (6)

Down

1 - Fighter (7)
2 - Noise (6)
3 - Fasten together (3)
4 - Lie (9)
5 - Hold position (6)
6 - Established in advance (1,6)
10 - Emaciated (9)
14 - Unfortunate (7)
16 - Smear (7)
17 - Respiratory disorder (6)
18 - Substitute (6)
23 - Flee (3)

No 282

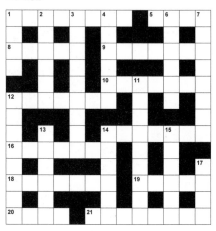

Across

1 - Driven to (8)
5 - Surprise (4)
8 - Throw away (5)
9 - Practicing great self-denial (7)
10 - Hearing range (7)
12 - Disobedient (7)
14 - Unconscious (7)
16 - Continue talking (5,2)
18 - Machine workers (7)
19 - Accustom (5)
20 - Ruin (4)
21 - Cuddles up (8)

Down

1 - Doubtful (4)
2 - Demurely (6)
3 - Rationally (9)
4 - Overjoyed (6)
6 - Irritable (6)
7 - Addictive tobacco drug (8)
11 - Gratifying (9)
12 - Greeted warmly (8)
13 - Examination (6)
14 - Occurring together (6)
15 - Yearly (6)
17 - Realizes (4)

No 283

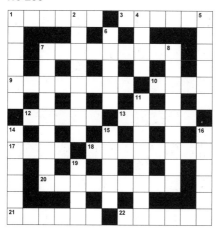

Across

1 - Domains (6)
3 - Rigid support (6)
7 - Involuntary (9)
9 - Word for word (8)
10 - Bedouin (4)
12 - Fiercely (5)
13 - Thighbone (5)
17 - Strokes (4)
18 - Witty reply (8)
20 - Twenty-four hours ago (9)
21 - Spatter (6)
22 - Time of widespread glaciation (3,3)

Down

1 - Take away (6)
2 - Reciprocally (8)
4 - Essential substance (4)
5 - Hat (6)
6 - Electronic communication (1-4)
7 - Fit to fly (9)
8 - In a depraved manner (9)
11 - Armorial (8)
14 - Fruits with pips (6)
15 - Biological sequences (5)
16 - Sell purchased goods (6)
19 - Egyptian goddess of fertility (4)

No 284

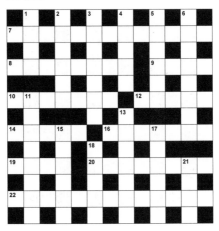

Across

7 - In a tolerant manner (5-8)
8 - Country bordering Spain (8)
9 - Solid (4)
10 - Caters for (7)
12 - Exhaust (5)
14 - Chart (5)
16 - Fact (7)
19 - Poultry enclosure (2-2)
20 - Throughout the world (8)
22 - Uncaring (13)

Down

1 - Therefore (4)
2 - Touched lightly (6)
3 - Representational process (7)
4 - Hill (5)
5 - Lower (6)
6 - Unselfish person (8)
11 - Flying (8)
13 - Hotels (7)
15 - Fruit tree (6)
17 - Lender (6)
18 - Country in NE Africa (5)
21 - Cut of meat (4)

No 285

Across
1 - Give away (4)
3 - In good spirits (8)
9 - Interest (7)
10 - Frighten (5)
11 - Having an acrid wit (5-7)
14 - Involuntary spasm (3)
16 - Come in (5)
17 - Hip (anag) (3)
18 - Associated by chance (12)
21 - Diacritical mark (5)
22 - Habitable (7)
23 - Plan anew (8)
24 - Type of poker game (4)

Down
1 - Wood preserver (8)
2 - School of thought (5)
4 - Belonging to him (3)
5 - Given to overstatement (12)
6 - Erupt suddenly (5,2)
7 - Torch (4)
8 - Entirety (12)
12 - Group of eight (5)
13 - Squander (8)
15 - Caressed (7)
19 - Path; route (5)
20 - Agitate (4)
22 - Follow behind (3)

No 286

Across
- 7 - Morals (6)
- 8 - Canvas covering (6)
- 10 - Raging fire (7)
- 11 - Golf clubs (5)
- 12 - Vale (4)
- 13 - Sphere (5)
- 17 - Small fragment (5)
- 18 - Pace (4)
- 22 - Play a guitar (5)
- 23 - Part of a gun (7)
- 24 - Shifty deceptive person (6)
- 25 - Irascibility; organ (6)

Down
- 1 - Time spells (7)
- 2 - Scramble the order (7)
- 3 - Fruit of the oak (5)
- 4 - Musical instrument (7)
- 5 - Pigmentation (5)
- 6 - Itinerant (5)
- 9 - Place side by side (9)
- 14 - Locked down (7)
- 15 - Walk with difficulty (7)
- 16 - Candid (7)
- 19 - Apart from (5)
- 20 - Newlywed (5)
- 21 - 60's free spirit (5)

No 287

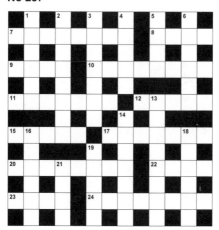

Across

7 - Period during which you live (8)
8 - Graphic symbol (4)
9 - Capital of the Ukraine (4)
10 - Monocle (8)
11 - Conducted (7)
12 - Turn (5)
15 - Circumference (5)
17 - Confinement (7)
20 - Joint (8)
22 - Fibber (4)
23 - The wise men (4)
24 - Sharply (8)

Down

1 - Small birds (6)
2 - Weighing the most (8)
3 - Increased the gap (7)
4 - Lumberjack (5)
5 - Legal document (4)
6 - Make less tight (6)
13 - Clattering (8)
14 - Places of business (7)
16 - Line of pressure (6)
18 - With affection (6)
19 - Young sheep (5)
21 - Leave (4)

No 288

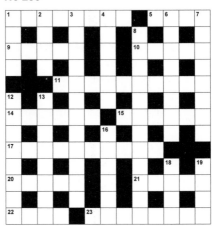

Across
1 - Sinfully (8)
5 - Parched (4)
9 - Smell (5)
10 - Bird houses (5)
11 - Propitious (10)
14 - Not uniform (6)
15 - Filling nourishment (6)
17 - Exaggerate (10)
20 - Looking tired (5)
21 - Bunches (5)
22 - Flower (4)
23 - Informer (8)

Down
1 - Insect (4)
2 - Stylish (4)
3 - Bubbling (12)
4 - Princely (6)
6 - Replies (8)
7 - Catastrophe (8)
8 - Examiner (12)
12 - Taxonomic group (8)
13 - Experienced soldiers (8)
16 - Talk nonsense (6)
18 - Doubtful (4)
19 - Star (anag) (4)

No 289

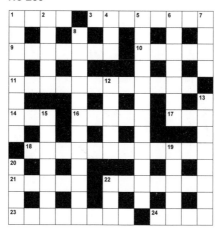

Across
1 - Deciduous trees (4)
3 - Edge of the ocean (8)
9 - Subjugate (7)
10 - Kingdom (5)
11 - Convalescence (12)
14 - Saw (anag) (3)
16 - Donates (5)
17 - Where a pig lives (3)
18 - Orcas (6,6)
21 - Impersonator (5)
22 - Riding the waves (7)
23 - Delaying (8)
24 - Modify (4)

Down
1 - Ridges above the eyes (8)
2 - Agreeable sound (5)
4 - Female sheep (3)
5 - Atmospheric layer (12)
6 - Speakers (7)
7 - TV award (4)
8 - Carefree (5-2-5)
12 - Body of water (5)
13 - Vision (8)
15 - Glisten (7)
19 - Property owner (5)
20 - Soot particle (4)
22 - Star (3)

No 290

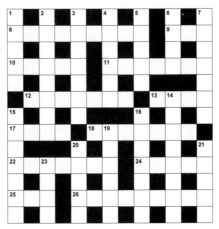

Across

8 - Footsoldier (9)
9 - Utilize (3)
10 - Group of eight (5)
11 - Put in place (7)
12 - Causes (7)
13 - Short tail (4)
17 - Electromagnetic radiation (1-3)
18 - Person in general (7)
22 - Lasted longer than expected (7)
24 - Robbery (5)
25 - Extremity of foot (3)
26 - Unable to move (9)

Down

1 - Ice hut (5)
2 - Segment of the spinal column (8)
3 - Skipper (7)
4 - Act between parties (6)
5 - Lock of hair (5)
6 - Brass instrument (4)
7 - One more than sixth (7)
14 - Is composed of (8)
15 - Sells abroad (7)
16 - Type of precision surgery (7)
19 - Possessors (6)
20 - Fruit of the vine (5)
21 - Unable to move (5)
23 - Not odd (4)

No 291

Across
1 - Eg T S Eliot (4)
3 - Principles (8)
9 - Period of government (7)
10 - Boat (5)
11 - Exemption (12)
14 - Antelope (3)
16 - Hurled (5)
17 - Night bird (3)
18 - Dishonesty (12)
21 - Protective garment (5)
22 - Body of troops (7)
23 - Fence formed by bushes (8)
24 - Moved through water (4)

Down
1 - An example (8)
2 - Borders (5)
4 - Beam of light (3)
5 - Science of deciphering codes (12)
6 - Flute (7)
7 - Hardens (4)
8 - Meddling (12)
12 - Underwater breathing device (5)
13 - Metal (8)
15 - Conducted (7)
19 - Relative by marriage (5)
20 - Run quickly (4)
22 - Personal pride (3)

No 292

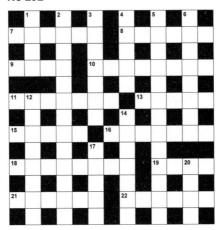

Across

7 - Duplicator (6)
8 - A parent's Mom (6)
9 - White soft mineral (4)
10 - Malicious (8)
11 - Immoderately vehement (7)
13 - Catches (5)
15 - Animal bedding (5)
16 - Stories in song (7)
18 - Ingoing (8)
19 - Utters (4)
21 - Hit (6)
22 - Nasal (6)

Down

1 - Musical finale (4)
2 - Of mixed character (13)
3 - Coming up (7)
4 - Once more (5)
5 - Benevolent (13)
6 - Pampered (8)
12 - Chant (8)
14 - Perils (7)
17 - Finicky (5)
20 - 365 days (4)

No 293

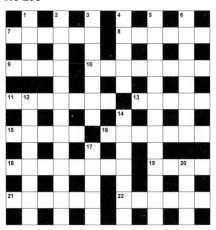

Across
7 - Dangerous snake (6)
8 - Jumbling up (6)
9 - Poker stake (4)
10 - Religious residences (8)
11 - More saccharine (7)
13 - Oblivion (5)
15 - Piece of land (5)
16 - Burns (7)
18 - Singer (8)
19 - Christmas (4)
21 - Tranquil (6)
22 - Flourish (6)

Down
1 - Blue-green color (4)
2 - Scheming person (7,6)
3 - Played out (7)
4 - ___ acid: protein building block (5)
5 - Designed for a journey (13)
6 - Unsteady (8)
12 - Easy victory (8)
14 - Disturb (7)
17 - Shuffles (5)
20 - Jealousy (4)

No 294

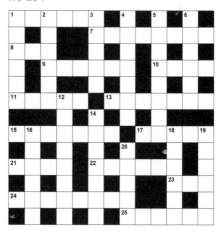

Across

1 - Earnest opinion (6)
7 - Substituted (8)
8 - Mother (3)
9 - Flat-bottomed rowboat (6)
10 - Nuisance (4)
11 - Courage (5)
13 - Eternal (7)
15 - Hurtful (7)
17 - Rocky (5)
21 - Partly open (4)
22 - Afternoon sleep (6)
23 - ___ Thumb: folklore hero (3)
24 - Extremely happy (8)
25 - Concealed (6)

Down

1 - Lament (6)
2 - Cut timber (6)
3 - Emancipated (5)
4 - Sudden increase (7)
5 - Booklet (8)
6 - Lines of poetry (6)
12 - Revere (8)
14 - Groups within (7)
16 - Showing utter resignation (6)
18 - Gave a speech (6)
19 - Sycophant (3-3)
20 - Soft fruit (5)

No 295

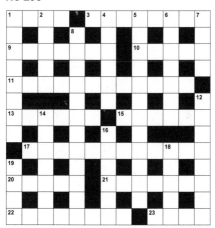

Across

1 - Team (4)
3 - Simultaneously (8)
9 - Pure (7)
10 - Apply pressure (5)
11 - Form of deception (12)
13 - Walk heavily (6)
15 - Part of eye (6)
17 - Sagacity (12)
20 - Lounge (5)
21 - Set down on paper (7)
22 - Straddle (8)
23 - Modify (4)

Down

1 - Ideal counterpart (4,4)
2 - Concave shapes (5)
4 - Large quantity (6)
5 - Chemical decomposition (12)
6 - Dancing party (7)
7 - Religious custom (4)
8 - Device for putting out fires (12)
12 - A hard-shelled nut (8)
14 - Diacritical marks (7)
16 - Declared (6)
18 - Observed (5)
19 - Protective crust (4)

No 296

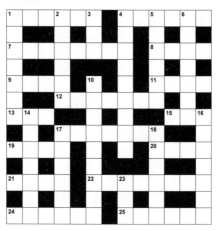

Across
1 - Wander; craftsman (6)
4 - Sheepskin (6)
7 - Assume command (4,4)
8 - Fruit pie (4)
9 - Egypt's river (4)
11 - Steals from (4)
12 - Enactment (7)
13 - Burnt wood (3)
15 - Broken equipment (3)
17 - Coincide (7)
19 - Among (4)
20 - Seabirds (4)
21 - Alone (4)
22 - Extra large (4-4)
24 - Hot spring (6)
25 - Preserved (6)

Down
1 - Garden flower (7)
2 - Topics (6)
3 - Increase the running speed (3)
4 - In an angry manner (9)
5 - Complete (6)
6 - Deer (7)
10 - Device to control heartbeats (9)
14 - A person (7)
16 - Lower (7)
17 - Detestable (6)
18 - Reverend (6)
23 - Seed (3)

No 297

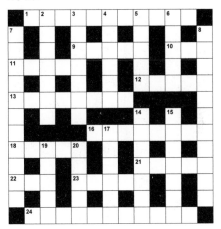

Across

1 - Citizenship (11)
9 - Spike (5)
10 - Round bread roll (3)
11 - Laud (5)
12 - Philosophical (5)
13 - Goes before (8)
16 - Person with shaved hair (8)
18 - Espresso and steamed milk (5)
21 - Pertaining to the ear (5)
22 - Largest deer (3)
23 - Needs (5)
24 - Items that make music (11)

Down

2 - One more (7)
3 - Hinted at (7)
4 - Stinging weed (6)
5 - Gives temporarily (5)
6 - Prejudice (5)
7 - Somnambulist (11)
8 - Irregular (11)
14 - All together (2,5)
15 - Thaw (7)
17 - Martial art (4,2)
19 - Symbol (5)
20 - Show triumphant joy (5)

No 298

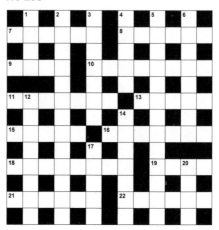

Across
7 - Intersection of two streets (6)
8 - Beat with the fists (6)
9 - Not stereo (4)
10 - Space rock (8)
11 - Waterlessness (7)
13 - Hankered after (5)
15 - Completely (5)
16 - Military force (7)
18 - Warn (8)
19 - Curves (4)
21 - Child (6)
22 - Church platform (6)

Down
1 - Indifferent (2-2)
2 - Absolute (13)
3 - A dimension (7)
4 - Malice (5)
5 - Unfeasible (13)
6 - Disease (8)
12 - Shaping (8)
14 - Accidents (7)
17 - Ski run (5)
20 - First son of Adam and Eve (4)

No 299

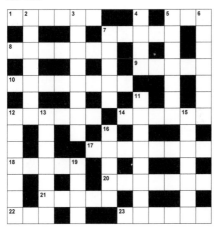

Across

1 - Sailor (6)
5 - Gear (3)
7 - Torn apart (5)
8 - Small bone (7)
9 - Stretches (5)
10 - Available source of wealth (8)
12 - Noses (6)
14 - Catch (6)
17 - Cavalrymen (8)
18 - Floral leaf (5)
20 - Take away from (7)
21 - Fertile area in a desert (5)
22 - Cooking utensil (3)
23 - Changes (6)

Down

2 - Oriental (7)
3 - Lists of transactions (8)
4 - Affirm with confidence (4)
5 - Device attached to a door (7)
6 - Ballroom dance (3-4)
7 - Change state (5)
11 - Not categorized (8)
12 - Temporary measure (7)
13 - Speech (7)
15 - Pink tinged with yellow (7)
16 - Networks (5)
19 - Failure (4)

No 300

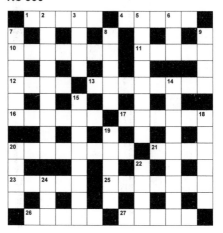

Across
1 - Lookout (5)
4 - Willow twig (5)
10 - Diminish (7)
11 - Male aristocrat (5)
12 - Bats (anag) (4)
13 - New York (3,5)
16 - Groups of animals (6)
17 - Graphs (6)
20 - Given without the normal duties (8)
21 - Closing section of music (4)
23 - Utilizing (5)
25 - Acted (7)
26 - Sudden constriction (5)
27 - Bony structure in the head (5)

Down
2 - Withdrawal (5-4)
3 - Official language of Pakistan (4)
5 - Bask (8)
6 - Recede (3)
7 - Changed (6)
8 - Start (5)
9 - Small pond (4)
14 - Employees (9)
15 - Titles such as Duke or Earl (8)
18 - Holds one's ground (6)
19 - Line of work (5)
20 - Sixty minutes (4)
22 - Hog sound (4)
24 - Elf (3)

No 301

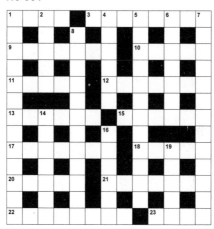

Across

1 - Child's word for mother (4)
3 - Dispersion of people (8)
9 - Official sitting (7)
10 - To be (5)
11 - Nook (5)
12 - Beer store (7)
13 - Overjoyed (6)
15 - Pious (6)
17 - Cynic (7)
18 - Disturbance (5)
20 - Ancient (5)
21 - Nasal opening (7)
22 - Separate (8)
23 - Conscription (4)

Down

1 - Misinterpreted (13)
2 - Agreeable sound (5)
4 - Burn (6)
5 - Horse race (12)
6 - River in N South America (7)
7 - Not manually (13)
8 - Jail term without end (4,8)
14 - Plans (7)
16 - Perfumes (6)
19 - Poem (5)

No 302

Across

7 - Unmarried young woman (6)
8 - Archimedes' insight (6)
10 - Aromatic herb (7)
11 - Waste matter (5)
12 - Parched (4)
13 - Attach to (5)
17 - Certain to fail (2-3)
18 - Dice (anag) (4)
22 - Crawl (5)
23 - Coat; decorate lavishly (7)
24 - Eye protector (6)
25 - Ratio of reflected light (6)

Down

1 - Licentious (7)
2 - Republic in W Africa (7)
3 - Relating to the kidneys (5)
4 - Someone who steals livestock (7)
5 - Litter (5)
6 - Tortilla topped with cheese (5)
9 - With the current (9)
14 - Marine mammal (7)
15 - Blames (7)
16 - Impression (7)
19 - Group of eight (5)
20 - Number of deadly sins (5)
21 - Burn with hot liquid (5)

No 303

Across

1 - Mend with rows of stitches (4)
3 - Elastic (8)
9 - Baltic country (7)
10 - Have knowledge of (5)
11 - Device for aligning (12)
13 - Make worse (6)
15 - Backward direction (6)
17 - Incredible (12)
20 - Apart from (5)
21 - Religious traveler (7)
22 - Preoccupies (8)
23 - Dairy product (4)

Down

1 - Leather (8)
2 - Generator part (5)
4 - Of inferior quality (6)
5 - Eloquently (12)
6 - Eg from Beijing (7)
7 - Toy (4)
8 - Sharpness (12)
12 - Indecent (8)
14 - Highly knowledgeable people (7)
16 - Small wave (6)
18 - Whip (5)
19 - Starch (4)

No 304

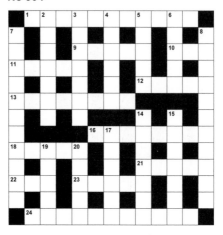

Across
1 - Oversee (11)
9 - Native American tent (5)
10 - Measure of length (3)
11 - Syntactic category (5)
12 - Agreeable sound (5)
13 - Hitting hard (8)
16 - Paper thrown at weddings (8)
18 - Neck warmer (5)
21 - Proof of vindication (5)
22 - Body's vital life force (3)
23 - Promotional wording (5)
24 - Political institutions (11)

Down
2 - Radioactive element (7)
3 - Pushes back a deadline (7)
4 - Cast doubt upon (6)
5 - Unit of heat (5)
6 - Requirements (5)
7 - Abstract talk (11)
8 - Form of energy (11)
14 - Friendly (7)
15 - Rattish (anag) (7)
17 - Dispute (6)
19 - Spanish friend (5)
20 - Legend (5)

No 305

Across
1 - Simple song (6)
5 - Enemy (3)
7 - Create or call forth (5)
8 - High spirits (7)
9 - Destiny; fate (5)
10 - 7 sided polygon (8)
12 - Tiny ear bone (6)
14 - Innocence (6)
17 - Control (8)
18 - Illustration (5)
20 - Country whose capital is Dublin (7)
21 - Spring tree (5)
22 - Purchase (3)
23 - Shun (6)

Down
2 - Disorder (7)
3 - Gives life to (8)
4 - Cry of a goose (4)
5 - Italian fast racing car (7)
6 - Understanding of another (7)
7 - Representative (5)
11 - Commerce (8)
12 - Yield (7)
13 - Affably (7)
15 - Beat easily (7)
16 - Plane figure (5)
19 - Lofty (4)

No 306

Across

1 - Indifferent (2-2)
3 - Card game (8)
9 - Give too much money (7)
10 - Strongly advised (5)
11 - Order (12)
14 - Antelope (3)
16 - Harass (5)
17 - Expert (3)
18 - Untruthfully (12)
21 - Fleshy (5)
22 - Cereal (7)
23 - Magnificence (8)
24 - Criticize strongly (4)

Down

1 - Obstruction (8)
2 - Blockage (5)
4 - Some (3)
5 - Female fellow national (12)
6 - Organize anew (7)
7 - Make neat (4)
8 - Conspicuously new (5-3-4)
12 - Greek building style (5)
13 - Having many spouses (8)
15 - Not level (7)
19 - Ruin (5)
20 - Mocks (4)
22 - Sticky substance (3)

No 307

Across

1 - Bird claw (5)
4 - Fragmentary (7)
7 - Role model (5)
8 - Person who goes to bed late (5,3)
9 - Spy (5)
11 - Pithy saying (8)
15 - Frozen dessert (3,5)
17 - Announcement (5)
19 - Compassionate (8)
20 - Piece of cloth (5)
21 - Overlooked (7)
22 - Not as expected (5)

Down

1 - Possible (9)
2 - Distances (7)
3 - Bring up (7)
4 - Pashminas (6)
5 - Increasing (6)
6 - Keyboard instrument (5)
10 - Telling fortunes (9)
12 - Frozen water spears (7)
13 - Plant (7)
14 - Metamorphic rock (6)
16 - Damned (6)
18 - Piece of information (5)

No 308

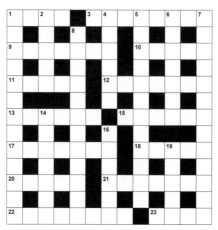

Across

1 - Shine (4)
3 - Machines (8)
9 - Release (7)
10 - Noblemen (5)
11 - Movements of water (5)
12 - Sheltered side (7)
13 - Passion (6)
15 - Workplace (6)
17 - Garment worn by dancers (7)
18 - Repasts (5)
20 - Absent from country (5)
21 - Genuine (7)
22 - Sprinkling with water (8)
23 - Poems (4)

Down

1 - Copious abundance (13)
2 - Smoothed nails (5)
4 - Maintain (6)
5 - First part of the Bible (3,9)
6 - Clumsy (7)
7 - Constant diligence (13)
8 - Enthusiastically (12)
14 - More spacious (7)
16 - More likely than not (4-2)
19 - In front (5)

No 309

Across

1 - Aide (8)
6 - Droops (4)
8 - Unconsciousness (6)
9 - Change gradually (6)
10 - Bloom (3)
11 - Republic in W Africa (4)
12 - Figure of speech (6)
13 - Chairs (6)
15 - Stick of wax (6)
17 - Ablaze (6)
20 - Utters (4)
21 - Compete for (3)
22 - Number of Apostles (6)
23 - Concept (6)
24 - Cleopatra's snakes (4)
25 - Longing (8)

Down

2 - Obtain (7)
3 - Island in the Bay of Naples (5)
4 - Little balls; children's game (7)
5 - Requires (5)
6 - Icy statue (7)
7 - Mallet (5)
14 - Diviners (7)
15 - Showy solo passage (7)
16 - Surrender a weapon (3,4)
18 - Young deer (5)
19 - All (5)
20 - Fabric (5)

No 310

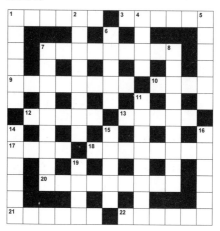

Across
1 - Patient (6)
3 - Stableman (6)
7 - Sweetened beverage (9)
9 - Wonderful (8)
10 - Watering device (4)
12 - Country in NE Africa (5)
13 - Textile (5)
17 - Microscopic arachnid (4)
18 - Divide (8)
20 - Variety of peach (9)
21 - Preserved (6)
22 - Irresolute (6)

Down
1 - Invade in large numbers (6)
2 - Eating places (8)
4 - Con (4)
5 - Dared (6)
6 - Cause (5)
7 - Long-armed ape (9)
8 - Use frugally (9)
11 - Rotation (8)
14 - Urges or forces (6)
15 - This date (5)
16 - Harass (6)
19 - Mace (anag) (4)

No 311

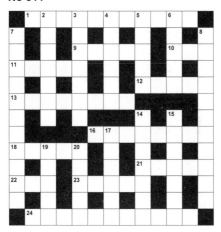

Across
1 - Earthly (11)
9 - Small explosive (5)
10 - Bristlelike appendage (3)
11 - Capital of Vietnam (5)
12 - Musical times (5)
13 - Stretched out (8)
16 - Volcanic glass (8)
18 - In the middle of (5)
21 - Finite sequence of terms (5)
22 - Born (3)
23 - Compare (5)
24 - Stargazers (11)

Down
2 - Issue forth (7)
3 - Departs (7)
4 - Slush (6)
5 - Machine (5)
6 - Warn (5)
7 - Something accomplished (11)
8 - Natural surroundings (11)
14 - Country in SE Asia (7)
15 - More straightforward (7)
17 - Small sharp-pointed tool (6)
19 - Sediment (5)
20 - Roof ceramics worker (5)

No 312

Across

1 - Small oval plum (6)
5 - Irritates (6)
8 - Facial feature (4)
9 - Mental attitudes (8)
10 - Score (5)
11 - Conducted (7)
14 - Worldly-wise (13)
16 - Normally (7)
18 - Moan (5)
20 - Horse of light tan color (8)
22 - Consumes (4)
23 - Among (6)
24 - Examines (6)

Down

2 - Irregular (9)
3 - Furtiveness (7)
4 - Cranny (4)
5 - Creative (8)
6 - Trap (5)
7 - Ox (3)
12 - Stylishly (9)
13 - Eg King David (8)
15 - Lacking air (7)
17 - Audibly (5)
19 - Legume (4)
21 - Goal (3)

No 313

Across

1 - Falls back (8)
5 - South American Indian (4)
8 - Sufficiently (5)
9 - Short hairs (7)
10 - Caresses (7)
12 - Phrasing (7)
14 - Newspaper (7)
16 - Sunshade (7)
18 - Hot fire (7)
19 - Rise (3,2)
20 - Coat with gold (4)
21 - Pattern of symptoms (8)

Down

1 - Large quantity (4)
2 - Type of hat (6)
3 - Eg residents of Cairo (9)
4 - Setting up (6)
6 - Almost (6)
7 - Glue (8)
11 - Made short and sharp turns (9)
12 - Paper covering (8)
13 - Tricky (6)
14 - Depressing (6)
15 - Stain skin with ink (6)
17 - Fencing sword (4)

No 314

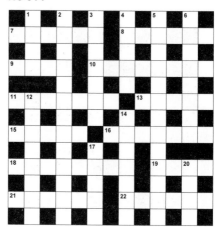

Across
7 - Encourages (6)
8 - Attach (6)
9 - Company emblem (4)
10 - Vigorously (8)
11 - Caresses (7)
13 - Battle (5)
15 - Attempted to achieve (5)
16 - Relaxes (7)
18 - Catastrophe (8)
19 - River in central England (4)
21 - Brawn (6)
22 - Choose (6)

Down
1 - Drive away (4)
2 - Tough enforcement policy (4,9)
3 - Took the place of (7)
4 - Cat (5)
5 - Intermittently (13)
6 - Surrounded (8)
12 - Station (8)
14 - Coat; decorate lavishly (7)
17 - Spread by scattering (5)
20 - Killer whale (4)

No 315

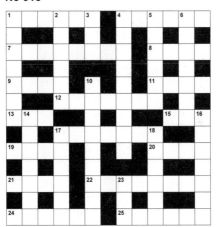

Across

1 - Gain (6)
4 - Expect (6)
7 - Masonry support (8)
8 - Lofty (4)
9 - Look at amorously (4)
11 - Outer covering (4)
12 - Round building (7)
13 - Cobra (3)
15 - Posed (3)
17 - Fixing (7)
19 - Republic in W Africa (4)
20 - Highest level (4)
21 - Well-behaved (4)
22 - Curiosity (8)
24 - Evaluate (6)
25 - Country (6)

Down

1 - Mechanical keyboard (7)
2 - Male parent (6)
3 - Definite article (3)
4 - Genuine (9)
5 - Desert in N Africa (6)
6 - Purplish red (7)
10 - Rankings (9)
14 - Eg spring and summer (7)
16 - Treachery (7)
17 - Center (6)
18 - Hard glassy mineral (6)
23 - Male offspring (3)

No 316

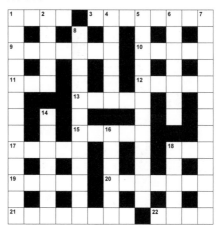

Across

1 - Crimp (4)
3 - Influenced positively (8)
9 - Green with vegetation (7)
10 - Tests (5)
11 - Put down (3)
12 - Additional (5)
13 - Hushed (5)
15 - Tines (anag) (5)
17 - Killer whales (5)
18 - Sum charged (3)
19 - Pastoral poem (5)
20 - Ugly thing (7)
21 - Ragged (8)
22 - Ignore correction (4)

Down

1 - Rebel (13)
2 - Attractively shaped (5)
4 - Floating (6)
5 - Planned in advance (12)
6 - Responded to (7)
7 - Denigration (13)
8 - Unmarried French woman (12)
14 - Decipher (7)
16 - Ball-shaped object (6)
18 - Ice (5)

No 317

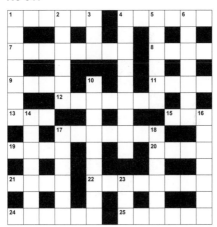

Across
1 - Nothing (6)
4 - Compare (6)
7 - Noble title (8)
8 - Adds (4)
9 - Fibber (4)
11 - Bread (4)
12 - Instructed (7)
13 - Title of a Turkish noble (3)
15 - Nervous twitch (3)
17 - Pushing in a direction (7)
19 - In place of; stead (4)
20 - Midwestern state (4)
21 - Poem (4)
22 - Linguistic system (8)
24 - Extract meaning from (6)
25 - Start fire (6)

Down
1 - Short story (7)
2 - Small racing car (2-4)
3 - Nineteenth Greek letter (3)
4 - Not inherent (9)
5 - Not purchased (6)
6 - Percussion instruments (7)
10 - Destroy wantonly (9)
14 - A look (7)
16 - Laughter (7)
17 - Papal representative (6)
18 - Evil-tempered spirit (6)
23 - Variety (3)

No 318

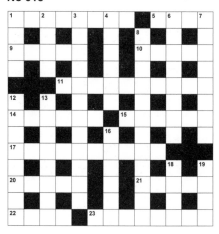

Across
1 - Yellowing of the skin (8)
5 - Character; sort (4)
9 - Leaves (5)
10 - Senseless (5)
11 - Having similar disposition (10)
14 - Yellow citrus fruits (6)
15 - Put to the test (3,3)
17 - Working class (4-6)
20 - Strike out (5)
21 - Distinguishing characteristic (5)
22 - Toy (2-2)
23 - Inherited property (8)

Down
1 - Young kangaroo (4)
2 - One part (4)
3 - Divided (12)
4 - Muslim ruler (6)
6 - Annual (8)
7 - Coming next after tenth (8)
8 - Rain gently (6-6)
12 - Swollen with fat (8)
13 - Pollutant (8)
16 - Recess (6)
18 - Starch (4)
19 - Moat (anag) (4)

No 319

Across
1 - In a slow tempo (6)
5 - Part of pen (3)
7 - Greeting (5)
8 - Experienced (7)
9 - Short high tone (5)
10 - Associating towns (8)
12 - Recurs in sequences (6)
14 - Empty (6)
17 - Young hares (8)
18 - Produces tones (5)
20 - Building cover (7)
21 - Tall and thin (5)
22 - Weep (3)
23 - Long legged waders (6)

Down
2 - Entry (7)
3 - Set in from margin (8)
4 - Stone block (4)
5 - Short story (7)
6 - Best pod (anag) (7)
7 - Songs of praise (5)
11 - Without shoes (8)
12 - Traditional example (7)
13 - With foresight (7)
15 - Communication system (7)
16 - Boat (5)
19 - Exposes to natural light (4)

No 320

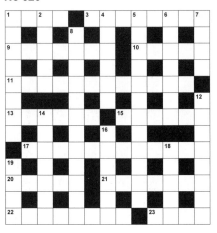

Across
1 - Overfill (4)
3 - Lineage (8)
9 - Hanging drapery (7)
10 - Operatic stars (5)
11 - Condemnation (12)
13 - Surface quality (6)
15 - Environmental condition (6)
17 - Sarcastically (12)
20 - Supplementary component (3-2)
21 - Military person (7)
22 - Pointers (anag) (8)
23 - Lazy (4)

Down
1 - Loose-fitting protective garment (8)
2 - Spring flower akin to the primrose (
4 - Small hole (6)
5 - Dimly (12)
6 - Pasta pockets (7)
7 - Relaxation (4)
8 - Freedom from control (12)
12 - Exempt from tax (4-4)
14 - A placeholder name (2-3-2)
16 - Occurring together (6)
18 - Property owner (5)
19 - Moist (4)

No 321

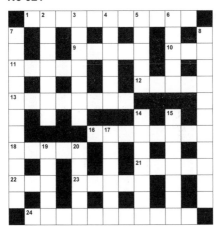

Across
1 - Desire for wealth (11)
9 - Dog like mammal (5)
10 - Inflated feeling of pride (3)
11 - Group of shots (5)
12 - Relating to a person (5)
13 - Decade of four score (8)
16 - Watcher (8)
18 - Stroll (5)
21 - Clean (5)
22 - Legal rule (3)
23 - Journeys (5)
24 - Indistinguishably (11)

Down
2 - Comparison (7)
3 - Spurs on (7)
4 - Time of widespread glaciation (3,3)
5 - Animal restraint (5)
6 - Water vapor (5)
7 - Indescribable (11)
8 - Forged (11)
14 - Ocean (4-3)
15 - Generally (7)
17 - Bathing suit (6)
19 - Bent; bandy (5)
20 - Consumed (5)

No 322

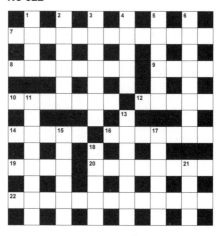

Across
7 - Perfect likeness or counterpart (8,5)
8 - Pink wading bird (8)
9 - Hog sound (4)
10 - Charging tax (7)
12 - Belonging to them (5)
14 - Facial hair (5)
16 - Trash (7)
19 - Short end or section (4)
20 - Commotion (8)
22 - Well-known or eminent (13)

Down
1 - Mineral (4)
2 - Stocky (6)
3 - Singing (anag) (7)
4 - Softly radiant (5)
5 - Caress; kiss (6)
6 - Business organizations (8)
11 - Using current (8)
13 - Prompting device (7)
15 - Mechanical devices (6)
17 - Bidding (6)
18 - Dark wood (5)
21 - Color properties (4)

No 323

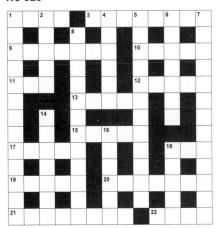

Across
1 - Breathe convulsively (4)
3 - The art of drawing (8)
9 - Bath brushes (7)
10 - More timid (5)
11 - Sprite (3)
12 - Departing (5)
13 - Bring on oneself (5)
15 - Strongly advised (5)
17 - Sleeping berths (5)
18 - Penultimate Greek letter (3)
19 - Money; revenues (5)
20 - Marsh gas (7)
21 - Passing (8)
22 - Supplements (4)

Down
1 - Monarch's 50th anniversary (6,7)
2 - Eat quickly (5)
4 - Countrified; unsophisticated (6)
5 - Person studying after a degree (12)
6 - Metal similar to platinum (7)
7 - Liveliness (13)
8 - Judiciousness (12)
14 - Cure all (7)
16 - Language spoken in Berlin (6)
18 - Silly trick (5)

No 324

Across
1 - Warning (6)
4 - Line of equal pressure (6)
9 - Ice cream flavor (7)
10 - European deer (7)
11 - Correct (5)
12 - Eg heart or liver (5)
14 - Relative by marriage (2-3)
15 - Repay (anag) (5)
17 - Ire (5)
18 - Blamed (7)
20 - Protective skins (7)
21 - Long pin (6)
22 - Customs (6)

Down
1 - Prance (6)
2 - Sour tasting (8)
3 - Dole out (5)
5 - In an unspecified manner (7)
6 - Attractive man; boyfriend (4)
7 - Calculate (6)
8 - Passionate (4-7)
13 - Burbling (8)
14 - Annoying (7)
15 - Jewels (6)
16 - Expects confidently (6)
17 - Regions (5)
19 - Give up (4)

No 325

Across
1 - Irregular (6)
5 - Salt water (3)
7 - Data received (5)
8 - Without weapons (7)
9 - Run away with a lover (5)
10 - Overabundances (8)
12 - Characteristic (6)
14 - Reddish brown (6)
17 - Engine part (8)
18 - Perform without preparation (2-3)
20 - Arachnids (7)
21 - Social ban (5)
22 - Stimulus (3)
23 - Exit (6)

Down
2 - Captures (7)
3 - Unhappy at being away (8)
4 - Fencing sword (4)
5 - Walks (7)
6 - Nonbeliever (7)
7 - Layabout (5)
11 - Making up an answer (8)
12 - From the East (7)
13 - Priest (7)
15 - Labors (7)
16 - Rope (5)
19 - Moves up and down (4)

No 326

Across
1 - Indian dresses (5)
4 - Mix a deck of cards (7)
7 - Pretend (5)
8 - The end of a sports match (4-4)
9 - Redden (5)
11 - Replies (8)
15 - Devilment (8)
17 - Welcome (5)
19 - Moderately rich (4-2-2)
20 - Farewell remark (5)
21 - Get back together (7)
22 - Derive (5)

Down
1 - Experiencing pain (9)
2 - Pragmatist (7)
3 - Felt hat (7)
4 - Dishonored (6)
5 - Without constraint (6)
6 - Company emblems (5)
10 - Six (4-5)
12 - Measuring (7)
13 - Retaliatory action (7)
14 - Revived or regenerated (6)
16 - Time of widespread glaciation (3,3)
18 - Natural elevation (5)

No 327

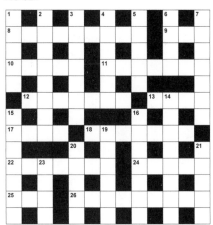

Across
8 - Speech sound that is not a vowel (9)
9 - Influenza (abbrev) (3)
10 - Pinch; squeeze (5)
11 - Not artificial (7)
12 - Companion (7)
13 - Individual (4)
17 - Enemies (4)
18 - Refrigerator (7)
22 - Huge coniferous tree (7)
24 - Judged (5)
25 - Every (3)
26 - Clotting agent (9)

Down
1 - Type of angle (5)
2 - Wrapper (8)
3 - Derision (7)
4 - Acquired (6)
5 - Utter (5)
6 - From a distance (4)
7 - Render legally void (7)
14 - Ultimate (8)
15 - Away from the highway (3-4)
16 - Anxious (7)
19 - Type of tire construction (6)
20 - Small moneybag (5)
21 - Modifies (5)
23 - Punctually (4)

No 328

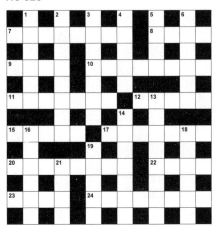

Across
7 - Refer to famous people (8)
8 - Merriment (4)
9 - Lose grip (4)
10 - Metrical analysis of verse (8)
11 - Pertaining to the skull (7)
12 - Clever (5)
15 - Republic in N Africa (5)
17 - Followed after (7)
20 - Got hold of (8)
22 - Too (4)
23 - Encourage in wrongdoing (4)
24 - Prestigious (8)

Down
1 - Blight (6)
2 - Inclination (8)
3 - ___ ball: used by clairvoyants (7)
4 - Flatten on impact (5)
5 - Chickens lay them (4)
6 - French painter (6)
13 - Notes (8)
14 - Highly knowledgeable people (7)
16 - Drink (6)
18 - Christian festival (6)
19 - Mountain range (5)
21 - Small social insects (4)

No 329

Across
8 - Finish (6,3)
9 - Lyric poem (3)
10 - Genuflect (5)
11 - Solvent; adhesive (7)
12 - Polish (7)
13 - Abominable snowman (4)
17 - Wildly (4)
18 - Informed (7)
22 - Scale; French mathematician (7)
24 - Reason for innocence (5)
25 - Draw in (3)
26 - With profound love (9)

Down
1 - Prickly (5)
2 - Alternate personality (5,3)
3 - Incapable of functioning (7)
4 - Piece of music (6)
5 - Suggest (5)
6 - Extinct bird (4)
7 - Abstraction (7)
14 - Latter part of days (8)
15 - Innocence (7)
16 - Extreme enthusiast (7)
19 - Portion of time (6)
20 - Stringed instrument (5)
21 - Plastic (5)
23 - Pieces of cloth (4)

No 330

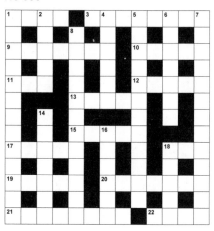

Across

1 - Long tube (4)
3 - Appetizing drink (8)
9 - Eg flies and beetles (7)
10 - Fish dish (5)
11 - Mother of the ancient Irish gods (3)
12 - Smallest quantity (5)
13 - Mix up (5)
15 - Approaches (5)
17 - Cook joint of meat (5)
18 - Court (3)
19 - Apparent (5)
20 - Samplers (7)
21 - Leniency (8)
22 - Linger (4)

Down

1 - Benevolent (13)
2 - Italian food (5)
4 - Urged (6)
5 - Uneasiness (12)
6 - Having a valid will (7)
7 - Teasingly (13)
8 - Someone you know (12)
14 - Issue forth (7)
16 - Pertaining to vinegar (6)
18 - Food grain (5)

No 331

Across
1 - Rushes (6)
7 - Power unit (8)
8 - Nay (anag) (3)
9 - Fictional (4-2)
10 - Row (4)
11 - Seabird (5)
13 - Least difficult (7)
15 - Silver-white metal (7)
17 - Suffering (5)
21 - Totals (4)
22 - Small stones (6)
23 - Goal (3)
24 - Traffic jam (8)
25 - Not noticed (6)

Down
1 - Conversation (6)
2 - Obstruct (6)
3 - Traveled on snow runners (5)
4 - Boat launcher (7)
5 - Abode (8)
6 - Large pebbles (6)
12 - Rump (8)
14 - Feeling of indignation (7)
16 - Snakes (6)
18 - Dedicated person (6)
19 - Sycophant (3-3)
20 - Verse form (5)

No 332

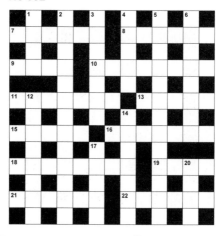

Across
7 - Emanating from God (6)
8 - Punctuation mark (6)
9 - Unit of measure (4)
10 - Thrust forward (8)
11 - Speculate (7)
13 - Inquired (5)
15 - Attach (5)
16 - Large island of Indonesia (7)
18 - Refuge for an animal (4-4)
19 - Recreational water-based facility (4)
21 - Stopped (6)
22 - Cosmetics (4,2)

Down
1 - High fidelity (abbrev) (2,2)
2 - Unsatisfactory (13)
3 - Scorn (7)
4 - Vibrated (5)
5 - Showing fair play (13)
6 - Protective clothing (8)
12 - Thawed (8)
14 - Repositories of antiques (7)
17 - Solids (5)
20 - Sullen (4)

No 333

Across
1 - Indecent (6)
3 - Lived by (6)
7 - Leading (9)
9 - Imagines to be the case (8)
10 - Sudden explosive noise (4)
12 - Dyed fabric (5)
13 - Yield (5)
17 - Religious order (4)
18 - Industrious (8)
20 - Drabness (9)
21 - Less quiet (6)
22 - Backward direction (6)

Down
1 - Self interest (6)
2 - Completely sealed (8)
4 - Remove water from a boat (4)
5 - Injure (6)
6 - Accent mark (5)
7 - Held at arms length (9)
8 - Seriousness (9)
11 - Sound units (8)
14 - Republic in SW Asia (6)
15 - Brilliant (5)
16 - Stress; pull a muscle (6)
19 - Poker stake (4)

No 334

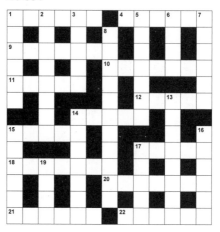

Across
1 - Superior of a nunnery (6)
4 - Relating to the backbone (6)
9 - Luck or chance (7)
10 - Cheese on toast dish (7)
11 - Governed (5)
12 - Enthusiastic (5)
14 - Watch (5)
15 - Raw fish dish (5)
17 - Clod of turf (5)
18 - The Windy City (7)
20 - Impassive (7)
21 - Setting up (6)
22 - Far from the intended target (6)

Down
1 - Declare (6)
2 - Thieves (8)
3 - Noise (5)
5 - Department distributing wages (7)
6 - Deprived of sensation (4)
7 - Finally (6)
8 - Spinning (11)
13 - Someone who lives (8)
14 - Organic nutrient (7)
15 - Tiny bag (6)
16 - Heavy and starchy (6)
17 - Low value coins (5)
19 - Lazy (4)

No 335

Across
1 - Run quickly (4)
3 - Free from error (8)
9 - General idea (7)
10 - Excess (5)
11 - Mouth; trap (3)
12 - Fork (5)
13 - Folded back part of a coat (5)
15 - Impudent (5)
17 - Narrow openings (5)
18 - Spot (3)
19 - Important question (5)
20 - Worm (7)
21 - Called the same (8)
22 - Catch sight of (4)

Down
1 - Expansion (13)
2 - Connective tissue (5)
4 - Doze (6)
5 - Joblessness (12)
6 - All illustrated material (7)
7 - In an inflated manner (13)
8 - Uneasiness (12)
14 - Floating wreckage (7)
16 - Diminished in size (6)
18 - Reduces the shine (5)

No 336

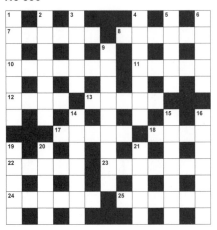

Across

7 - Of the eye (6)
8 - Open type of footwear (6)
10 - Purplish red shrub (7)
11 - Subject (5)
12 - Deprived of sensation (4)
13 - Farm (5)
17 - Flavoring (5)
18 - Movable barrier (4)
22 - Island in the Bay of Naples (5)
23 - Featured (7)
24 - Essential qualities (6)
25 - Doze (6)

Down

1 - Place limits on (7)
2 - End result (7)
3 - Lift up (5)
4 - Thrown away (4,3)
5 - Ticks over (5)
6 - Pilot (5)
9 - Universe as a whole (9)
14 - Established in advance (1,6)
15 - Stronghold (7)
16 - Provoked or teased (7)
19 - Perfume (5)
20 - Large indefinite amount (5)
21 - Circular shape (5)

No 337

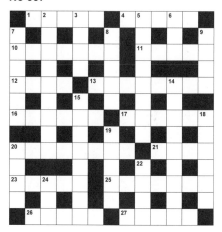

Across

1 - Yellow-orange pigment (5)
4 - Taken ___ : surprised (5)
10 - Structures that span a river (7)
11 - Uptight (5)
12 - Get rid of (4)
13 - Immediately after this (8)
16 - Metal grating (6)
17 - Evening meal (6)
20 - Summary (8)
21 - Brave person (4)
23 - Reasoned judgment (5)
25 - Larva of frogs (7)
26 - Implant (5)
27 - Gelatin (5)

Down

2 - Find fault with (9)
3 - Nervy (4)
5 - Flatter (6,2)
6 - Cheat (3)
7 - Elongated rectangle (6)
8 - Twisted to one side (5)
9 - Plant having fronds (4)
14 - Pork and beef sausage (9)
15 - Collarbone (8)
18 - Covered (6)
19 - Conquers (5)
20 - Capital of Norway (4)
22 - Chances of winning (4)
24 - Athletic facility (3)

No 338

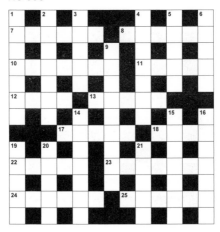

Across

7 - Make worse (6)
8 - Specify (6)
10 - Non-believer (7)
11 - Compact (5)
12 - Saw; observed (4)
13 - Relating to the kidneys (5)
17 - Dirty (5)
18 - Group of three (4)
22 - Anxiety (5)
23 - Vacationers (7)
24 - Widen (6)
25 - Spirited horses (6)

Down

1 - Ignition device (7)
2 - Informed (7)
3 - Opposite of day (5)
4 - Progress; forward motion (7)
5 - Very tall (5)
6 - Unit of measurement (5)
9 - Forbid (9)
14 - Sarcastic (7)
15 - Commanded (7)
16 - Composed of (7)
19 - Escapade (5)
20 - Semiprecious quartz (5)
21 - Gives out (5)

No 339

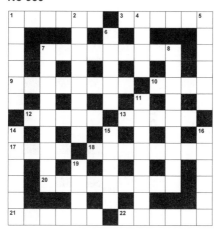

Across
1 - Take away (6)
3 - Princely (6)
7 - Unharmed (9)
9 - Dangerous; severe (8)
10 - Hero (4)
12 - Villain (5)
13 - Block (5)
17 - Ammunition (abbrev) (4)
18 - Sharply (8)
20 - Sailor (9)
21 - Bits of bread (6)
22 - Gastropods (6)

Down
1 - Step down (6)
2 - Volcano near Naples (8)
4 - Yearn for (4)
5 - Modest (6)
6 - Not clearly stated (5)
7 - Consistently (9)
8 - Polygon having 12 sides (9)
11 - Presiding officer (8)
14 - Verse pentameter (6)
15 - Grime and dirt (5)
16 - Wildcats (6)
19 - Protective crust (4)

Solutions

No 1

```
I N D U C E . . S . E G G
A . H . G A W K Y . E . .
E S T U A R Y . A . E . N
T . . P . P . N O B L E .
L I G H T E S T . R . . S
L . . E . Y . A . O . I .
B Y W O R D . S C O W L S
A . R . S . N . O . I . .
Y . E . S A L U T I N G .
O U S T S . T . S . . G .
N . T . A . A N T I Q U E
E . L E G A L . I . . A .
T I E . A . . S C U L L S
```

No 2

```
R E C Y C L E S . C H E F
A . O . O . N . S . O . U
R O M A N . D . T I T A N
E . B . S . U . O . H . N
. . R E F R A C T O R Y .
A . S . Q . E . K . U . M
D I C T U M . S I E S T A
M . I . E . C . N . E . N
I N S A N D O U T S . . .
T . S . T . R . R . L . V
T W I L L . O . . A B I D E
E . O . Y . N . D . L . R
D I N E . T A P E S T R Y
```

No 3

```
J E S T E R . F A M I S H
O . I . I . I . E . . . T
C I N N A M O N . D A R T
U . G . . . A . I . O . .
L O S E . C . N . A I L S
A . . S T O I C A L . L .
R A N . . R . I . . U S E
. C . A W K W A R D . X .
S T U B S . S . L . E T C H
U . B . C . . . A . A . A
G A V E . R E S I D U A L
T . S . E . I . L . . . E
S E E S A W . R H Y M E D
```

No 4

```
T U T U . I M M I N E N T
R . R . D . A . N . C . R
A C U T E L Y . V I L L A
N . L . D . E . I . N . .
S T Y L I . A P R O P O S
C . . . C . Y . T . S . P
R A S C A L . G E N E V A
I . U . . . T . A . B . R
P E N D E N T . R O G U E
T . B . S . T . A . R . N
I T E M S . E N T R A N T
O . A . E . S . E . T . L
N O M I N A T E . D E N Y
```

No 5

```
. P A R C H . G R A S P .
R . X . R . V . E . O . S
O R I G A M I . J A B O T
C . O . B . G . E . . . I
O H M S . D I S C O V E R
C . . A . A . L . T . I .
O P T I M A . S E L D O M
. I . E . I . D . E . E .
Y A C H T I N G . F O I L
O . . H . G . B . T . O .
G L O R Y . O P E R A N D
A . V . S . T . N . P . Y
. P A C T S . S T E E D .
```

No 6

```
P . P . C . S . C . F
S I E R R A . C H O I R S
. L . E . S . A . N . E
B L O C . T O M A T O E S
. O . . O . P . R . W .
R E U N I F Y . Q A T A R
. P . C . F . D . D . R
F I R E D . V I S I T E D
. T . P . U . O . C . .
R H Y T H M I C . T I M E
. E . I . B . E . I . E
O T I O S E . S C O R N S
. S . N . R . E . N . D
```

No 7

```
C A F E . D A Y D R E A M
O . A . F . S . I . P . I
R E L O A D S . S N I P S
R . S . I . I . P . S . C
E V E N T . S P L O T C H
S . . H . T . A . L . I .
P A C I F Y . A C C E D E
O . A . U . A . E . . . V
N E E D L E D . M E T R O
D . S . N . V . E . H . U
E X U D E . I N N A R D S
N . R . S . C . T . E . L
T R A N S F E R . R E L Y
```

No 8

```
N E W E S T . A . S . L
O . E . . O B S E R V E R
B O A . X . I . I . A .
L . S I L I C A . L A V A
E . E . N . T . A . E .
S P L A Y . D I M N E S S
. B . A . C . K . . . .
B R I S T L E . E A R E D
O . O . G . O . A . E .
T O L L . E M B A R K . J
. T . V . R . O . I C E
T E N E R I F E . S . C
. D . S . A . S A C H E T
```

No 9

```
D E W Y E Y E D . S C A R
I . O . P . R . D . O . E
M A O R I . O . I R O N S
E . S . S . D . L . . . I
. . H O M E M A K I N G .
E . U . D . S . P . D . N
L E N T I L . M I N G L E
I . L . C . M . D . E . D
T R I L A T E R A L . . .
I . K . L . R . T . M . L
S P E L L . I . . I N U R E
T . L . Y . N . O . T . N
S A Y S . Y O U N G E S T
```

Solutions

No 10

```
A S T H M A   E S S A Y S
L     E   V   W       O
  E N D E A R I N G     O
E   X   I   U   G   R   T
G R E A T E N S   L A T H
E   M     A   T   D   C E
S P O T S   A I D E D
E   L   E   C   S     L A
V E I N   S H A T T E R S
O   F   T   U     A   S S
K   Y E A R N I N G S   A
E     L     K   C   Y
S H R I K E   D E B U T S
```

No 11

```
A S T R A L   O U S T E D
C   A   E   B   O     M
C A R P   A D D E N D U M
R   P   N   U   I
D E P O T   P R E C E D E
  C   R   E   A     E
A R I T H M E T I C I A N
  O     U   E   H   T
T W I D D L E   Y A C H T
  U   S     O   O   T
S T I C K I N G   T A R T
A   A   O   L   I   A
M U T T O N   E S C A P E
```

No 12

```
  F   L   P   A A   C
B U R E A U   M A T R O N
  S   T   N   E   T   R
P E R T   C O N T E M P T
  E   H   D   N     O
S C A R P E R   S T O R Y
  U   P   S M   I   A
S P R E E   M A R V E L S
  B   R   S   R     E
C O N F E T T I   N O N E
  A   E   R M   E   I
O R A C L E   B A S A L T
  D   T   W   A S   E
```

No 13

```
O B E D I E N T   A P S E
G   N   N   E   O   S
L I V I D   I S L A N D S
E   I   O   G   C   A
  E L   H A U G H T Y
R E D R E S S   N   O   I
E   N     M       S
C E C   I N E X A C T
E A S T E R N   R   L
I   C   J   I   B   F
P A R V E N U   T H E S E
T   O   R   E   D   T
S A W S   S Y N D R O M E
```

No 14

```
L A I D B A C K   C O C A
  M   O   G   I   U   L
N U C L E I   T I P T O E
  L   L   L E T   C   U
K E Y S   E   Y E A S T S
  T   L       K
A S T R A Y   B L E A C H
  E       O       L
W A R P E D   N   U T A H
  H   L   E W E   P   S
R E V A M P   D I S U S E
  A Y T   R   R   E   I
O D D S   H A Y S T A C K
```

No 15

```
S W I T C H E D   V E N D
A   B   I   N   D   P   I
S M E A R   R   E M I T S
H   X   C   O N S   S
  A U T O N O M O U S
L   C   M   T   U D   T
A G H A S T   E N T I C E
C   E   T   O   C   C   R
  R E S E A R C H E D
O   T   N   C   M L   D
S O N I C   U   E R A S E
S   U   E   L   N   M   F
E A T S   S T A T U A R Y
```

No 16

```
W I S H E S   A   P   U
A   C   O R D E R I N G
L E A   L   O   O   S
L   M E T E O R   P E A S
O   P   S   I   E   I
P R I N T   I N T R U D E
  E     B     G   T
B L O W O U T   T Y I N G
  I   S   L   M   N   A
E P I C   B I O N I C   R
O   A   O   T   I N N
M I S S O U R I   T   E
D   T   S   F O M E N T
```

No 17

```
  N S   T T Y   M S
I N T E R V E N E   A L E
P   A   I   E   A L   L
P I L A U   M A S T I F F
Y   K   M   E T   I
  K E Y P A D S   W H Y S
M   R   H   F   A   H
A L S O   A B A L O N E
E     R   L   O U   K
S O P R A N O   W A K E N
T   I   D T   E K   I
R U T   A C C O R D A N T
O   Y   R H S   H S
```

No 18

```
  H T W     C P   T
A V O W A L   C H A I S E
R   U G C   I   A   E
P E R S O N A   N I N O N
I   E N T   W O   S
S I R E   S C R A M
T   S B   H G L   S
  C L A W S   G U R U
A   R O O C   M   B
B L O A T   R H O M B U S
B   L T D   L A   E
O P E N E R   F O R G E T
T   S R     N O   S
```

343

Solutions

No 19

No 20

No 21

No 22

No 23

No 24

No 25

No 26

No 27

Solutions

No 28

SNAPPY LAUREL
KIWI TONEDEAF
NOWHERE PIVOT
DEALT UNRAVEL
SCENARIO EAVE
AMUSES CHAIRS

No 29

VICTOR LAZULI
ALLEGRO RALLY
OBEY SNACK
CALLS PAIR
DEISM TUTORED
LATENT PLYING

No 30

RETINA
COOLNESS
CAR REFORM EELS
LORDS ANYTIME
IGNEOUS IDIOM
WARM GLYPHS
AMP BEDLINEN
ALLEGE

No 31

KEEN RHAPSODY
NAIROBI ERECT
DISAGREEABLE
MIGHTY DIVERS
COLDSHOULDER
WAGON FOLLOWS
SMALLEST ZERO

No 32

LOCALE EVICTS
POCKETING
RECLINER POET
PASSE LEMON
PAIL MERIDIAN
GREATCOAT
ERRAND STARVE

No 33

FIRST MAPPING
SAN FIEND
NATIVITY
STAYS NAUTICAL
NAMEDROP
SKUAS THANKYOU
INCUR
GORILLA EASES

No 34

INTERCHANGE
VERGE REX
DOPEY SIDLE
SQUANDER
STARGAZE
ICING IONIC
URN IVIES
PROLIFERATE

No 35

UPTOTHEMINUTE
EXCESSES LEGO
JUSTICE USUAL
STEPS COUNTED
EDIT UNIQUELY
SLEIGHTOFHAND

No 36

PROOFS AWN
ENDED DREADED
RAIDS OBDURACY
STARTS OUTRUN
UNSTABLE
TUDOR PREDICT
FAINT
RAY TSETSE

345

Solutions

No 37

No 38

No 39

No 40

No 41

No 42

No 43

No 44

No 45

Solutions

No 46

```
DEER ESPRESSO
WORKMEN SLAKE
PERIODICALLY
UNTIDY WRITHE
UNPROFITABLE
THROB OCULIST
AILMENTS SKID
```

No 47

```
VULCAN CREAMY
CONCERTO VERB
URDU EROS
SMACKED
SHY HIS
ITALICS
HUES INTO
BARB OVERHEAT
YEARNS MADDEN
```

No 48

```
LAGER HANDSET
IMMINENT AFIRE
INSCRIBE MENSA
LITERATI
AGAIN
UNEFFUSIVE
ASTIR
USUALLY DRYER
```

No 49

```
SWIVEL THORNY
ODOR SHABBILY
FIREMEN ASIDE
NORSE WAVIEST
CASTAWAY ABET
CRAVEN UNLOAD
```

No 50

```
CHRYSANTHEMUM
EPIPHANY STOP
CLOSEUP ADDIS
UMBRA REPORTS
GNAT RAINFALL
ATTENTIVENESS
```

No 51

```
MAT APB
LIQUOR STAIRS
PITH MEDITATE
SCORNED SCORE
TROTS NIPPING
MADRIGAL TONE
POMADE SWOONS
```

No 52

```
VERIFY EGRETS
PLATITUDE
ROLEPLAY ACHY
OVULE ENJOY
AGUE CALIGULA
TURNSTILE
PILLAR AGEOLD
```

No 53

```
NAUGHTIER BOA
OFTEN ALLOYED
UPRAISE EPIC
ONES IMMORAL
CARAVAN TROTS
CHI RETENTION
```

No 54

```
FIDDLE MAVERICK
YES CARETS NOUS
GASES EVOLVED
SCEPTER ADOPT
SILO ATOMIC
YULETIDE RONDOS
```

Solutions

No 55

```
B S S . . . G A D . . . .
O T T A W A . B R O W S E
Y . R A P . I . A . I . .
C H I A N T I . F I R S T
O . P . S K . F . D Y . .
T E E D . H E L I X . . .
T . S . M . S N . L H . .
. . T E S T S . L O G O .
S T D . A . A . T . T . .
T I R E D . F A B R I C S
R . A . L . F . B O P . .
A R C H E S . L E A N T O
W . T . R . Y S T . . . .
```

No 56

```
. A S I D E . A D M I T .
E . U . E . T . O . N . C
D E C L A R E . C O N G O
I . C . L . S . T . O . .
B L U R . S T A R S H I P
L . L . A Y . I . A . . .
E L E C T S . E N T R A P
. N . T . C . E . M . L .
O N T H E J O B . N O N E
V . N . O . D . N . D . .
I D L E D . L O O P I N G
D . O . E . S . J . U . E
S P I E S . P O E M S . .
```

No 57

```
H Y G I E N I C . I F F Y
E . L . E . H . N . O . .
P A G E R S . A F F O R D
R . U . T O T . U . U . .
A D A M . I . S E S A M E
O . . . N . E . . . . . .
S T R I N G . R E S U M E
. N . . . E . . . E . . .
T O F F E E . D . C A L M
F . L . N E W . A . . . .
E F F O R T . I N S A N E
E . W . R . N . E . I . .
U R N S . Y I E L D I N G
```

No 58

```
E Q U I T Y . W O M B A T
U . N . A . E . O . Y . .
A I D S . R E S T O R E D
N . U . D . T . S . . . .
S T I L L . D E S E R V E
U . A . S . R . O . . . .
A P P R E H E N S I B L E
L . . I . S . N . U . . .
R E S H A P E . C H U N K
A . M . H . A . T . . . .
M O U S S A K A . L E A N
W . T . T . H . E . R . .
E N Z Y M E . A R R A Y S
```

No 59

```
R I D I C U L E . T R A P
I . R . A . O . . O . A .
N E E D S . N E T B A L L
D . S . T . G . . M . I .
S . S I . E S C H E W S .
V O Y A G E R . O D . A .
A . A . A . R . A . D . .
N G T . A S K A N C E . .
G A R D E N S . S A . A .
U . I . . P . C R A . . .
A C T U A T E . R U R A L
R . T . . C E O . L . . .
D A Y S . S T O W A W A Y
```

No 60

```
. S G . S . R . R . P . .
U N F A S H I O N A B L Y
. A . M . R . U . G . A .
S P E E D I N G . O A T H
. . T . N . E . U . Y . .
S Q U E A K Y . S T O P S
U . S . I . . . U . . . .
N E W T S . K N A V I S H
S . H . C . I . U . . . .
S T I R . A N T E L O P E
I . E . R . I . C . U . .
N O N A P P E A R A N C E
N . D . S . L . N . E . .
```

No 61

```
O C C U R S . S . C H I .
L . . A . V A P O R . S .
B E G U I N E . A . I . T
A . N . . N I . R A N C H
S N O W F A L L . G . M .
S . . A . S . F . E . U .
F E E B L Y . S L I D E S
E . A . L . U . A . X . .
R S . K N I T W E A R . .
R E E F S . T . F . M . .
U . O . A . I D I O T I C
L . F U G U E S . S . N .
E L F . A . S H A R E D .
```

No 62

```
B A B E . S C A L L O P S
O . A . D . O . O . B . E
M A D N E S S . N A S A L
B . G . L . I . G . C . F
A R E . I N . I N U R E .
S . . C H E S T . R . V .
T . D . A . . U . E . I .
I I . T A P E D . . D . .
C O P S E . R . I . A Y E
A L L . S . O N . M . N .
L O O P S . V I A D U C T
L . M . E . E . L . S . L
Y E A R N I N G . D E F Y
```

No 63

```
. S . M . S . A . S . E .
A T T A C K E D . T I N Y
A . D . E . D . O . T . .
I T C H . W O O D W O R M
U . O . E . N . . E . . .
E S Q U I R E . S H E E P
. S . S . E . O . . . . .
A L I E N . P L O T T E D
E . R . E . E . N . . . .
R A T T L I N G . L O C O
S . O . N . A . I . A . .
N E O N . S U N B E A M S
D . S . E . T . R . P . .
```

348

Solutions

No 64

	G	E	N	T	L	E	M	A	N	L	Y	
P		M		R	L	D			I	A		
A	B		U	S	U	A	L		C	E	P	
S	A	L	O	N		D	I		K	O		
S		E	D	E		B	A	S	I	C		A
T	I	M	E	L	E	S	S				A	
H		S	E					C	C	L		
E				J	E	A	L	O	U	S	Y	
B	U	S	E	S		N		A	R	P		
U		I		I	R		S	W	E	E	T	
C	A	N		L	I	O	N	S		A	I	
K		C	O	L		E	L	C				
S	E	N	S	E	L	E	S	S	L	Y		

No 65

SHAKES — POUNDS
Y R E A N O
ADZE — ACRIDITY
R M R M U
TOOLS — HERETIC
F I R S N
COUNTERACTIVE
I D N Y E
PLAYPEN — SPASM
E P I E T
INTAGLIO — SOON
U R O T E R
STINGY — ATTEST

No 66

PRINCELY — OSLO
I M E E H B
TYPES — VENEERS
H O S I K E
S A ENAMELS
AVERTED B L S
N I S E
G C O AMOROUS
SCANNED R P
T L H B T S
RELEASE — EXIST
O U R N O U
MOPS — DESTINED

No 67

MIGHTY — TRENCH
I E H I A O I
CONCEAL — N U K
R I I LICENSE
OUTER M H R
N I A EXAMS I
V HONOR I S
HYENA N L S
O L E GREAT
PROFFER E R E
P P W ENCLOSE
E A A D K N D
DELAYS — TOSSES

No 68

FUMES — PROSAIC
R A T R Y T
U G A E IDEAL
INNATELY N L
T I U I BERYL
LIFETIME Y I
E Y E S M T
S A SKITTISH
SHADY I U S E
A V GRANDSON
FRAIL S N I E
S C C E O S
CHEETAH — RANTS

No 69

RIPPLE — INTONE
N A B N H O
ABET — BISCUITS
E E T S T D
STEEP — MISSIVE
W R D N E
REINFORCEMENT
E E W T I G
UNDOING — INNER
R R P L E A
BROCCOLI — RINK
O A U S A C
LESSER — PELLET

No 70

BONSAI — A P M
A O DEFERRAL
NOR L F O R
A MAKEDO PROP
N A D R E O
ALLOT — ADORING
V O S L
DECEIVE — MYRRH
S R E M I E
SCAR — REASON R
R I L L GOO
COLDCALL E N
W E Y STORMS

No 71

DUNCE — ORBITAL
I A M F N P
S G A F SCARF
PAGANISM O I
L I A E SMELL
ANNOTATE E O
Y G E N E L
E G OPTIONAL
DIVER E T T I
R M STARSHIP
DIGIT N L U O
S N L T S P
CHOICES — EVENS

No 72

LORD — PHYSIQUE
Y A M E I U L
RIVIERA — MEALS
I E R U R E
CONGRATULATE
I Y S T E D
SAVAGE — TATTOO
T A O S N D
INFREQUENTLY
O I O U I H W
PILAU — ARTDECO
U L N T Y T R
STARDUST — BACK

349

Solutions

No 73

```
O W I N G   F O O T M A N
P   N   L   O     R   C
E   C   A   R   M E R R Y
R A I N C O A T     M   I
A   T   I   G   G O A D S
T E E N A G E R     R   O
I   S   L     S   T   C
N     A   B R O C C O L I
G R A D E   A   E   C   A
U   V   A T Y P I C A L
A S T I R   T   T   A   I
T   S   L   E   T   S
E S S E N C E     R E A L M
```

No 74

```
  G   S   G   N   N   G
B I T T E R L Y   O V A L
  V   R   A   L   U   M
Z E B U   D O O R N A I L
  U   G   U   N     N
E P I G R A M   A L I G N
  L   L   D   I
U P S E T   T R U F F L E
  O     C   A   E   O
H E D G E H O G   B A L M
  T   A   I   O   O   L
B R O W   M A N D A T E S
  Y   P   E   S   T   D
```

No 75

```
D E S K   O B L I G A T E
I   E   C   I   M Q   X
S A T R A P S   P L U M P
S   T   P   H   O   A   E
E G O   I   O   N O T E D
M     T A P E D   I   I
I   E   A     E   C   T
N   V   L A Y E R     I
A L I B I   E   A   R H O
T   D   S   O   B E   U
I N E R T   M I L L E R S
O   N   I   E   E   V   L
N O T I C I N G   B E V Y
```

No 76

```
B O Y I S H   S C H O O L
R     C   V   U     A
O   S C A R E C R O W   D
W   T   R   N   B   H   I
S T A C C A T O   S I T E
E   U   I   S   R   T   S
K N I T S   V A L E S
E   C   Y   K   D   L   T
J O H N   U N T I D I L Y
E   L   P   O   A   E   P
C   Y E A R L I N G S   I
T   L   C   L   C
S T I N K Y   V E R I F Y
```

No 77

```
D I A T O N I C   P O S E
C   R   A   O   O   H
G E M I N I   M A R V E L
P   M   V I M C E
M I S S   E   A L I G N S
C       L       N
S K I M P Y   P L E N T Y
  A       R       A
T H O R A X   O   H E R B
Y   K   Y E T   I   G
R E T E L L   E Y R I E S
  N   T   E   C   E   T
L A Y S   M O T O R I S T
```

No 78

```
A B A C U S     A   P E N
U   N   V A C U A   E
F I N E S S E   H   T   G
L   T   R   Y U C C A
S T O N E A G E   H   T
U   A   E   P   E   E
U P S I D E   P L U S E S
P   C   Y   V   E
H   H   S O F T S P O T
O V E R T   D   H   N
L   R   U   K N O W H O W
D   Z E B R A   R   M
S K I   E   D A C T Y L
```

No 79

```
S W A T C H   B E S T O W
R   U   O   A   T   W
H O A R   S O C I A B L E
N   N   E   I   I
A G L O W   F L O R I S T
D   U   D   L   A
C O N T R I B U T I O N S
E     V   S   N   D
T R A N S I T   A G A P E
A   D   L   R   A
A N A T H E M A   A L P S
E   A   N   I   E
S T O L I D   P E N U R Y
```

No 80

```
H A S S L E   A D R I F T
A   L   U   E   O   D   I
P H O E N I X   D   L   T
P   G   G   P I G M E N T
E D G E S   E   E   E
N   I   R   M I S E R
  N   S W I M S   A
B E G E T   E   L   A
R   A   N   B A I L S
I D I O T I C   R   V   S
C   N   U   E M I R A T E
K   N   T S   N   T   S
S A S H E S   R E N E W S
```

No 81

```
  F   B   S   L   B   F
I L L U S T R I O U S L Y
  I   Y   R   M   T   O
O P T I M I Z E   A G U E
  N   D   S   N   R
T R I G G E R   R E L I C
  H     S   D   S
N Y M P H   W E A L T H Y
  T   O   B   S   U
S H U N   E M I S S I V E
  M   C   E   G   T   E
L I G H T F I N G E R E D
  C   O   Y   S   R   R
```

Solutions

No 82

```
L U P I N E   V I R T U E
I   A   E   B   N   O   X
S A S H I M I   D   G   O
T   T   G   R E E N A C T
E A R T H   D   P   I
D   A   W   T U N I C   O
  M   A W A S H   O
C A I R N   T   F   A
O   N   C   Y A R D S
R E T O U C H   A   I   I
N   I   L   E X H A L E D
E   E   A   R   O   L   E
R O S A R Y   N O O S E S
```

No 83

```
  J   A C   S   A   M
T A T T O O   C E N T E R
  V   T   M   A T A
M A G E   M U L T I P L Y
  N   U   D   H   T
I N S T A T E   M I N I M
  A   I   E   S S M
G R A V Y   C H A T T E L
  R   E   S   O   A
B A R N A C L E   M U L E
  T   E   O   B   I U
M E S S U P   O W N E R S
  S   S   E X   E   K
```

No 84

```
  G H I   S   S   A
I N Q U I S I T I V E L Y
  A D S   A   E L L
S T A D I U M S   L A C K
  L   I   H   T L
S O M E O N E   N E W E R
  B   G   A   A A
F L U F F   A D J O U R N
  I   U   T   J C
A V E R   H O U S E M A N
  I   O   E D L L
B O A R D I N G H O U S E
  N   E R E T O
```

No 85

```
P O T A T O   R A P I D S
A   G   A E   O   E   E
N A M E D R O P   P E A L
A   O   U   P   D
C O O L   L B   E A S T
H   D O U B L E D   E
E L L   X   I   R A J
A   C O U R S E S   U
U S E R   R H   C H A R
T   E   I   A   Y
L I M A   O P T I M I S M
N   T   U   I   P   E
E G R E T S   E D I S O N
```

No 86

```
C   S B   C I R
H E C K L E   T R I V I A
E   H E   P   E I F
A V O C A D O   W R E S T
T   O T   R C S S
E E L S   S T R U M
D   S S R   T C H
  S T R A Y   N A P E
P R A Y   T P I
R E A L M   A V O W I N G
O V M   L U T H
N E E D E D   E R R A N T
G L R   S L S
```

No 87

```
T   A G O   O   V
B U I L D E R S   D U E L
R   T O   I   O R
M E S H   R Y E G R A S S
E   O   G   R   E
I N S U L I N   P H A S E
G   A   A   A
S I G H S   G A I N I N G
M   G   U   D O
S P I L L I N G   R I T E
A O V   H A I
E C H O   E Y E P I E C E
T P N   D L E
```

No 88

```
F   R S   V U A
U N I O N S   J E T S A M
L G A S   N U U
S C H E R Z I   T E A R S
O T E   L U L E
M U L E   S K I R T
E Y C I E   A C
  F R A N C   A S I A
T S E   S U R
A T T I C   S E M I N A R
T I K S   A D O
T I N S E L   A R G E N T
Y T T   T R S
```

No 89

```
L O U D N E S S   S H E D
I T E   E C I I
K H A K I   V   H U N T S
E H G E E   D A
    C H A R A C T E R S
H A B S K   R T
O P T I O N   D E L E T E
S T R Z R D R
P E A C H M E L B A
I I O N O S T
T A N G O   I   A L T E R
A E D T R O O
L A D S   S H A D O W E D
```

No 90

```
O B E Y E D   S   I R E
A   D   U N T I L   M
A N T H I L L   A   L P
N   T   T   G R I P E
T E R T I A R Y   C R
R   O   A D I O
A S S E N T   P A T T E R
N N S F R M
Y I   P I C K M E U P
T O P A Z   N R L
I P E   A R O U S A L
M   E A S E L O T
E A T T   S M I L E D
```

Solutions

No 91

A	N	G	E	R	S		B	L	A	Z	E	R
L		E	E	G		E		I		A		
C	U	R	A	B	L	E		C	N		I	
O		A	E		N	O	T	I	C	E	S	
V	I	N	Y	L		T		E		I		
E	I		L		R	E	S	I	N			
	U		T	I	E	I	N		C			
C	O	M	M	A		W		R		C		
A		C	O		B	R	I	E	R			
E	R	R	A	T	U	M		R	P	O		
S	O		I	A	Q	U	A	T	I	C		
A	O	C		N		S	E	U				
R	E	F	U	S	E		S	H	A	D	E	S

No 92

S	I	L	I	C	A		S	K	·	S
W	A		D	E	T	O	N	A	T	E
I	C	Y		I	E	O	A			
R		O	R	I	O	L	E		C	A	V	Y
L	U		S		P	K	E			
S	E	T	U	P		H	E	R	O	I	S	M
	N	K	N	U						
W	O	R	N	O	U	T		S	T	O	O	D
R	E	M	M		U	E				
T	I	D	E		Q	U	A	I	N	T
G	D	U	N		R	I	M			
L	I	T	E	R	A	T	I		U	A	
N	D	T		C	H	A	N	E	L	

No 93

G	I	V	E	A	N	D	T	A	K	E
C	M	G	U	H	A	A				
H	M	M	O	R	D	E	R		R	I	G
A	F	O	O	T	G	O	T	G		
I	R	I	E		B	A	S	I	L
R	E	A	S	S	E	S	S		O
P	L	T		P	S	M			
E		R	A	D	I	A	N	C	E
R	I	D	E	S	L	R	O	R	
S	U	E	U	A	T	R	I	A	
O	N	E	D	E	M	O	N	K	T
N	T	G	N	H	E	E			
A	S	C	E	T	I	C	A	L	L	Y

No 94

I	G	U	A	N	A		I	F	A
M	N	B	A	C	K	L	A	S	H
P	A	R	Y	I	O	P			
A	E	D	I	S	O	N	E	I	C
R	S	S	E	I	C				
T	I	T	E	R	I	S	O	L	A	T	E
X	C	S	L						
A	D	A	P	T	E	D	C	A	P	R	I
O	L	S	P	O	S				
O	U	Z	O	S	P	H	E	R	E	
B	I	I	A	T	A	U			
S	T	A	T	I	O	N	S	I	E
S	S	N	E	L	E	C	T	S	

No 95

S	P	A	D	E	S		U	P	T	O	W	N
R	R	W	P	A	E				
L	I	D	O	A	N	T	I	B	O	D	Y
V	P	P	H	L					
B	A	T	O	N	F	R	E	E	Z	E	S
T	F	W	U	L				
S	E	L	F	P	O	S	S	E	S	S	E	D
L	O	T	T	C				
E	Y	E	L	I	D	S	F	R	O	T	H
L	W	R	I	R				
M	A	C	A	R	O	N	I	V	E	I	N
S	M	R	F	E	C			
S	H	R	A	N	K	F	I	N	I	S	H

No 96

O	P	P	O	S	I	T	E	O	V	I	D
N	U	U	H	S	I	I			
T	I	M	E	R	R	U	R	G	E	S
O	A	R	O	B	N	B	A		
Y	O	U	N	G	S	T	E	R	S
R	R	U	G	T	T	T		
E	T	H	A	N	E	T	I	P	T	O	E
V	A	D	F	T	E	R		
A	M	P	H	I	B	I	O	U	S
M	S	N	R	T	I	A		
P	R	O	N	G	M	I	N	N	E	R
E	D	S	L	O	N	K		
D	A	Y	S	H	Y	P	N	O	S	I	S

No 97

S	S	S	A	S	E				
F	O	R	E	S	T	S	W	E	R	V	E
S	M	O	I	L	E			
G	O	B	I	R	E	D	E	F	I	N	E
P	A	E	A	T			
L	I	N	E	A	G	E	S	W	I	F	T
L	R	E	S	A	U			
B	L	A	M	E	S	H	A	R	P	L	Y
F	E	P	R	E			
C	A	L	A	M	A	R	I	N	O	U	N
T	B	R	M	E	S			
S	E	L	L	E	R	P	E	S	T	E	R
D	E	Y	S	S	S			

No 98

S	H	A	R	D	S		B	E	L	I	E	F
P	I	P	P	L					
A	S	I	L	L	I	N	E	S	S	A
R	I	U	A	E	Y	B			
S	I	G	H	T	I	N	G	S	C	A	B
E	H	I	O	E	O	Y			
S	T	O	O	D	A	G	A	P	E	
R	N	S	G	H	C			
P	L	E	A	E	P	I	P	H	A	N	Y
E	A	L	O	L	N	B			
E	D	E	O	D	O	R	A	N	T	O
C	O	K	N	R			
H	O	P	I	N	G	S	T	R	O	N	G

No 99

S	C	A	N	T	Y		S	S	O	W
L	W	M	A	C	A	W	H		
A	D	T	T	I	L	L	S	E	I
A	N	E	C	D	O	T	E	T	K
E	L	L	E	S	E	E		
E	D	D	I	E	S	Q	U	I	R	K	Y
X	I	D	O	B	I			
P	S	O	B	D	U	R	A	C	Y
I	N	T	R	O	E	R	K		
A	U	V	S	U	B	S	O	I	L
T	R	A	I	S	E	I	N		
E	B	B	D	S	A	V	A	G	E

Solutions

No 100

```
O D D S O N ■ S Q U I R M
E ■ C ■ O ■ P ■ N ■ H ■ ■
A S I A ■ O V E R F L O W
T ■ ■ R ■ K ■ C ■ I ■ ■ ■
G I L L S ■ S I T T I N G
T ■ E ■ T ■ ■ O ■ ■ O ■ ■
C U T T H E M U S T A R D
T ■ ■ M ■ ■ S ■ I ■ ■ M ■
P E R H A P S ■ S T E A K
■ E ■ O ■ C ■ A ■ ■ L ■ ■
R E S E A R C H ■ N A I L
R ■ L ■ A ■ I ■ I ■ ■ T ■
T A S S E L ■ C O C C Y X
```

No 101

```
■ R ■ T ■ H ■ M ■ M ■ A ■
R E C R E A T E ■ A R M Y
■ P ■ E ■ T ■ T ■ L ■ E ■
P U M A ■ C U R D L I N G
■ T ■ ■ T ■ H ■ O ■ D ■ ■
R E V I S E D ■ C R A S S
■ ■ S ■ T ■ ■ H ■ O ■ ■ ■
S T E E D ■ H A R S H L Y
■ R ■ ■ T ■ N ■ I ■ A ■ ■
N U R T U R E D ■ N O T E
D ■ A ■ U ■ S ■ E ■ E ■ ■
A G E S ■ C O A R S E L Y
■ E ■ K ■ K ■ W ■ S ■ Y ■
```

No 102

```
E X P L O D E D ■ S P E D
C ■ I ■ T ■ X ■ I ■ O ■ I
H U N C H ■ P ■ N E W T S
O ■ K ■ E ■ A ■ S ■ D ■ S
■ A R T N O U V E A U ■ ■
A ■ R ■ W ■ D ■ F ■ R ■ A
I C E B O X ■ O F F E N D
R ■ S ■ R ■ M ■ I ■ D ■ ■
■ B R I L L I A N C E ■ ■
R ■ D ■ D ■ N ■ I ■ O ■ ■
U S U A L ■ I ■ E A S E S
S ■ A ■ Y ■ L ■ N ■ L ■ E
H A L E ■ F A S T F O O D
```

No 103

```
D E J E C T E D ■ R A K E
A ■ N ■ R ■ O ■ E ■ ■ N ■
G R U D G E ■ S T A T E S
T ■ O ■ L Y E ■ C ■ ■ E ■
S H O W ■ L ■ S C H I S T
L ■ ■ ■ I ■ ■ ■ ■ E ■ ■ ■
H Y E N A S ■ M I S U S E
E ■ ■ ■ A ■ ■ ■ A ■ ■ ■ ■
T S E T S E ■ R ■ M I F F
A ■ W ■ N U T ■ U ■ ■ U ■
A L L O T S ■ I N F E R S
S ■ R ■ U ■ N ■ T ■ ■ O ■
T A S K ■ E D I T I O N S
```

No 104

```
■ S ■ I ■ S ■ M ■ P ■ P ■
G A D G E T R Y ■ L A U D
H ■ N ■ O ■ R ■ A ■ R ■ ■
M A G I ■ R A R E N E S S
R ■ T ■ I ■ ■ H ■ ■ U ■ ■
R A D I A N T ■ J E W E L
■ N ■ ■ G ■ E ■ N ■ ■ ■ ■
L I E G E ■ M Y S T I F Y
N ■ ■ ■ O ■ E ■ R ■ L ■ ■
A F F L I C T S ■ E L A N
O ■ O ■ H ■ O ■ N ■ ■ M ■
E R A S ■ E N R I C H E S
M ■ S ■ R ■ E ■ H ■ ■ S ■
```

No 105

```
E N D S ■ T R O U B L E D
N ■ R ■ P ■ U ■ N ■ E ■ I
C H A L E T S ■ M A S K S
O ■ M ■ R ■ S ■ I ■ S ■ A
U S A ■ M ■ I ■ S C O O P
R ■ ■ I N A P T ■ N ■ ■ P
A ■ C ■ S ■ ■ A ■ S ■ E ■
G ■ O ■ S P E C K ■ ■ A ■
E N N U I ■ N ■ A ■ C U R
M ■ T ■ V ■ J ■ B ■ A ■ A
E R O D E ■ O I L S K I N
N ■ U ■ L ■ L ■ Y ■ E ■ C
T A R R Y I N G ■ I S L E
```

No 106

```
O W L S ■ B L A C K T I E
P ■ I ■ C ■ O ■ A ■ O ■ X
P U N C H E D ■ T R U M P
O ■ E ■ I ■ G ■ E ■ R ■ E
R A D A R ■ E A R L I E R
T ■ O ■ R ■ P ■ S ■ ■ I ■
U N R I P E ■ D I C T U M
N ■ E ■ R ■ F ■ L ■ ■ E ■
I M I T A T E ■ L I K E N
T ■ S ■ C ■ S ■ A ■ R ■ T
I N S E T ■ T E R M I N I
E ■ U ■ O ■ E ■ S ■ L ■ N
S H E A R E R S ■ F L O G
```

No 107

```
S E T S ■ A B A C U S E S
E ■ W ■ R ■ I ■ L ■ O ■ U
L O A F E R S ■ O X L I P
F ■ N ■ S ■ T ■ S ■ I ■ E
C O G ■ T ■ R E I D E R ■
O ■ A L O O F ■ U ■ ■ F ■
N ■ E ■ U ■ I ■ S ■ L ■ ■
T ■ C ■ R E S E T ■ U ■ ■
A L O H A ■ T T ■ M O O ■
I ■ L ■ T ■ A ■ I ■ A ■ U
N O O N E ■ N A N N I E S
E ■ G ■ U ■ Z ■ G ■ D ■ L
D A Y B R E A K ■ E S P Y
```

No 108

```
P O M P ■ S L I P P E R S
U ■ U ■ O ■ A ■ E ■ X ■ E
R E F I N E S ■ D R A W L
P ■ T ■ O ■ T ■ I ■ C ■ F
O D I U M ■ E L A S T I C
S ■ A ■ D ■ T ■ L ■ O ■ ■
E N T I T Y ■ C R A Y O N
L ■ R ■ O ■ I ■ I ■ ■ F ■
E X E M P T S ■ C H I L I
S ■ M ■ O ■ O ■ I ■ M ■ D
S P O K E ■ B R A M B L E
L ■ L ■ I ■ A ■ N ■ U ■ N
Y E O M A N R Y ■ R E N T
```

Solutions

No 109

```
D I S S O L V E ▓ P A S T
M ▓ T ▓ I ▓ B ▓ I ▓ W ▓
F A R O F F ▓ O U T L E T
G ▓ N ▓ T O N ▓ F ▓ L ▓
M E R E ▓ I ▓ Y E A R L Y
R ▓ ▓ N ▓ ▓ L ▓ ▓ ▓ ▓
D Y E I N G ▓ D U L C E T
▓ ▓ N ▓ R ▓ ▓ X ▓ ▓ ▓
P E A K E D ▓ E ▓ K E E P
N ▓ W ▓ O L D ▓ E ▓ C ▓
U N S E A T ▓ G E N I U S
U ▓ L ▓ E ▓ E ▓ Y ▓ T ▓
G I L L ▓ S E R R A T E D
```

No 110

```
W E S T ▓ S C O R N F U L
O ▓ Q ▓ T ▓ A ▓ H ▓ O ▓ E
R O U G H E N ▓ Y A R D S
S ▓ I ▓ O ▓ V ▓ T ▓ E ▓ S
H A B E R D A S H E R Y ▓
I ▓ ▓ O ▓ S ▓ M ▓ U ▓ B ▓
P O S S U M ▓ V I E N N A
S ▓ P ▓ G ▓ C ▓ C ▓ B ▓
T E C H N I C A L I T Y ▓
C ▓ C ▓ B ▓ R ▓ L ▓ M ▓ H
O T T E R ▓ C A L Y P S O
M ▓ R ▓ E ▓ L ▓ Y ▓ E ▓ O
B R A N D N E W ▓ S L I D
```

No 111

```
A D V E R B ▓ U ▓ C ▓ A
R ▓ E ▓ ▓ A N G E L I C A
C U R ▓ S ▓ L ▓ E ▓ C ▓
H ▓ G E M I N I ▓ A N E W
E ▓ E ▓ L ▓ E ▓ N ▓ D ▓
D A R T S ▓ A S P I R E S
▓ R ▓ B ▓ T ▓ N ▓ ▓ ▓
A R S E N A L ▓ A G R E E
U ▓ M ▓ S ▓ S ▓ E ▓ I ▓
S N U B ▓ H A T I N G ▓
W ▓ L ▓ I ▓ Y ▓ A S H
M A T E R N A L ▓ L ▓ T
Y ▓ D ▓ G ▓ E N M E S H
```

No 112

```
T H I R T E E N ▓ U N D O
A ▓ O ▓ M ▓ I ▓ N ▓ R ▓
M I K A D O ▓ N O T I O N
R ▓ D ▓ T U T ▓ A ▓ L ▓
O N E S ▓ I ▓ H O M E L Y
E ▓ ▓ V ▓ ▓ E ▓ ▓ ▓ ▓
O T I O S E ▓ L A D D E R
A ▓ ▓ ▓ E ▓ ▓ S ▓ ▓ ▓
E M B R Y O ▓ O ▓ R O T A
U ▓ S ▓ A C T ▓ U ▓ O ▓
S T A M P S ▓ A L M O N D
E ▓ E ▓ I ▓ R ▓ O ▓ I ▓
E D E N ▓ S I D E R E A L
```

No 113

```
F ▓ L ▓ I ▓ A ▓ I ▓ P
P A T E R N A L I S T I C
I ▓ A ▓ T ▓ A ▓ S ▓ V ▓
G R A N D E U R ▓ U P O N
▓ T ▓ N ▓ M ▓ E ▓ T ▓
E S P O U S E ▓ A D L I B
K ▓ ▓ E ▓ C ▓ ▓ N ▓ ▓
D I S K S ▓ F O R E I G N
R ▓ A ▓ A ▓ N ▓ N ▓
O M E N ▓ M A G A Z I N E
I ▓ S ▓ P ▓ E ▓ Y ▓ O ▓
E S T A B L I S H M E N T
H ▓ S ▓ Y ▓ T ▓ E ▓ E ▓
```

No 114

```
D I C T U M ▓ L O S S E S
W ▓ N ▓ C ▓ W ▓ ▓ N ▓
A ▓ A F T E R G L O W ▓ E
R ▓ P ▓ I ▓ O ▓ S ▓ H ▓ A
F R A C T I O N ▓ M I L K
S ▓ R ▓ L ▓ N ▓ R ▓ T ▓ Y
▓ S T E E P ▓ G E N E S ▓
A ▓ M ▓ D ▓ S ▓ F ▓ L ▓ P
C R E W ▓ I M P E R I A L
U ▓ N ▓ Y ▓ E ▓ R ▓ E ▓ A
I ▓ T H E S A U R U S ▓ N
T ▓ ▓ R ▓ A ▓ A ▓ ▓ ▓
Y U P P I E ▓ P L A Y E R
```

No 115

```
B U M P E R ▓ G L A R E D
I ▓ O ▓ X ▓ M ▓ I ▓ I ▓ R
S U M A T R A ▓ M ▓ L ▓ U
E ▓ E ▓ O ▓ R I P P L E D
C A N A L ▓ K ▓ E ▓ ▓
T ▓ T ▓ E ▓ T E P E E ▓
▓ U ▓ P U T T S ▓ U ▓
T E M P I ▓ P ▓ L ▓ E ▓
U ▓ V ▓ L ▓ A L L A Y ▓
S E Q U O I A ▓ O ▓ B ▓ E
S ▓ U ▓ T ▓ C U R E A L L
L ▓ I ▓ A ▓ E ▓ T ▓ C ▓ E
E X P E L S ▓ R A C K E T
```

No 116

```
A S I D E S ▓ P O P L A R
▓ T ▓ R ▓ W ▓ E ▓ E ▓ W
A R E A ▓ A R R E S T E D
▓ U ▓ S ▓ G ▓ S ▓ T ▓ ▓
A G A T E ▓ G U M S H O E
▓ G ▓ I ▓ F ▓ A ▓ ▓ U ▓
B L A C K A N D W H I T E
▓ E ▓ ▓ L ▓ E ▓ E ▓ A ▓
E S S E N C E ▓ L A W N S
▓ X ▓ O ▓ O ▓ T ▓ ▓ D ▓
A S S I G N E D ▓ I C O N
P ▓ S ▓ R ▓ O ▓ N ▓ U ▓
P A S T R Y ▓ R I G H T S
```

No 117

```
C L O Y ▓ A C C I D E N T
A ▓ C ▓ C ▓ A ▓ N ▓ X ▓ I
N A T I O N S ▓ C A P E D
B ▓ E ▓ I ▓ T ▓ O ▓ A ▓ Y
E N T A N G L E M E N T ▓
R ▓ ▓ C ▓ E ▓ P ▓ S ▓ B ▓
R E P A I D ▓ C A R E E R
A ▓ R ▓ D ▓ S ▓ R ▓ ▓ U ▓
▓ D E C E L E R A T I O N
T ▓ P ▓ N ▓ A ▓ B ▓ M ▓ E
A L L O T ▓ B A L L A S T
L ▓ A ▓ A ▓ E ▓ E ▓ G ▓ T
L A N D L A D Y ▓ C E D E
```

354

Solutions

No 118

```
B A C K U P . F . P . D .
R . H . . . R E L I E V E S
E T A . . . O . A . N . L .
A . N I T W I T . A N T S .
T E . . L . . . O . L . A .
H I L L Y . B U S I E S T .
. . A . . . O . T . Z . . .
O D D N E S S . R E C A P .
O . D . T . F . . . A . L .
B R I M . R E A L M S . A .
. S . A . I . R . . . K E Y
C A P S I C U M . . . E . E
. L . S . H . . . S A L T E D
```

No 119

```
T I C K . O B D U R A T E
R . O . M . R . N . U . A .
A I R B A S E . P A T E R .
N . G . T . A . R . O . L .
Q U I N T E S S E N C E . .
U . E . . . T . J . U . P .
I N S E R T . T U X E D O .
L . C . O . P . D . . . L .
. C O M F O R T I N G L Y .
S U F . I . C . I . G . . .
T E R R A . C H E R V I L .
A . G . C . E . D . E . O .
G R E A T E S T . . K N I T
```

No 120

```
D Y A D . C L A P T R A P
O . T . K . A . H . E . R .
U N T W I S T . I G L O O .
B . I . N . E . L . A . P .
L U C I D . S H A M P O O .
E . E . E . T . N . S . R .
C H E E R Y . S T R E E T .
H . L . G . N . H . . . I .
E L E V A T E . R O D E O .
C . M . R . W . O . I . N .
K N E L T . E M P O R I A .
E . N . E . S . Y . G . T .
D E T O N A T E . G E N E .
```

No 121

```
M U S H E S . A . R . S .
E . E . . . C O N S I S T S
W I N . O . Y . D . R . .
I . S U B U R B . I D O L .
N O . . R . O . C . N . .
G O R G E . A D J U D G E .
. . E . S . Y . L . . . .
S P I R I T S . V E S T S .
O . A . A . L . H . U . .
S K I N . R I O T E R . N .
E . I . C . U . . . I L L .
D R A U G H T S . . N . I .
. S . M . Y . E X T E N T .
```

No 122

```
A S T R A Y . S C A M P I
W . D . L . A . . . S . D .
A S Y M B I O S I S . S D .
R . H . I . M . T . U . I .
D I A T R I B E . E P I C .
S . P . E . S . S . P . T .
. R E T R O . S T O O L . .
S . L . S . G . A . S . A .
E D E N . T R A M P I N G .
A . A . U . P . N . N . H .
D . S I M M E R I N G . A .
O . . . E . L . N . . . S .
G R O U N D . E G O I S T .
```

No 123

```
J . M M . S . D . E .
D O M I N A N T . E O N S
. G . D . N . A . M . M .
E G O S . A I R L I N E S
. E . H . G . . . E . S .
A R B I T E R . E I G H T
. P . D . P . D . P . L .
P U R S E . I R E L A N D
. N . L . A . T . E . .
G L I T T E R Y . I T E M
. O . U . A . I . M . D .
V A I N . C O N C E D E D
. D . A . H . G . D . D .
```

No 124

```
S H E E T S . R E S U L T
H . O . A . V . . . R .
A . M I N E F I E L D . O .
B E E . E . I . R . I . I .
B U R G L A R S . R A N K .
Y . R . E . E . S . G . A .
. T I P S Y . D O W N Y . .
B . M . S . O . U . O . B .
O V E N . G U E R N S E Y .
N . N . G . T . N . I . P .
G . T I R E D N E S S . L .
O . O . . . O . O . S . .
S C R E W S . A S T R A Y .
```

No 125

```
G A L A C T I C . L A M B
R . I . O . N . C . N . A .
I L E U M . S . O P T I C .
D . N . M . T . N . I . K .
. . R E P E A T E D L Y . .
A . L . N . P . R . O . A .
C R O U C H . T A R T A R .
E . N . E . O . R . E . D .
R A G A M U F F I N . . . .
B . H . F . W . F . B . .
A C O R N . K . I D E A L .
T . R . E . S . T . O . .
E O N S . T Y P E C A S T .
```

No 126

```
S . T . C . . . A . G . C
O R A L L Y . A M O R A L
J . F . U . R . O . O . A
O F F E N S E . U S U R Y
U . E . K . I . N . T . S
R A T E . S T A T E . .
N . A . L . E . S . N . B
. . W E A R S . L A M A .
R . P . I . A . S . I . S
E T H O S . N A T I V E S
A . O . U . T . I . E . I
D I N E R S . S C O L D S
S . E . E . . . K . Y . T
```

355

Solutions

No 127

No 128

No 129

No 130

No 131

No 132

No 133

No 134

No 135

Solutions

No 136

```
R   N   S       H B   S
U S U R P S   F A R R O W
B   M   A B   S O   E
B R E E D E R   T R I C E
I   R   E   E   I   L P
N E A R   T A L L Y
G   L   C   K Y   C   S
    T R I A L   M Y T H
A A   U   W   G N Y
C A P R I   A R R A I G N
I   H   S Y   E   C   E
D R I V E S   P E D A L S
S   D   S       K L   S
```

No 137

```
B O R E R S   R   W P
E   I   P R E S I D E S
S U N   L   D N   R
T   S P R I T E   D E S K
O   E   T E B O   O
W I D T H   I M P U G N S
    R   N S   R
E R R A T A   K N A C K
A   V M S     R N
E D G E   B I K I N I   O
I   R E   I       S E C
O U T S T R I P   E   K
M E S   S T A S I S
```

No 138

```
S U C K S   A P P E A R S
O   A   C S   X   O
L   T   R T   P I L O T
I L L F A T E D   L   T
T I I W R   R E U S E
A L K A L I N E   D   X
I   E   S   C P C
R   A   C A L A M A R I
E X A L T   P R R T
Y P   O P E R E T T A
C L E A T   L I   I B
E C   E   E E A L
I M P A L E S   S O L V E
```

No 139

```
P   P C       M I   J
R U E F U L   B I L B A O
O   R   P U D S U   I
S E S S I O N   W E E D S
A   O   D S I N T
I N N S   S C O F F
C   A   C R   E C G
    T R I E D   T R I O
O S O   W   E A D
B L I T Z   E S S A Y E D
O   N   I D T O E
E L U D E S   F E I N T S
S   S S R     R S   S
```

No 140

```
T D   B   A S   D
D O C U M E N T A T I O N
  F L Q O E C
P U N C T U A L   P I T H
  E   E L U O
B R I T I S H   S P U R S
  E   T D   E
S L Y L Y   T R A G E D Y
  A   A C I E
S T O P   L O V I N G L Y
  I   T O I R O
I N C O N V E N I E N C E
  G P E G S   H
```

No 141

```
H O C K   P R O D U C E D
O   U A U O   I   A I
M O R O C C O   N O U N S
E   I Q F N   S   K
M E A S U R E M E N T S
A   A D R   I E
D A H L I A   E J E C T S
E   A N A A     T
U N A T T R A C T I V E
T D A   M K D E
A R G O N   P R E M I U M
L U C   I   T O E
C O N V E N T S   A M I D
```

No 142

```
I R O N I C   P O R O U S
N   A   N A R   C
V   E X C U S A B L Y   H
E U U   C S A I
S U P E R I O R   E R A S
T   H R T O M T
C E D E D   S C R U B
A   M D U C L A
B L I P   U N M A R K E D
A S   R I S E O
T   M O U N T A I N S R
E   M E O   E
S W A M P Y   U N B E N D
```

No 143

```
S   A E   P F P S
T E L E P H O N E   A P T
U   T I T W I   A
N E E D S   I D E A L L Y
G   R O O R   I I
  T E N D I N G   L O I N
P G E   R V G
R O O K   O F F I C E S
E   M A S R S
C H E M I S T   O X B O W
I S S H T E E
S U P   S H O R T C A K E
E Y Y M O R P
```

No 144

```
A R T F U L L Y   N O T E
E L   I   A A H
U N L O C K   C R I S E S
E U A A H   R T
S W A T B   T H O R A X
E L   B
A D H E R E   F E I N T S
L U U   O
S T E E D S   C A I R Y
I C A S H D P
E A R T H S   S A L V E R
R E S I I D
P A I D   Y E A R B O O K
```

Solutions

No 145

```
H E A D T E A C H E R
U N O R   R N   A
N L   D R A M A   D U G
C L I N G   S   S   O G
A   S E E   H E W E R
L I T E R A R Y     E
L   S   S     A S G
E       O P E R E T T A
D E P T H   O   M U T
F   I A O   R A B B I
O I L   V E R S E   B O
R   A O E     S E E N
P U L C H R I T U D E
```

No 146

```
S R F     A O A
H E A D O N   A M A Z O N
A U R C   I O K
D E C I M A L   A N N U L
I O S   O B E   E
N O U S   C A L L S
G S N K E D S
      L E E R S   D I S H
O R U O A V U
P L A I T   O F F B E A T
E   T R M   I R E
R A T I O N   C R A G G Y
A Y N     E E E
```

No 147

```
D A R E D   B E H A V E D
E O O L   B B P
U O L L E   P L A I D
T U M B L I N G   O C
E I A D   B O O S T
R Y E G R A S S   M A
I R S     L E R
U S   H A C I E N D A
M I N K S   B G A N
D U   P R O H I B I T
L I O N S   O T L U
O K   A U E L
A M A S S E D   P A S T A
```

No 148

```
H O G S   O B S O L E T E
Y R S   L   C N X
P R E S U M E   C H E A P
E E P   A A M A
R A N G E   R U S S I A N
C   R Y   I E S
R E T I N A   B O N S A I
I E A N N V
T O L S T O Y   A T O N E
I A U M L V N
C O V E R   P U L S A T E
A I A H Y L S
L O V E L E S S   U S E S
```

No 149

```
R E L I G I O U S L Y
C N M O N A E
O C M I N E D R A N
M E R G E   I E G L
M U N Z   R I O J A
O B S E S S E D   R
N T E L R G
S     A B S O L U T E
E X C E L   A C N M
N A O S   U N D U E
S A G O A S I S O N
E E S E T T W T
A D V E R T I S I N G
```

No 150

```
I P R U S S
I N V A S I O N   N U T S
N T P C U O
M A C H   C A L I G U L A
T E O E I
V E N T U R E   B R I D E
I D P O
L A R C H   B E E S W A X
L D R E X
L U S C I O U S   T R I M
M O U O T O
I N T O   S U N B E A M S
I S E S S S
```

No 151

```
B J P U O U
J U N I O R   S E V E R E
R G I U E B
B R A G   C H A I R M A N
E K L S N
S P A R K L E   E T H I C
R Y E T A Z
P O P P Y   K E T T L E S
P O A M E
W O R K E D U P   M A R K
U E E E E O
U N W R A P   S A N I T Y
D Y T T T S
```

No 152

```
O B L   C G L
N E U R O N   D E L U D E
E S C D N I A
S T I M U L I   T A L K S
E E S S R D E
L I S P   C A B A L
F T F V L S P
    A R B O R   S O Y A
P A E W G U R
U N C U T   A M O U N T S
L U F L D D L
P U T O U T   F L E E C E
Y E L Y D Y
```

No 153

```
S S S F P W T G
W A T E R P O L O   U S E
A O O S R B Y
M A I L S   T H R E A D S
P C T A Y E
  F I R E F L Y   F A I R
T S S D F N S
R O M E   O S P R E Y S
A A O E P C
S C R E W E D   I N L A Y
H I F D G A C
E G G   U N E T H I C A L
D S L N T E E
```

Solutions

No 154

```
C L O W N S █ R O A S T S
H █ O █ K █ E █ W █ I █
A N G E L I C A █ H O M E
N █ F █ R █ █ █ I █ P █
T O F U █ D G █ L E A N █
E █ █ L E I S U R E █ N █
D A M █ V █ A █ █ A I L █
█ Q █ E Y E B R O W █ A █
R U I N █ R D █ A L E S █
A █ O █ S █ S █ █ A █ █
U R D U █ E A R T H I N G
I █ G █ L █ A █ E █ █ N █
S A S H A Y █ M A R I N A
```

No 155

```
S A B E R S █ A D V E R B
C █ A █ E █ P █ R █ T █ I
A L C H E M Y █ I N █ O █
R █ K █ V █ R E F R A I N
F U D G E █ O T █ █ I █
S █ R █ T █ E T H I C █
C O P S E █ C █ L █ S █
█ H █ N █ H █ R E S I N
U N C H A I N █ E █ I █ E
K █ O █ T █ I M M E N S E
K █ I █ O █ C █ I █ K █ R
A L L U R E █ S T R I P S
```

No 156

```
V O L U M E █ L █ P U T
R █ O █ S L I M Y █ H █
B I V O U A C █ M █ R █ E
G █ █ N █ O █ P L A Z A
S I G H T I N G █ M █ T █
N █ A E █ R █ I █ E █
A S S A I L █ F O L D E R
B █ U █ N █ O █ B █ N █
I █ C █ O B D U R A C Y
D E C O R █ O █ S █ O █
I █ U █ E █ E S T U A R Y
N █ M E E T S █ L █ E █
G A B █ D █ █ T Y P I S T
```

No 157

```
M █ T █ O █ █ S █ S E
A B R A D E █ D U P L E X
G █ I █ I █ S █ R █ Y █ T
N U R T U R E █ F O L I O
E █ E █ M █ C █ E █ Y █ L
T O M E █ V E E R S █
S E T █ S █ S █ C █ W █
█ W H I S T █ L A M A
W █ A █ E █ I █ S █ R █ R
R E F E R █ O U T C R O P
A █ F █ A █ N █ A █ I █ A
C H I R P S █ A F L O A T
K █ X █ Y █ █ F █ N █ H
```

No 158

```
█ P █ J █ W █ S █ I █ J
L A Z U L I █ T O N G U E
█ N █ X █ S █ I █ C █ V
█ P E L T █ H O L L O W E D
█ █ A █ F █ L █ R █ N █
P O M P O U S █ B R A I N
█ V █ O █ L █ B █ U █ L
M E S S Y █ C R O P P E D
█ R █ I █ T █ I █ T █
P L O T T I N G █ I D L E
█ O █ I █ L █ A █ B █ E
T R Y O U T █ D E L U G E
█ D █ N █ S █ E █ E █ O
```

No 159

```
C R O W D S █ U P S E T S
H █ A █ A █ N █ C █ A █
A F F L I C T S █ R U B Y
T █ L █ L █ C █ I █ L █
E C H O █ C █ R █ B E E F
A █ █ P H O N E M E █ A █
U S E █ M █ W █ █ J U G
T █ O P P R E S S █ U █
R E A R █ O █ D █ T E R M
E █ E █ D █ N █ O █ S █
A P S E █ E Y E T O O T H
E █ A █ N █ A █ G █ O █
A N K L E T █ T W E L V E
```

No 160

```
K I M O N O █ M I D █
R █ E █ D W I N D L E D
A F T █ I █ X █ E █ T █
K █ R E S U M E █ N O A H
E █ I █ M █ D █ T █ I █
N A C R E █ A U D I B L E
█ E █ P █ P █ T █ █
U N C L E A N █ S Y L P H
O █ I █ R █ S █ U █ I █
D R U G █ B O T T O M █ D
M █ I █ O █ █ █ B I D
P A L O M I N O █ E █ E █
█ L █ N █ L █ P A T R O N
```

No 161

```
T E E N Y █ C R O Q U E T
R █ T █ E █ A █ U █ L █
A E L T █ I T █ M I N I M
D E R E L I C T █ C █ T █
I █ N █ O █ H █ S H R E W
T R A M W A Y S █ E █ O █
I █ L █ S █ █ T █ I █ O
O █ S █ A P P R I S E D
N I F T Y █ O █ E █ O █ C
█ N █ U █ S T R A I N E R
O D O R S █ E █ D █ O █ A
█ I █ D █ N █ L █ M █ F
B A B Y S I T █ E G Y P T
```

No 162

```
S T A N C E █ L █ T A P
R █ █ A █ E V O K E █ O
W A T E R E D █ T █ L █ I
█ D █ O █ D █ S T A I N
P E R F U M E S █ V █ T █
I █ █ S █ S █ D █ I █ E
E N D E A R █ B E A V E R
X █ E █ L █ S █ R █ █ P
P █ V █ D A T A B A S E
O V E R T █ I █ N █ █ I
R █ L █ A █ N I G H T L Y
T █ O N S E T █ E █ █ O
S I P █ K █ █ I D L I N G
```

Solutions

No 163

```
M . S L . S A N . . . .
M I L I E U . T O U P E E
N . L . M U T . . X . . .
K I E V . B O B W H I T E
. E . . A . S . O . D . .
O U T R A G E . D R O O P
P . W . O . V . I . O . .
A S H E S . S E I Z U R E
. T . D . A . R . A . . .
S A D D E N E D . T E E D
R . I . . I . I . . . P .
S T I N T S . C H O P I N
. S . G . E . T . N . C .
```

No 164

```
M . P B . . M R G . . . .
A S Y L U M . L I K E L Y
N . R R E N . N . I . . P
H O A R S E N . D U N E S
O . M . A . D S S . . . Y
O M I T . G A S E S . . .
D . D . L . N . T . L . A
. . . . T O N G S . T A L C
A . K . Y . E S C R . . .
M E N S A . R E P R O V E
B . O . L . S . O . . N A
L O C A L S . S K I I N G
E . K . Y . . . E . C E .
```

No 165

```
S . A H . I . P . . E .
R O U G H A N D R E A D Y
. S . E . L . Y . D . G .
C O L O R F U L . A R I A
. L . . W . L . N . N . .
H A N D B A G . S T E E R
. I . . Y . B . . . S . .
B R O I L . O U T M O S T
. F . N . P . F . A . . .
M I N G . I N F O R M E D
. E . E . P . E . K . X .
F L A S H I N T H E P A N
. D . T . T . S . T . M .
```

No 166

```
. D S . O . S F D . . . .
L E V E R S . C L O V E S
. M . M . P A R . C . . .
G O B I . R E L I G I O N
. . . C . E . E . E . R .
A C R O N Y M . S T R A P
O . N . S . S . F . T . .
A M U S E . S C O U R E R
. M . C . D . R . L . . .
C A L I G U L A . N U L L
. N . O . E . G . E . A .
A D J U S T . G O S S I P
. O . S . S . Y . S . R .
```

No 167

```
E . L H . P O E . . . .
S T R I V E . R O B O T S
. N . G . R O J H . . . .
M A S H . S O U V E N I R
. . . T . E . D . C . O .
T R U F F L E . S T E P S
. E . I . F . E . I . I .
S P I N S . A C R O B A T
. R . G . G . O N . . . .
D O V E T A I L . A X E D
. A . R . M . O . B . K .
A C C E D E . G U L P E D
. H . D . S . Y . E S .
```

No 168

```
A G E N D A . S T O W E D
T . . . . A . S . W . . E
T . C A T E C H I Z E . .
E . L . E . O . N . N . E
S E A P L A N E . A J A R
T . M . E . E . D O S . .
. N O R S E . F R A Y S .
C . R . S . H . I . . A F
L O O T . F A L L I B L E
A . U . V . S . L . L . N
R . S L A N T W I S E . C
E . . I . Y . N . . . . E
T Y P I N G . U G L I E R
```

No 169

```
P A P A L . S Q U E E Z E
O . A . O . E . X . A . .
R . C . G X . S T A I N .
T A I L G A T E . E . R .
R . F . I . E . A N N E X
A L I E N A T E . T . . Y
Y . C . G . . . I . E . L
A . . G . F L A M E N C O
L O V E S . Y . P . G . P
V . M . E N C R O A C H .
T E P I D . X . E . G . O
N . N . E . S . E N . N .
A S S I S T S . S I D L E
```

No 170

```
I C I C L E . B E A R D S
O . O . K . E G O . . . .
F L E X . E X A M I N E R
L . C . S . U N . . . . .
D O D O S . S T A G G E R
. C . M . I . . . X . . .
C A R B O N I F E R O U S
. T . . S . Y . O . B . .
R E A C H E S . F U M E S
. . . O . C . C . G R . .
B A D M O U T H . H O A X
. D . E . R . I . L . N .
B O T T L E . C O Y O T E
```

No 171

```
. L . A H . C . E . R .
R U S S I A . O F F S E T
. M . C . R U F . P . . .
E P E E . V E N D E T T A
. . . R . E . T C . I . .
L O U T I S H . S T I L L
. F . A . T . C . I . E .
A F F I X . P R O V O S T
. E . N . F . A . E . . .
A N N A L I S T . N A V Y
. D . B . F . E . E . E .
P E L L E T . R O S A R Y
. D . E . H . S . S . Y .
```

Solutions

No 172

```
HOPS  SHRUGGED
A E H U N R   I
RECLAIM DOOMS
D A U   E A K
CONSTRUCTING
O   E R E E D
PAR CIGAR DUO
Y E U E M   G
AWEINSPIRING
S A S   N N E
CORGI GREETED
A D N E D R L
MASTERLY POSY
```

No 173

```
SAYS TRICYCLE
C A N E A H A
ATHEIST BRIMS
B O G U I C E
BROTHERINLAW
A T N E G C
RAUNCH STROLL
D P L T M   I
DENOMINATION
O N T R K M I
WIDTH ACERBIC
N E E D R U A
SIDESTEP VEIL
```

No 174

```
R C T S A E
NETHER PANAMA
D O E A T P
BOAR BASTILLE
E L M H O
INTONED VINYL
I G D L S E
WHERE VICTORY
I A C M A
FLIPFLOP MIND
I H A O I E
ASSETS PANTRY
M R H O E O
```

No 175

```
WREATHES IPSO
E I O V A V
AUGUR OUTSIZE
K H M K N R
T E   EMITTED
SAYINGS R S R
U T A A A
B S O BESTREW
JAKARTA C E
E A S I M B
CUTBACK BROKE
T E E L V T
SORE ETCETERA
```

No 176

```
SAFARI U W F
I A SENSIBLE
GNU L D L A
H COMELY DESK
T E S I F H
SATIN ANTONYM
N S G W
PASSOUT ALLEY
V E B C E E
TALC SCHISM L
T U I E OIL
LACROSSE N E
R E T PHASED
```

No 177

```
SCAVENGE SCAM
E C X A I O I
CATCH R NOTES
T S I L T T D
ILLITERATE
OTHERS AFIELD
P R A C E S S
SWEATSHIRT
I A I O E A B
DITTO S NACRE
E E N E C I R
DUNG UNDERDOG
```

No 178

```
S D E   E G L
TWELVE INDIGO
A T O A C A C
BREAKUP RANCH
L S E P Y T S
EATS PROPS
S S V O T N L
NERVE PUCE
M G R I S C I
ATLAS NETTLES
C E I G I E U
HEADON AFFAIR
O M N F R E
```

No 179

```
FOURSOME ROTE
S A U D E I
STRICT GOSPEL
R N LYE I R
NIPS O RUDEST
C O E
SHRANK LADDER
L U V
DOLLOP L SWAG
B E I L L T C
MATRON ASYLUM
M G C B L E
VARY HAYFEVER
```

No 180

```
APART ADORE
S S O M E U L
THERAPY MANIA
I U M R O I
LADS ARMCHAIR
L O T H R C
SONNET TATTOO
Y A A T U S
LIMERICK GAWP
A D T D L R
CHAIR ORIFICE
K P O R P Z Y
HELPS ASSET
```

Solutions

No 181

No 182

No 183

No 184

No 185

No 186

No 187

No 188

No 189

Grid solution

Solutions

No 190

```
A C N E _ K N I T W E A R
C I B E R M O
C O N G E A L _ A T O L L
I O L S F T L
D I N G O _ O F F L I N E
E W N I O R
N I C E T Y _ I C O N I C
T U H S L O
P A T I E N T _ I N D I A
R T B R G I S
O L I V E _ I N H E R I T
N N L D T G E
E I G H T E E N _ B E E R
```

No 191

```
O U T B U R S T _ A P S E
N U E A N E
S T Y L U S _ P A G O D A
R G C U E E A
D U K E _ I _ D A R I N G
T N E E
T H R E A D _ C O D D L E
N A O
A V I D L Y _ R _ F I Z Z
O U A G E A E
B U R R O W _ F A C I N G
C E N U T G
T H U S _ S P L A S H E S
```

No 192

```
I N T O _ O P P O S I N G
M W D I B N R
P R E M I E R _ S O F I A
E E S A C L V
R A D A R _ T S U N A M I
C E E R M T
E X C E P T _ G A L E N A
P H U H N T
T R E S T L E _ T E M P I
I R A A I A O
B L U R B _ R U S S I A N
L B L T M Z A
E S S A Y I S T _ S E A L
```

No 193

```
S S S I E S T
C A T A M A R A N _ P R O
O R A I E U O
F L A I R _ S E M I N A L
F G T E Y B
A G E L E S S _ E C H O
W L Y D H X
H E E L _ O B L I G E S
I T L L R M
P L A C E B O _ A Z U R E
P U N W T B T
E L K _ C A U T E R I Z E
T S H P S C R
```

No 194

```
S F S G W A
B E F O U L _ E N O U G H
M L I N R R
G I R L _ P A R O D I E S
O O W E P E
S N O W M A N _ B R A I D
A T Y C O N
C U S H Y _ C H I C A G O
S R K E E
H E D O N I S M _ S I F T
A U N I S I
S T A G E D _ S T O O L S
E H S T R L
```

No 195

```
F A L S V A
L O B B Y I S T _ I D L E
R R N A S M
Z E B U _ E M B L A Z O N
G P A S S
M O N T A G E _ M O U T H
L E T P
P L A Y S _ C A P E R E D
I Z N N N
E V O L V I N G _ E D D Y
E A P L Y I
C L A D _ P R E S E R V E
Y Y Y D D D E
```

No 196

```
T R E A T I N G _ B E E F
W L I E V A
I N E P T _ S A L O O N S
G V R T L T
E A _ E N L I V E N
I G N I T E D _ O E E
G I C S S
N S O _ T E A C H E S
I M P I N G E _ T A
T R A I W B
I T A L I C S _ O V A T E
O W E N I R
N I L E _ P R E S S I N G
```

No 197

```
S E W E R _ I M P O S E S
H O E N C T
A U C D _ P U S H Y
P O L K A D O T _ L I
E D S O _ R A N C H
L O B S T E R S _ R Y
E E S A C P
S P _ B L U D G E O N
S T R U M _ O J D O
H M _ F U T U R I S T
R U M M Y _ N D L I
M E G G L Z
A B A L O N E _ E V A D E
```

No 198

```
G R U M P Y _ A F F I R M
O R B A O
B _ E G O M A N I A C _ U
L X T C R A S
I S C A R I O T _ I B I S
N H U N L R E
W E E D S _ L U R I D
A Q E S N O T
S C U D _ S T I C K L E R
S E A A H E U
A _ R E C U R R E N T _ D
I N K O G
L A T T E R _ U N W I S E
```

Solutions

No 199

No 200

No 201

No 202

No 203

No 204

No 205

No 206

No 207

Solutions

No 208

```
EASY PROGRESS
X  T  B  U  R  A  E
PURSUIT APRON
E  U  R     P  A  T
DEMOGRAPHICS
   L  T  O  H  H
TWO ATOLL EVE
E  I  R  M  O     A
CLEARSIGHTED
D  S  L     I  W  I
OMEGA SUSTAIN
G  E  R  O  T  I  G
SEDIMENT GNUS
```

No 209

```
 FLIRTATIOUS
P  O  E  R  N  N  I
EW VIGIL DON
R ADII U A U E
F  O  SE WEEKS
UNWIELDY   S
N  N  S    PA E
C    EMULSION
TRASH I A R T
O  B EL TEMPI
ROB ARISE A A
Y  O  V  E  A  I  L
 STRENUOUSLY
```

No 210

```
SQUAWK F CUE
U  O  INLAY P
DISCORD A C I
E DY YOLKS
STENCILS O T
L O L UNL
LYRICS SLEEVE
O E K L T U
O C LOVINGLY
KRILL C M G
I T O HEADWAY
N AUNTS T T
GEL E  SETTER
```

No 211

```
REMEMBER STAB
N  M  U  I  H  S
STAPES STITCH
E  T  ICE A O
PREY E NOTATE
E  S  S  S
ADVERT THUMBS
   M  O  O
DOUBLE R MAUL
A  A  SIP O D
USURPS ESCROW
I  K  A  D  H  I
ASKS YEOMANRY
```

No 212

```
MAGNATES CLEF
I I R R O U
LEVER RUCTION
D I OA T N
NW NAIVELY
AUGURED M R M
N O P A
I E O BROADEN
MINUTIA T E
A T T ESE
TWINKLE NAILS
E C A CG P
SEEP BUOYANCY
```

No 213

```
K S P T D D
ENDEAR HOOTER
E L E E U C
DEAF SCRUBBED
 C A E L M
OBLONGS HERBS
A N E TC E
EDIFY BEARERS
G I E N O
VENDETTA SPAR
R E U N S V
LEANED THESIS
D T E S D D
```

No 214

```
THORNY DECEIT
O E O I H L
PLAT GASWORKS
O I A C I
AGING CORRUPT
R U S L E
WATERPROOFING
P R R O I
CHEETAH FRANK
L W E E S
TRAVELED SMUT
Y I E G T L
VERSED YESMAN
```

No 215

```
RENDER E PUB
X L CAMEL E
PARVENU U A L
C C R SISAL
STARTERS T B
L I Y BIO
PYTHON PATCHY
E A N A L O
E M SCALLOPS
VIPER I R E
I E A DROPOFF
S RAINS O U
HIS D IMPELS
```

No 216

```
DIVORCEMENT
I R F O E A I
MA FUMES INN
MOTHS E S V A
E E I O YIELD
DELUDING V
I Y E T A E
A ENGRAVER
TAPER E A O T
E I A C NICHE
LYE LUTES A N
Y C L A I D T
DEHYDRATION
```

Solutions

No 217

```
G A R L I C ▓ P ▓ T ▓ T
O ▓ E ▓ H A R D W A R E
G A S ▓ U ▓ E ▓ E ▓ O ▓
G ▓ C H A R T S ▓ A X L E
L U ▓ N ▓ S ▓ K ▓ L ▓
E L E G Y ▓ B U S I E S T
▓ A ▓ W ▓ P ▓ N ▓
P L U M M E T ▓ A G O N Y
U ▓ E ▓ E ▓ L ▓ F ▓ E
E L A N ▓ P A Y O F F ▓ L
L ▓ E ▓ I ▓ R ▓ I L L
H E L S I N K I ▓ S ▓ O
D ▓ S ▓ G ▓ C A S H E W
```

No 218

```
B O W M A N ▓ Z ▓ S A P
U ▓ G ▓ I D I O T ▓ R
S T A T I O N ▓ N ▓ A E
W ▓ T ▓ N ▓ C O M E S
D O G E A R E D ▓ M ▓ I
R ▓ T ▓ R ▓ S ▓ E ▓ D
S K E W E D ▓ S C A R C E
C ▓ Y ▓ D ▓ S ▓ H ▓ A
A E ▓ A T R O C I T Y
P A W E D ▓ U ▓ O ▓ H
U ▓ A ▓ U ▓ B A N G K O K
L ▓ S E C T S ▓ E ▓ D
A A H ▓ T ▓ P R I V E T
```

No 219

```
T ▓ O B ▓ G ▓ A ▓ O
G R A V E L ▓ R I P O F F
E ▓ E ▓ U ▓ O ▓ A ▓ F
L E E R ▓ F O U N T A I N
▓ S ▓ F ▓ P ▓ H ▓ C
W R I T T E N ▓ N E W E R
E ▓ A ▓ R ▓ T ▓ T ▓ R
S L O T S ▓ B U S I E S T
I ▓ E ▓ U ▓ R ▓ C ▓
P A R M E S A N ▓ A U N T
B ▓ E ▓ U ▓ I ▓ L ▓ I
P L A N A R ▓ P A L A C E
Y ▓ T ▓ Y ▓ S ▓ Y ▓ E
```

No 220

```
F U R Y ▓ A T Y P I C A L
O ▓ U ▓ F ▓ E ▓ R U E
R I P C O R D ▓ E G R E T
T ▓ E ▓ R ▓ I ▓ P R T
I N E P T ▓ U N A W A R E
F ▓ H ▓ M ▓ R ▓ N R
I N S E R T ▓ P E N T U P
C ▓ W ▓ I ▓ A ▓ D E
A M A L G A M ▓ N A D I R
T ▓ L ▓ H ▓ P E R F
I N L E T ▓ E N S N A R E
O ▓ O ▓ L ▓ R ▓ S K C
N E W L Y W E D ▓ L E S T
```

No 221

```
I S L A N D ▓ C L E F T S
N ▓ E ▓ E ▓ I ▓ T
D ▓ T A X O N O M I C ▓ O
I ▓ A ▓ T ▓ A ▓ E H R
A Q U E D U C T ▓ W O R M
N ▓ T ▓ O ▓ T ▓ F P S
▓ D O N O R ▓ B L U S H
W ▓ L ▓ R ▓ F A T A
R I O T ▓ C L A S H I N G
A ▓ G ▓ D ▓ A H C E
P ▓ Y A R D S T I C K ▓ H
U ▓ A ▓ H ▓ L ▓ T
P I P I T S ▓ S Y R U P S
```

No 222

```
L ▓ O A ▓ I ▓ S H
D I S S E M I N A T I O N
E ▓ P ▓ A ▓ A ▓ U R
U N F R O Z E N ▓ P O R T
E ▓ I ▓ E ▓ O ▓ I
S W A Y I N G ▓ P R O B E
A ▓ ▓ G ▓ G ▓ L
A S T I R ▓ C R E A S E S
T ▓ N ▓ W ▓ A D
V E N D ▓ O P T I M I S M
F ▓ O ▓ R ▓ I ▓ I P
S U B O R D I N A T I O N
L ▓ R ▓ Y ▓ G S T
```

No 223

```
E S T I M A T E ▓ G A W P
D ▓ O ▓ A ▓ I ▓ S N A
G R O W N ▓ G ▓ O D D L Y
Y ▓ T ▓ E ▓ H M R M
▓ B U T T O N H O L E ▓
R F ▓ V ▓ S ▓ A I N
E A R N E D ▓ A M I D S T
I ▓ E ▓ R M ▓ B S S
G R E G A R I O U S ▓
N ▓ Z ▓ B ▓ Z L B M
I D E A L ▓ Z ▓ I R O N Y
T ▓ R ▓ E ▓ L S O T
E A S T ▓ B E S M I R C H
```

No 224

```
▓ H T ▓ I ▓ C R H
P Y T H O N ▓ O P E N E D
▓ M ▓ U ▓ T P F L
A N O N ▓ R E S T R A I N
▓ D ▓ U E ▓ I ▓ P
A D D E N D A ▓ A G L O W
E ▓ R ▓ E M E R ▓
S T A S H ▓ M I G R A T E
E ▓ T ▓ A ▓ S A
S C O R N F U L ▓ T A X I
T ▓ U ▓ O E ▓ I R
P O N C H O ▓ A M O R A L
R K T ▓ D ▓ N Y
```

No 225

```
O H M S ▓ S H R I V E L S
B ▓ O ▓ E A ▓ N X N
S T R I V E S ▓ C O C O A
E ▓ A ▓ O ▓ O U P
S E L F L E S S N E S S ▓
S ▓ U T V ▓ E M
E V E ▓ T R U C E ▓ S P A
D ▓ N I N ▓ N N
S T R O N G W I L L E D ▓
A ▓ E N ▓ E O A
P A N D A ▓ S E N A T O R
S ▓ T R E ▓ T T I
E V E R Y D A Y ▓ L O O N
```

Solutions

No 226

```
D E E P N E S S . . H I T S
A . I . N . P . O . E . .
C R A Z E D . E Q U I N E
N . . Z O R C . S . C . .
L I Z A . R . K N I G H T
N . . S . . . N . . . . .
I G N O R E . S I G N E D
. L . . . H . . . S . . .
S A W Y E R . I . M O P E
N . M E L M . O . . O . .
S N I P E R . M O C K U P
O . U . U . E . H . S . .
E Y E S . N A R R A T E S
```

No 227

```
F R O T H Y . R A M M E D
E . A . U . E . A . W . .
K I C K . A D V A N C E S
N . E . N . E . T . . . .
A F O O T . B R E A T H E
. O . F . E . S . . . O .
C R A F T S M A N S H I P
. C . . P . L . T . . P .
S E S S I O N . P I L O T
. . T . U . U . R . L . .
M O L A S S E S . R E L Y
H . I . A . E . U . O . .
A M O R A L . S O P H I A
```

No 228

```
A T T E S T . A B S O R B
C . A . L . A . U . R . E
C O X C O M B . G . B . S
E . A . T . B A B Y S I T
D U T C H . R . E . . . O
E . I . . . E . A S K E W
. O . L O V E R . A . . .
G E N I I . I . . N . P .
U . . B . A . A U G E R .
F E R M E N T . S . A . E
F . E . R . E X H O R T S
A . A . A . D . E . O . E
W A R B L E . . A S S O R T
```

No 229

```
U G L Y . A D J U T A N T
N . Y . M . I . N . W . A
S E I Z U R E . F U E L S
Y . N . L . S . L . S . T
M U G . T . E . A L O N E
P . . I N L E T . M . L .
A . A . L . . . T . E . E
T . R . A W A R E . . S . S
H A B I T . B . R . C O S
E . I . E . A . I . R . N
T U T O R . C O N F I D E
I . E . A U G . S . S . S
C O R D L E S S . A P E S
```

No 230

```
B . S . A . . S . I . L .
R A T T L E . S T U D I O
A . I . B . P . E . . N .
V E R D U R E . E R A S E
E . R . M . R . P . S . R
R O U T . S K U L L . . .
Y . P . S . I . E . S . P
. . G O I N G . L O G O .
C . H . M . E . E . J . L
L O O S E . S O M E O N E
U . K . H . S . A . U . C
C O U P O N . S I E R R A
K . M . W . . L . N . T .
```

No 231

```
L . I . A . O . A . O .
L I N N E T . S Y R U P S
M . E . H . C . G . E . .
W A I F . I N A H U R R Y
. F . R . R . M . A . . .
A D V E R S E . D E R B Y
A . C . T . T . N . L . .
S I X T H . C H A T T E R
Q . I . T . E . A . . . .
S U R V E Y O R . T R A P
I . E . P . E . I . D . .
G R I L L E . B L O N D S
I . Y . S . Y . N . S . .
```

No 232

```
A C H E . E S C A L A T E
P . I . S . H . F . M . C
R U N A W A Y . T O U G H
I . G . A . E . L . O . .
C H E E S E B U R G E R .
O . H . L . T . T . L . .
T I C . B E E C H . S E A
S . O . U . E . O . D . .
. C O N C E P T U A L L Y
S . P . K . G . U . L . .
K N E L L . S C H E R Z I
I . R . E . A . T . C . K
D I S C R E T E . S H O E
```

No 233

```
C L I M B S . A B A T E S
H . L . O . C . A . O . E
A L L E G R O . D . F . N
P . T . U . M E D I U M S
E M I T S . P . E . . E .
L . M . L . B O U T S . .
. E . D R A F T . N . . .
A R D O R . I . F . O . .
W . . I . N . G O A D S .
A L G E B R A . R . I . T
R . I . L . N E U T R A L
D . R . L . T . E . L . E
S U D D E N . P L A Y E R
```

No 234

```
F L A P P I N G . S P U R
A . U . E . E . H . E . E
C O N G A . G . O W N E D
T . T . C . A . M . C . E
. . G E T T H E C H O P .
B . P . K . E . L . A . L
E R A S E D . L E A N T O
A . R . E . G . S . T . Y
R E A P P R A I S E . . .
S . N . I . Z . N . D . A
K N O W N . E . E D I T S
I . I . G . B . S . C . P
N E A P . M O N S T E R S
```

Solutions

No 235

No 236

No 237

No 238
```
UNITS SOPHISM
N N C I   A P
D SR M KNEEL
EPIDEMIC G L
F G A MAPLE
INHUMANE R X
N T S   A T T
E S ASPIRATE
DOWEL H R P N
D Q FIRMNESS
VIRUS M A I
U E   M I E V
AMPLIFY LEDGE
```

No 239
```
QUAY OBSESSED
U R F A X A I
ECONOMY PUTTS
S S R I L C C
THERM NEITHER
I   A G C EE
OCCULT VIOLET
N O D T T   I
NURSERY NACHO
A D H R E A N
ITALY AUSTRIA
R T D N S O R
ELEMENTS PLAY
```

No 240

No 241

No 242

No 243

Solutions

No 244

```
B L O G G E R S   A M M O
I   O   A     I   B
B E Z E L   N O V E N A S
S   I   D   G     I   E
  N   M   E X P E N D S
R E G R E S S   E   G   S
E       D     P     E
S   A   A   P A P Y R U S
P A D D L E R   E   E
O   D   A   R   V   U
N A U G H T Y   O B E Y S
D   C     E   N   R   E
S E E S   A D D I C T E D
```

No 245

```
F L O U R I S H   G O O F
  I   L   G   E   A   Z
B A T T E N   W A L L O P
  I   R   I C E   I   N
A S I A   T R O L L E R
  O     E     E
K N O C K S   S L O G A N
  A     A   V
M A N T R A   R   S E E M
N   C   S I C P   N
M I S H A P   A L L E G E
O   U   E   S   I   E
S N I P   N E M A T O D E
```

No 246

```
  A P P L Y   A M B L E
A   E   I   B   I   E   D
M A R I M B A   D R A K E
U   T   A   S   N   E
S O U P   C I V I L W A R
E   R   W   L   G   A
S U B W A Y   C H A T T Y
  E   R   S   T   E   U
O B D U R A T E   T R I P
N     I   E G P P
L I M B O   M A R C O N I
Y   O   R   S   A   L   E
  B O O S T   A B H O R
```

No 247

```
C L E M A T I S   T S A R
A   N   U   G   T   E
G A L L S   L I Z A R D S
E   I   T   O   O   T
  S   R   O C T O B E R
B E T R A Y S   I   E   I
R     L   M     C
E   F I   S N I P P E T
A B R E A S T   D   E
K   I     U   N W U
O R G A N I C   E N T E R
U   H     C   S   E   G
T U T U   C O N S T R U E
```

No 248

```
H   M V S M   M M W
A R A B E S Q U E   I C E
R   I   T U N   N   I
S I N C E   E L U D I N G
H   T   R A A S   N
  C A P A B L E   A B U T
A   I N     P R S
R U N S   J A V E L I N
R   P B   R   E   T
A C C R U A L   M U F T I
I   L L O U I L
G N U   S H O R T E N E D
N   B   E M E G E
```

No 249

```
F U S S   A R G U A B L E
O   H   D E   N   O   X
O C A R I N A   C L A S P
L   R   S   R O T   E
H O P   C E   N O M A D
A     R I D E S E   I
R   I E     I N   T
D   K   E G G E D   I
I N E P T   A E   W H O
N   B   N U R R E U
E L A T E   C L E R I C S
S   N   S H D G   L
S N A P S H O T   W H E Y
```

No 250

```
O U T M O D E D   C L A D
P   H   B   L   E   R
E M I T S   E S T O N I A
N   E   E V   T   U
V   S   E T C H I N G
T R E A S O N   O   L   H
H   I   L     T
O   O V   U N L O C K S
R E D D E N S   O H
O   E     H   C E V
U P S C A L E   A G R E E
G   S     R   T   U   R
H O A R   A S S E M B L Y
```

No 251

```
  B   S E   E   C V
R A R I T Y   M O H A I R
  N   L   E   I R G
E D T V   S U R M O U N T
  E   O S N E
T E R R O R S   P O U T S
V   T E   P L T
B E F O G   D E C O D E D
N   N E E   G
S I N G U L A R   I C O N
N   U   U E   C O
A G R E E D   S N A Z Z Y
S   D E   S   L Y
```

No 252

```
H Y P E   F L Y P A P E R
O   A   H   A   E   R   I
L U S T I L Y   D R E A D
I   T   E     I   V   E
D I A G R A M M A T I C
A     A   I   T   E   A
Y A M   R A D A R   W A S
S   O   C   S   I     S
  A R C H I T E C T U R E
A   T   I     I   S   S
F R A N C   P E A N U T S
A   L   A   I   N   R   O
R E S O L V E S   S P U R
```

Solutions

No 253

P	R	O	P		E	N	D	O	R	S	E	S
E		P		P		A		L		T	A
R	E	T	R	E	A	T		D	R	A	I	N
F			I		R		I	F		R	G
O	C	C	A	S	I	O	N	A	L	L	Y
R		P		N		S		E		S	
M	I	S	F	I	T		S	H	U	T	U	P
S		P	R		A		I		A		
	C	A	T	A	S	T	R	O	P	H	I	C
D		N		T	O	N		U		I	
A	L	I	B	I		M	A	E	S	T	R	O
M	E		O		I		D		C		U
P	O	L	O	N	E	C	K		T	H	U	S

No 254

No 255

E	N	C	L	O	S	E	D		A	P	E	S
D		A		V		X		U		E	
G	E	N	I	E		I	N	S	U	R	E	R
Y		C		R		T		S		G	
A		W		E	X	C	R	E	T	E	
L	U	N	C	H	E	D		H		S	A
E			E		E			N			
I		G	L		A	T	H	E	I	S	T
S	H	R	I	M	P	S		U		N	
U		A			A		D	T			
R	I	C	H	T	E	R		H	A	I	R	Y
E		E		A		U		G		P	
D	A	S	H		S	Y	C	A	M	O	R	E

No 256

No 257

H	A	R	D	B	A	C	K		D	A	F	T
D		A		V		E	I	L	
B	A	F	F	L	E		M	A	S	C	O	T
M		F		N	A	P		O		O	
W	A	R	Y		G		T	O	W	E	R	S
N		E				N					
S	T	A	Y	E	D		H	A	S	S	L	E
O			E				A			
R	I	D	G	E	S		R		S	I	N	E
D		U		I	R	E		L		O	
H	Y	B	R	I	D		T	R	O	L	L	S
L		T		L		I		O		I	
A	L	M	S		E	S	C	A	P	I	N	G

No 258

S	P	O	T	T	Y		B	A	D	G	E	S
L		S		A		O		A		O	
B	E	A	U		R	E	N	A	M	I	N	G
N		N		D		H		E			
S	T	E	A	M		T	O	P	S	I	D	E
I			M		L		M		E		
E	F	F	I	C	A	C	I	O	U	S	L	Y
U			G		E		N			I	
P	L	U	M	A	G	E		S	I	E	V	E
	A		A		E		C		E		
B	A	C	K	D	R	O	P		O	U	R	S
F		E		D		I		R		E	
S	T	A	S	I	S		C	A	N	A	D	A

No 259

W	I	C	K		G	A	Z	P	A	C	H	O
E		O		T		N		E		L	U
D	I	V	E	R	G	E		N	E	E	D	S
D		E		A		M		N		A	T
I	N	T	E	N	S	I	F	Y	I	N	G
N			S		C		P		U		A
G	R	A	T	I	S		D	I	S	P	E	L
S		G		T		M		N			T
	R	E	M	I	N	I	S	C	E	N	C	E
D		N		O		D		H		E	R
O	L	D	E	N		G	R	E	N	A	D	E
D		A			A		E		R		G
O	B	S	O	L	E	T	E		O	S	L	O

No 260

T	R	E	N	D	Y		S	C	O	R	E	S
E		S		U		O		R		I	N
A	N	T	W	E	R	P		U		C	A
S		E		T		E	L	E	M	E	N	T
E	V	E	N	S		R		L			C
R		M			A			T	E	E	T	H
	E		B	I	T	T	Y			X	
G	I	D	D	Y		I		O		S	
O			O		G		O	C	T	E	T
C	A	R	T	O	O	N		N		E	U
A		O		N		A	S	S	U	R	E	D
R		T	E		L	E		I		
T	H	E	I	S	T		S	T	U	C	C	O

No 261

A	F	A	R		E	S	T	I	M	A	T	E
D		D		U		C		N		R	X
V	A	L	E	N	C	Y		G	R	I	S	T
E			I	P		T	R		Z		R
N	I	B		R		H		A	R	O	M	A
T		U		E	J	E	C	T		N	O
U		L		J			I		A		R
R	I		U	M	B	R	A			D	
E	D	G	E	D		O		T		P	H	I
S		H			I		B	I	A	N	
O	P	T	I	C		C	A	N	A	S	T	A
M	U		E		A		G	T		R	
E	X	P	E	D	I	T	E		W	A	R	Y

Solutions

No 262

```
T R E A D S   C R I M E A
E   M U G   O   I   P
T O B A C C O   A D O
C   A   H   D A S H I N G
H A R D Y   F   T   E
Y   K   O   E R O D E
  E   E A R E D   U
T I D E S   S   T T
I   C   A   D O S E S
B A R R A C K   R H E
I   A   P   E G O T I S T
A   I   E N   W N S
L E D G E R   S N E E Z E
```

No 263

```
C E I L I N G S   R O T E
Q   O   A   E   E
O U T L E T   V A C A N T
A   L   T O E   O   C
A B L Y   E   D O U G H S
L       R   N
F E A S T S   O U T F O X
  U       A   R
A I R B A G   T   W H A M
N   T R I M   I   T
A T H E N A   E N R O O T
  E   X   P   A   E R
W R I T   H O L I D A Y S
```

No 264

```
S U M M E R   S T U R D Y
W   Y   U   T   N   R
I N F O R M E R   L E A P
M   P   O   O   C
M A L I   C N   A C H E
E   C H A N G E D   M
R A G   L B   W A R
  F   M A M M O T H   E
E R N E   A   X   O P U S
I   L T   A   I
E C H O   I N V E R S E S
A   D   V   O   S   T
E N Z Y M E   W I E L D S
```

No 265

```
  I N S P I R A T I O N
C   A   U   I   A   M
O   I L I F T S   L E A
N A V E L   F   K E   S
V   E   I L   S O D A S
I N T E N D E D       P
V   Y   G   S O R
I   T O A N D F R O
A R B O R   C   I   F D
L   E   O   P I L A U
L O G   T U L I P   O C
Y   A   O   E   A E
  I N G R A T I T U D E
```

No 266

```
R A K E   A B N E G A T E
O   E B E   X   P   M
U N B O U N D   T H R O B
N   A   T   L   R   I
D E B I T   A X O L O T L
T   E   M   V   R   L
H A R A R E   G E M I N I
E   E S   A R       S
C H A U C E R   S L O S H
L   C   O   C I   S M
O C T E T   A T O M I Z E
C   O   N N   E   N
K E R C H I E F   B R A T
```

No 267

```
  G   V   S R   I   A
  I N S I D I O U S N E S S
  U   S M N   F   T
A S S U M I N G   A G E D
  A   L   S M R
S H E L V E S   L Y R I C
  E   S   C   S   S
C A U S E   B A Z O O K A
  D   T S D R
B L U R   C H E A P E S T
  A   A A N   H   H
U N A P P R E C I A T E D
  D   S F E N   D
```

No 268

```
  O R G A N   S C A L P
B   E   M   E   R   A P
L E A V I N G   I N D I A
O   D D   Y   T   C
W E I R   A P T I T U D E
U   N   S   T   Q N
P I E R C E   S U N S E T
  S   H D E   I   H
D I S C O V E R   O G L E
E   L   N E H R
M A N T A   S Y M P T O M
O   A R E   I L   S
  A B A S H   T R A Y S
```

No 269

```
C A R R Y I N G   L O T S
T   O   N   L A H
S H O U T S   O U S T E D
  I   N   P E R A   I N
P R O D   E   Y O G U R T
  S   C   N
U T M O S T   H E A V E N
  F   E   E   X
A R T F U L   R   M I C E
  I   S   A S S O L
A S L E E P   E X T R A S
  E   T E L E   I
E N D S   L I F E T I M E
```

No 270

```
D O R M A N C Y   A G E D
A   A   B R   R   E
M U R K Y   O R A T O R S
E   I S   W   U S
  T M   E X P U N G E
W A Y W A R D   E   D R
I   L   A   T
D   F L   E S C U D O S
E N J O Y E D   E R
N   O   I T A S
I N R O A D S   I N P U T
N   D   O   M E   A
G A S H   U N D E R D O G
```

Solutions

No 271

```
UNSTEADY   BACK
U   I   R   A   O   R
SLALOM   RHYMES
L   T   BID   C   E
DIPS   A   SLOPPY
T       N       T
BYROAD   DATING
    M       E     A
EFFIGY   S   RAID
A   T   AMP   A   R
CUSTER   INDOOR
N   E   N   S   I   B
BALD   SPECIFIC
```

No 272

```
A   G   G   T   A   E
OVERDO   EXPOSE
E   A   D   E   P   S
BRAT   SENTRIES
I   I   E   S   E   N
DEAFENS   CHECK
M   I   D   B   E   E
SPICE   DRYNESS
T   A   C   E   S
HYSTERIA   IRIS
I   I   A   K   B   N
INMOST   UNLIKE
G   N   E   P   E   S
```

No 273

```
S   H   I   P   D   G
SPLATTER   OVEN
H   R   C   U   V   N
PICA   HINDERED
N   N   I   E   V
EXIGENT   GREAT
O   U   G   L   E
AMBER   KARAOKE
O   G   W   S   E
ACHILLES   SAYS
K   D   E   U   I   I
HULL   BRINGING
P   E   E   T   N   G
```

No 274

```
F   C   O   A   U   T
BISHOP   GENTRY
R   R   A   E   D   A
AMMO   CONSERVE
N   I   T   R   E
ACCOSTS   STILL
O   L   Y   E   H   E
SNOOP   EXTENDS
T   G   O   P   T
MEDIEVAL   ARCS
M   C   A   O   B   R
SPRAWL   RELOAD
T   L   S   E   E   G
```

No 275

```
FENCED   AMBUSH
L   H   O   N   E   A
LAIR   CRIBBAGE
B   O   K   M   O
MOONS   RAMPAGE
R   I   V   T   R
SANCTIMONIOUS
T   L   R   L   F
KEYHOLE   ALOFT
A   A   P   E   N
EPILOGUE   GLEE
U   V   E   E   A   S
STRESS   RELISH
```

No 276

```
FACT   ABSOLUTE
E   R   R   A   B   P   S
RAIDERS   LISZT
O   S   N   S   I   U   A
CUP   O   E   THROB
I   UNTIE   G   L
O   P   N   R   E   I
U   E   CURIA   S
SPACE   I   T   ASH
N   F   M   P   I   W   M
EVOKE   PROBATE
S   W   N   E   N   I   N
SOLITUDE   STET
```

No 277

```
GRUBBY   O   RAM
A   O   IMBUE   I
SPELLED   E   V   D
P   T   E   YIELD
SOOTHSAY   R   L
R   O   S   S   T   E
STILLS   VERSUS
E   N   E   S   A   M
Q   H   BLOWPIPE
UNARM   A   A   T
O   B   A   BATCHES
I   IDLES   E   E
ART   I   ERRAND
```

No 278

```
TRACKRECORD
M   E   O   I   L   E   N
A   V   COCOA   ACE
LEECH   H   N   D   T
E   L   E   GLYPH
VERTEBRA       E
O   Y   A   S   H   R
L   MOTHBALL
EDUCE   G   I   N   A
N   M   V   R   ADDON
CUB   EVENT   F   D
E   E   R   S   S   U   S
GROTESQUELY
```

No 279

```
O   O   L   A   A   B
INOFFENSIVELY
Y   F   G   H   I   U
EXPEDITE   DABS
R   B   N   L   B
LOOSELY   LYRES
C   E   R   R
SCARP   DEPLOYS
U   E   A   D   A
IPSO   DOOMSDAY
A   P   L   U   T   R
UNRELIABILITY
T   N   B   T   Y   S
```

372

Solutions

No 280
```
S T A F F S . A D S O R B
T . O . S . E . . I . R
R . E U R O P E A N S . T
O X . E . O . N . I . T
B A C K S T O P . E D G E
E . L . T . R . M . E . R
G U A R D . R I N S E
H S . Y . H . S . T . A
E D I T . C O N Q U E S T
L . O . A . A . U . P . H
I . N E F A R I O U S . E
U . U . A . D . T . N
M A K E R S . P E S E T A
```

No 281
```
B I S H O P . F L O R A L
A . U . I . A . C . P
T R I B U N A L . C O R N
T . B . S . U . I
L I E U . B . E . P L O Y
E . B R A S H L Y . R
R H O . R . O . H I S
. A . A W E S O M E . P
O P U S . B . D . R O L L
L . T . O . S . O
M E S H . N A R R A T E D
S . M . E . U . T . G
I S L A N D . N U Z Z L E
```

No 282
```
I M P E L L E D . S T U N
F . R . O . L . E . I
F L I N G . A S C E T I C
Y . M . I . T . C . O
. L . C . E A R S H O T
W A Y W A R D . E . Y . I
E . L . W . N
L . P . L . U N A W A R E
C A R R Y O N . R . N
O E . I . D . N . S
M I L L E R S . I N U R E
E . I . O . N . A . E
D A M N . S N U G G L E S
```

No 283
```
R E A L M S . S P L I N T
E . U . E . I . R
M . A U T O M A T I C . I
O . I . U . A . H . O . L
V E R B A T I M . A R A B
E . W . L . H . R . Y
H O T L Y . F E M U R
A . R . Y . G . R . P . R
P A T S . R E P A R T E E
P . H . I . N . L . L . S
L . Y E S T E R D A Y . A
E . S . I . L
S P L A S H . I C E A G E
```

No 284
```
E . I . K . N . A
B R O A D M I N D E D L Y
G T . A . O . T . T
P O R T U G A L . H A R D
. E . E . L . E . U
P A N D E R S . D R A I N
I . Y . R . S
G R A P H . R E A L I T Y
B . A . E . S . O
C O O P . G L O B A L L Y
R . A . Y . R . N . O
U N S Y M P A T H E T I C
E . A . T . S . R . N
```

No 285
```
C E D E . C H E E R F U L
R . O . C . I . X . L . A
E N G R O S S . A L A R M
O . M . M . G . R . P
S H A R P T O N G U E D
O . L . C . E . U . M
T I C . E N T E R . P H I
E . U . T . E . A . S
. A D V E N T I T I O U S
S . D . N . I . R . P
T I L D E . L I V A B L E
I . E . S . A . E . I . N
R E D E S I G N . S T U D
```

No 286
```
P S A . M C G
E T H I C S . C A N O P Y
R . U . O . C . R . L . P
I N F E R N O . I R O N S
O . F . N . L . M . R . Y
D E L L . G L O B E
S . E . C . O . A . S . U
. F L E C K . S T E P
A . B . A . A . H . A . F
S T R U M . T R I G G E R
I . I . P . E . P . G . O
D O D G E R . S P L E E N
E . E . D . Y . R . T
```

No 287
```
P H W H . W L
L I F E T I M E . I C O N
P . A . D . W . L . O
K I E V . E Y E G L A S S
T . I . N . R . E
U S H E R E D . C R A N K
. S . D . O . A
G I R T H . C U S T O D Y
S . L . T . T . E
D O V E T A I L . L I A R
B . X . M . E . I . R
M A G I . B I T I N G L Y
R . T . S . S . G . Y
```

No 288
```
W I C K E D L Y . A R I D
A . H . F . A . I . E . I
S N I F F . V . N E S T S
P . C . E . I . V . P . A
. P R O S P E R O U S
S . V . V . H . S . N . T
U N E V E N . S T O D G E
B . T . S . W . I . S . R
O V E R C H A R G E
R . R . E . F . A . I . T
D R A W N . F . T U F T S
E . N . T . L . O . F . A
R O S E . B E T R A Y E R
```

Solutions

No 289

```
E L M S _ S E A S H O R E
Y _ U _ H _ W _ T _ R _ M
E N S L A V E _ R E A L M
B _ I _ P _ _ _ A _ T _ Y
R E C U P E R A T I O N _
O _ _ _ Y _ I _ O _ R _ E
W A S _ G I V E S _ S T Y
S _ H _ O _ E _ P _ _ _ E
_ K I L L E R W H A L E S
S _ M _ U _ _ _ E _ A _ I
M I M I C _ S U R F I N G
U _ E _ K _ U _ E _ R _ H
T A R R Y I N G _ E D I T
```

No 290

```
I _ V _ C _ L _ T _ T _ S
G R E N A D I E R _ U S E
L _ R _ P _ A _ E _ B _ V
O C T E T _ I N S T A T E
O _ E _ A _ S _ S _ _ _ N
O B L I G E S _ S C U T _
E _ R _ N _ _ _ K _ O _ H
X R A Y _ S O M E O N E _
P _ _ _ G _ W _ Y _ S S S
O V E R R A N _ H E I S T
R _ V _ A _ E _ O _ S _ U
T O E _ P A R A L Y T I C
S _ N _ E _ S _ E _ S _ K
```

No 291

```
P O E T _ P R E C E P T S
A _ D _ I _ A _ R _ I _ E
R E G E N C Y _ Y A C H T
A _ E _ T _ _ _ P _ C _ S
D I S P E N S A T I O N _
I _ _ _ R _ C _ O _ L _ A
G N U _ F L U N G _ O W L
M _ S _ E _ B _ R _ R _ _
_ C H A R L A T A N I S M
D _ E _ E _ _ _ P _ N _ I
A P R O N _ E C H E L O N
S _ E _ C _ G _ Y _ A _ U
H E D G E R O W _ S W A M
```

No 292

```
_ C _ M _ A _ A _ P _ I _
C O P I E R _ G R A N N Y
_ D _ S _ I _ A _ T _ D _
T A L C _ S P I T E F U L
_ E _ _ _ I _ N _ R _ L _
V I O L E N T _ S N A G S
N _ L _ G _ D _ A _ E _ _
S T R A W _ B A L L A D S
O _ N _ P _ N _ I _ I _ _
E N T E R I N G _ S A Y S
A _ O _ C _ E _ T _ E _ _
S T R U C K _ R H I N A L
E _ S _ Y _ S _ C _ R _ _
```

No 293

```
_ C _ W _ E _ A _ E _ U _
P Y T H O N _ M I X I N G
A _ E _ A _ I _ P _ S _ _
A N T E _ C O N V E N T S
L _ _ _ T _ O _ D _ A _ _
S W E E T E R _ L I M B O
A _ R _ D _ A _ T _ L _ _
G L A D E _ I G N I T E S
K _ E _ M _ _ _ I _ O _ _
V O C A L I S T _ N O E L
V _ L _ X _ A _ A _ N _ _
S E R E N E _ T H R I V E
R _ R _ S _ E _ Y _ Y _ _
```

No 294

```
B E L I E F _ U _ P _ V _
E _ U _ _ _ R E P L A C E D
M O M _ E _ S _ M _ R _ _
O _ B A T E A U _ P E S T
A _ E _ D _ R _ H _ E _ _
N E R V E _ A G E L E S S
_ _ E _ _ _ S _ E _ E _ _
P A I N F U L _ S T O N Y
B _ E _ B _ P _ R _ E _ _
A J A R _ S I E S T A _ _
E _ A _ E _ A _ _ _ T O M
E C S T A T I C _ E _ A _
_ T _ E _ S _ _ _ H I D D E N
```

No 295

```
S I D E _ T O G E T H E R
O _ O _ E _ O _ L _ O _ I
U N M I X E D _ E X E R T
L _ E _ T _ L _ C _ D _ E
M I S D I R E C T I O N _
A _ _ _ N _ S _ R _ W _ H
T R U D G E _ C O R N E A
E _ M _ U _ A _ L _ _ _ Z
C L A I R V O Y A N C E _
S _ A _ S _ O _ S _ O _ L
C O U C H _ W R I T T E N
A _ T _ E _ E _ S _ E _ U
B E S T R I D E _ E D I T
```

No 296

```
P O T T E R _ F L E E C E
E _ H _ E _ U _ N _ A _ _
T A K E O V E R _ T A R T
U _ M _ _ _ I _ I _ I _ _
N I L E _ P _ O _ R O B S
I _ _ _ S T A T U T E _ O
A S H _ C _ S _ _ _ D U D
O _ O V E R L A P _ _ _ E
A M I D _ M _ Y _ A U K S
E _ I _ A _ _ _ R _ C _ _
S O L O _ K I N G S I Z E
N _ U _ E _ U _ O _ N _ _
G E Y S E R _ T I N N E D
```

No 297

```
N A T I O N A L I T Y _
S _ N _ M _ E _ E _ A _ U
L _ O _ P I T O N _ B U N
E X T O L _ T _ D _ O _ S
_ E _ H _ I _ L _ S T O I C
P R E C E D E S _ _ _ H _
W _ R _ D _ _ _ E _ D E _
A _ _ _ S K I N H E A D _
L A T T E _ U _ M _ F _ U
K _ O _ X _ N _ A U R A L
E L K _ U R G E S _ O _ _
R _ E _ L _ F _ S _ S _ D
_ I N S T R U M E N T S _
```

Solutions

No 298

S	U	B		S			I		B
C	O	R	N	E	R		P	U	M	M	E	L

(Grid puzzle – answers)

Row 1: SUB · S · I · B
Row 2: CORNER · PUMMEL
Row 3: S · C · E · I · P · R
Row 4: MONO · ASTEROID
Row 5: N · D · E · A · B
Row 6: ARIDITY · ACHED
Row 7: O · I · H · M · T · R
Row 8: QUITE · MILITIA
Row 9: N · I · P · S · C
Row 10: ADMONISH · ARCS
Row 11: I · N · S · A · B · A
Row 12: INFANT · PULPIT
Row 13: G · L · E · S · E · N

No 299

Row 1: SEAMAN · A · KIT
Row 2: A · C · RIVEN · W
Row 3: OSSICLE · E · O · O
Row 4: T · O · A · RACKS
Row 5: RESOURCE · K · T
Row 6: R · N · T · U · E · E
Row 7: SNOUTS · ENTRAP
Row 8: T · R · S · G · S · P
Row 9: O · A · TROOPERS
Row 10: PETAL · I · R · I
Row 11: G · I · O · DETRACT
Row 12: A · OASIS · E · O
Row 13: PAN · S · ADAPTS

No 300

Row 1: SCOUT · OSIER
Row 2: E · L · R · B · U · B · M
Row 3: DWINDLE · NOBLE
Row 4: I · M · U · G · B · R
Row 5: TABS · BIGAPPLE
Row 6: E · D · P · N · T · E
Row 7: DROVES · CHARTS
Row 8: W · E · C · E · S · T
Row 9: HONORARY · CODA
Row 10: O · A · A · O · N · N
Row 11: USING · FEIGNED
Row 12: R · M · E · T · N · E · S
Row 13: SPASM · SKULL

No 301

Row 1: MAMA · DIASPORA
Row 2: I · U · L · G · T · R · U
Row 3: SESSION · EXIST
Row 4: U · I · F · I · E · N · O
Row 5: NICHE · TAPROOM
Row 6: D · S · E · L · C · A
Row 7: ELATED · DEVOUT
Row 8: R · G · N · S · C · I
Row 9: SKEPTIC · HAVOC
Row 10: T · N · E · A · E · A
Row 11: OLDEN · NOSTRIL
Row 12: O · A · C · T · E · S · L
Row 13: DISPERSE · LEVY

No 302

Row 1: I · L · R · R · S · N
Row 2: MAIDEN · EUREKA
Row 3: M · B · N · D · S · D · C
Row 4: OREGANO · TRASH
Row 5: R · R · L · W · L · N · O
Row 6: ARID · ANNEX
Row 7: L · A · D · R · R · A · E
Row 8: NOWIN · ICED
Row 9: O · S · L · V · S · C · I
Row 10: CREEP · ENCRUST
Row 11: T · V · H · R · A · S · I
Row 12: EYELID · ALBEDO
Row 13: T · N · N · D · S · N

No 303

Row 1: DARN · STRETCHY
Row 2: E · O · I · R · X · H · O
Row 3: ESTONIA · PRIVY
Row 4: R · O · C · S · R · N · O
Row 5: STRAIGHTENER
Row 6: K · S · Y · S · S · U
Row 7: IMPAIR · ASTERN
Row 8: N · U · V · R · I · S
Row 9: UNBELIEVABLE
Row 10: S · D · N · P · E · I · E
Row 11: ASIDE · PILGRIM
Row 12: G · T · S · L · Y · C · L
Row 13: OBSESSES · WHEY

No 304

Row 1: SUPERINTEND
Row 2: M · R · X · M · H · E · E
Row 3: E · A · TEPEE · ELL
Row 4: TENSE · U · R · D · E
Row 5: A · I · N · G · MUSIC
Row 6: POUNDING · T
Row 7: H · M · S · A · A · R
Row 8: Y · CONFETTI
Row 9: SCARF · P · F · H · C
Row 10: I · M · A · P · ALIBI
Row 11: CHI · BLURB · R · T
Row 12: S · G · L · G · L · S · Y
Row 13: GOVERNMENTS

No 305

Row 1: BALLAD · H · FOE
Row 2: I · N · EVOKE · M
Row 3: ELATION · N · R · P
Row 4: M · M · V · KARMA
Row 5: HEPTAGON · A · T
Row 6: N · T · Y · B · R · H
Row 7: STAPES · PURITY
Row 8: U · M · S · C · S · R
Row 9: C · I · DOMINION
Row 10: CHART · N · N · U
Row 11: B · A · IRELAND
Row 12: M · LILAC · S · C
Row 13: BUY · L · ESCHEW

No 306

Row 1: SOSO · BACCARAT
Row 2: T · I · S · N · O · E · I
Row 3: OVERPAY · URGED
Row 4: P · G · I · N · R · Y
Row 5: PRESCRIPTION
Row 6: A · K · O · R · U · P
Row 7: GNU · ANNOY · PRO
Row 8: E · N · N · I · W · L
Row 9: MENDACIOUSLY
Row 10: A · Q · S · M · P · G
Row 11: PLUMP · GRANOLA
Row 12: E · A · A · O · N · I · M
Row 13: SPLENDOR · FLAY

Solutions

No 307
No 308
No 309

No 310
No 311
No 312

No 313
No 314
No 315

Solutions

No 316

No 317

No 318

Solutions

No 319

A	D	A	G	I	O		S		N	I	B
O			N		H	E	L	L	O		E
W	O	R	L	D	L	Y		A	V		D
R		E		M		B	L	E	E	P	
T	W	I	N	N	I	N	G		L		O
A		T		S		B	L		S		S
C	Y	C	L	E	S		V	A	C	A	N	T
L		A		D		F		R		E	
A		N		L	E	V	E	R	E	T	S
S	I	N	G	S		R		F		W	
S		I		U		R	O	O	F	T	O	P
I		L	A	N	K	Y		O		R	
C	R	Y		S			S	T	O	R	K	S

No 320

C	L	O	G		P	E	D	I	G	R	E	E
O		X		I		Y		N		A		A
V	A	L	A	N	C	E		D	I	V	A	S
E		I		D		L		I		I		E
R	E	P	R	E	H	E	N	S	I	O	N	
A			P		T		T		L		D	
L	U	S	T	E	R		M	I	L	I	E	U
L		O		N		U		N				T
	S	A	R	D	O	N	I	C	A	L	L	Y
D		N	E		I		T		A		F	
A	D	D	O	N		S	O	L	D	I	E	R
M		S		C		O		Y		R		E
P	R	O	T	E	I	N	S		I	D	L	E

No 321

	M	A	T	E	R	I	A	L	I	S	M	
U		N		X		C	E		T		C	
N		A		H	Y	E	N	A		E	G	O
S	A	L	V	O		A		S		A		U
P		O		R	G		H	U	M	A	N	
E	I	G	H	T	I	E	S				T	
A		Y		S		D		D	O	E	
K			O	B	S	E	R	V	E	R	
A	M	B	L	E		I		E		E		F
B		O		A		K		P	U	R	G	E
L	A	W		T	R	I	P	S		A		I
E		E		E		N		E		L		T
	I	D	E	N	T	I	C	A	L	L	Y	

Solutions

No 322

No 323

No 324

Solutions

No 325

No 326

No 327

Solutions

No 328

No 329

No 330

Solutions

No 331

No 332

No 333